A Sociological Perspective

Understanding Organizations

A Sociological Perspective

FRANK E. JONES

Copp Clark Ltd.
Toronto

ISBN: 0-7730-5540-1

Publisher: Jeff Miller
Acquisitions editor: Danelle D'Alvise
Substantive editor: Andy Carroll
Copy editor/proofreader: Robyn Packard
Indexer: Kate Forster
Design: Kyle Gell
Typesetting: Marnie Benedict
Printing and binding: Metropole Litho Inc.

Canadian Cataloguing in Publication Data

Jones, Frank E. (Frank Edward), 1917–
   Understanding organizations: a sociological perspective

Includes bibliographical references and index.
ISBN 0-7730-5540-1

1. Organizational sociology.   I. Title

HM131.J65 1996   302.3'5   C96-930021-2

COPP CLARK LTD.
2775 Matheson Blvd. East
Mississauga, Ontario
L4W 4P7

Printed and bound in Canada

1 2 3 4 5   5540-1   00 99 98 97 96

*To Jean, for many years of
unconditional support*

Contents

Contents

Contents

REFACE

My sustained interest in organizations as social entities began at McGill University where Oswald Hall introduced me to the work of Max Weber and Talcott Parsons. In due course, Professor Hall directed my M.A. thesis, a study of the work organization of structural steelworkers. My interest deepened at Harvard where, at that time, Talcott Parsons was developing his theory of social systems. Parsons directed my Ph.D. thesis on infantry training in the Canadian Army. It gives me great pleasure to acknowledge my intellectual debt to Professors Hall and Parsons.

My later research included a study of workers' attitudes in a manufacturing company and other studies, centred on participatory structures, in psychiatric hospitals and treatment centres.

Thirty-odd years of interacting with undergraduates and graduates who took my courses in the sociology of organizations has honed my ability to clarify and to communicate my understanding of this field. Even so, I and the readers of this text are indebted to Andy Carroll, my editor, for his unflagging effort to ensure that I achieved these goals in this text. My teaching and researching experience underlies my aim in this text to explain what it means to study organizations from a sociological perspective and to convey the importance of such a perspective to understanding how organizations work.

$\mathscr{I}$NTRODUCTION

$\mathscr{T}$he objective of this text is to provide an account of the various ways of thinking about organizations as these have developed in sociology. Throughout the discussion of this development, a focus will be maintained on the concepts essential to a sociological perspective. Thus, organizations will be considered as systems of social relationships or social interaction that must be analyzed, at a minimum, in terms of a division of labour or role differentiation, in terms of the distribution and structure of authority, and in terms of the consensus and cohesion among the participants in these relationships.

As the study of organizations developed, various perspectives emerged from theory and research. While several of these are identified in the chapters to follow, the discussion will focus on three perspectives that have maintained a prominence in the field from its inception to the present: the *rational*, the *human relations*, and the *system* perspectives. These three chapters trace important developments in the study of organizations. For those beginning a study of the sociology of organizations, an understanding of the contributions of these early perspectives is important both for their historical significance and for understanding other perspectives that have emerged over the past twenty-five years.

The sociology of organizations began with Max Weber, whose name is associated with the rational perspective (Chapter Two). As we shall see, Weber formulated a model of bureaucracy that identified what he regarded as its fundamental characteristics or properties, such as a hierarchical authority structure and the presence of rules. One consequence of Weber's work was that, although Weber restricted his analysis to the administrative staff of the organization, bureaucratic structure came to be equated with organizational structure. An organization was a bureaucracy and vice versa. Research, however, led to the recognition that organizations could not be described exclusively in bureaucratic terms. Blau, Gouldner, and Selznick, who used Weber's analysis of the bureaucracy as a starting point for their researches, concluded, on the basis of their field observations, that there were different kinds of bureaucracies or that the presence of bureaucratic characteristics could vary in organizations. The attack on the single model was also carried forward by Burns and Stalker, who argued that organizations vary along a continuum from bureaucratic to what they called *organic*, that is, organizations that are virtually the opposite of bureaucratic. In reality, Burns and Stalker expected most organizations to be located along the continuum rather than at its extremes, and they identify several sub-continua along which organizations vary.

Work proceeding from these beginnings focused on the identification of the relevant variables, such as formalization, complexity, and centralization, that characterize organizations. The human relations perspective challenged the Weberian view by focusing on motivation, on informal relationships, and on variations in styles of exercising authority—concepts given limited attention or ignored by Weber and the rational perspective.[1] In the human relations perspective, motivation, viewed as essential to organizational effectiveness, is seen as varying in relation to employee participation in informal relationships and styles of exercising authority. The idea that a single model, the bureaucracy, was sufficient for the description and analysis of organizations was further weakened by the application of the system perspective (Chapter Four), which argued that goal-achievement was not the sole condition of organizational survival. The system perspective can be seen to merge the components of the rational and human relations perspectives. More important, this perspective emphasizes the systemic nature of organizations: the interdependence of its subsystems. In this perspective, organizational survival depends on the preservation of an organization's identity relative to its environment rather than depending exclusively on goal achievement.

The next four chapters identify analytical concepts that are addressed by a wide range of sociological perspectives on organizations. These concepts are used to identify system problems but also to define the narrower focuses of more recent perspectives.

Chapter Five provides a discussion of the relations between organizations and their environments. Strongly influenced by the idea that organizations are social systems involved in interchanges with their environments, sociologists identified "mechanisms" in organizations that served as defences against environmental threats. This approach led, in turn, to the concept of "open systems"—input-output models that portrayed organizations as both producing environmental change as well as reacting to environmental forces. In relation to the system problem of adaptation, Chapter Five also includes a consideration of technology, size, and societal values as forces for organizational change.

The internal order of organizations is the subject of Chapter Six. The central concerns are the variations in structure, the exercise of authority, and compliance with norms, rules, and decisions.

In Chapter Seven, the discussion centres on the significance to organizational functioning of consensus and dissensus, and cohesion and conflict among participants.

Finally, Chapter Eight is concerned with the goals or objectives of organizations. It provides an account of the problems in identifying such goals and in obtaining reliable, valid data on their achievement.

ENDNOTES

[1] The introduction of the human relations perspective preceded the work of such neo-Weberians as Blau and Gouldner, but both rational and human relations perspectives co-exist.

CHAPTER 1

*S*tudying Organizations

THE PREVALENCE OF ORGANIZATIONS

*I*t is commonplace to observe that we live in an organizational society.[1] The observation calls attention to the prominence of organizations in the lives of people in modern societies. However, while the idea that business is dominated by big corporations is familiar, there may be less awareness that all aspects of our lives, from birth to death, are likely to involve organizations. Many responsibilities and services, once accepted and provided by the immediate or extended family are now organized, that is, provided by the many private and public organizations. For example, babies, which at one time were delivered at home, are delivered in hospitals. The percentage of births taking place in Canadian hospitals increased from about 26 percent in 1930 to almost 100 percent in 1977 (Statistics Canada 1977a). Despite an increased interest in home births in more recent years, more than 95 percent continue to be born in hospitals.[2] Education and much of child care have been transferred to day-care centres and schools. To deal with problems that arise in the care of children, in marital relationships, and in the care of ageing parents, people turn to a host of private and public agencies that provide advice and support. At death, public mourning and burial ceremonies are more likely to take place in a funeral home than in the family home, where they would be arranged by the family. Leisure activities are pursued within frameworks established by organizations: this is true of plays, films, and music; sports, from Little Leagues to professional levels; and even hiking and other seemingly informal activities. Because the number of organizations has increased disproportionately to population increase and because organizations are increasing in size, the prominence and dominance of organizations in our lives will increase.

Organizations, viewed as distinct social forms, arouse sociological curiosity and stimulate attempts to study and understand them. Apart from academic interest, the fact that organizations are prominent, often dominant, forces in our lives is a compelling reason for trying to understand them. If human beings need to understand their environments to be able to survive and, even more, to live effective lives, they need to learn how organizations, which dominate these environments, work.

APPROACHES TO THE STUDY OF ORGANIZATIONS

Understanding organizations is no simple matter. Indeed, sociological study of organizations only began in the twentieth century, and while progress has been made, there is much more to be done before an understanding of the significance of organizations and the causes and consequences of their structures and functions nears completion.

There is more than one approach to understanding organizations. Each academic discipline that includes organizations as its subject matter contributes to an understanding of organizations, but none can claim to fully explain what goes on in organizations. In fact, as each discipline conceives of organizations in terms of its own basic concepts, partial understanding is the most we can expect. While it seems reasonable to combine these different conceptualizations in order to achieve a fuller understanding of organizations, it would be premature to adopt an interdisciplinary approach before each discipline's contribution is more fully developed.

Sociological interest in organizations has been evident throughout this century. This chapter is the first step toward describing and explaining how sociologists perceive and study organizations. Stated briefly, sociologists treat organizations as sociological phenomena—as social groups or as systems of relationships or interaction—rather than as administrative forms, as economic entities, or as political systems.

ORGANIZATIONS AS COLLECTIVITIES

Organizations are regarded by sociologists as social groups, or systems of social interaction, or, to use a more general term, as **collectivities**. This means that sociological description and analysis of organizations will use the same ideas and concepts as would be used to analyze other kinds of collectivity, such as families, groups of friends, or communities. In short, organizations, like these other kinds of collectivity, are regarded as having a social structure, which will manifest identifiable substructures, including one regulating authority, and some degree of role differentiation within the substructures. Norms or rules, accepted by the participants, will define expectations and regulate action. Interests and emotional ties between participants will define levels of conflict and cohesion.

One objective of sociologists studying organizations as systems of social relationships is to describe the relationships in terms of the ties that hold the relationship together, the conditions that generate tensions in the relationship, and the related conditions that promote stability or change. These relationships could be those among people who do different jobs in an organization, such as rank-and-file workers, line supervisors, and managers, or among people who are involved with each other as spouses, parents, or offspring.

It is central to this approach that analysis is focused on the *relationships* rather than on the individuals who are involved. The individual and the relationship are abstractions based on the observable actions of human beings as organisms.[3] Sociologists do not necessarily ignore the individualistic actions of human beings, but the emphasis is on such concepts as social structure, social relationship, and role, all of which are collectivity-oriented. In the sociological view, social action must be explained in terms of people's shared acceptance of specific values and of expectations of action in various situations. Furthermore, such shared values and expectations are assumed to transcend the lives of specific persons who at any one time belong to a social group, to an organization, or to a society. As a general beginning, then, it can be said that to understand organizations, it is necessary to describe and explain both the nature of the relationships in organizations and how conditions that bear on the organization affect these relationships.

Collectivities Are Variable

Although organizations are studied, sociologically, in the same way as other social groups or collectivities, this does not mean that organizations do not differ from these other social forms. In everyday language, "organization" is a word used to refer to such identifiable entities as business firms, labour unions, government departments and agencies, hospitals, schools and universities, and charitable and welfare agencies. More specifically, however, organization suggests the idea that people and resources are organized to provide some service or to achieve some goal. This idea implies that there is something about organizations that is different from other collectivities. When we speak of organizations, we are not, of course, referring to individuals, even though corporations are treated in law as though they were individuals and reference is made to the "corporate personality" or to "corporate citizenship"; nor are we referring to such collectivities as families, groups of friends, or gangs. And while we can easily distinguish between organizations and individuals and do not confuse a supermarket with a person, making conceptual distinctions between organizations and, for example, families, friendship groups, and communities, requires a little thinking.

At a general level, sociologists define organizations as a type of collectivity *created* to achieve some objective or objectives. Defined in this way, organizations stand in contrast to social groups, such as the family or the larger lineages and clans. Although social functions, such as the regulation of sexual and reproductive behaviour and the regulation of inheritance, may be attributed to family and kinship structures, there is no historical evidence that families were consciously established to meet these functions. In contrast, an enterprise established to exploit a natural resource, to manufacture goods, or to manage financial operations is the result of a conscious decision by one or more persons, as are the decisions concerning the distribution of rights and responsibilities to the organization's employees. Similarly, hospitals, schools, prisons, unions, and voluntary organizations come into being as instruments to achieve some objective or objectives—to provide health care, to provide education, etc. In short, organizations are seen as a conscious arrangement of material and human resources required for the achievement of a defined objective or objectives. On the whole, this definition holds up fairly well, although there may be enterprises whose structures developed with a minimum of conscious decision.

It is also possible to distinguish organizations from other collectivities in terms of differences in the relationships among members of the various collectivities. In organizations, people relate primarily in terms of their jobs, interests, or membership responsibilities. This is in contrast to families, where people relate primarily on the basis of ties of birth, affection, or both. While there is evidence to support this distinction, it will not be discussed in this book about organizations. Indeed, some sociologists with a special interest in organizations focus more on the differences between organizations than those between organizations and other types of collectivity.

Variations among Organizations

Although all organizations may share certain characteristics—there will be some degree of role differentiation, some structure of authority, some procedural similarities—there can be important differences between organizations depending on, for example, whether participation is voluntary or involuntary or the differences in objectives or services. It would certainly fly in the face of reality to argue that all organizations, whatever their purpose, are the same. It is fair to say that students of organizations are not of one mind in regarding how widely generalizations that apply to business organizations will apply, say, to hospitals or schools, or vice versa. The difficulty arises because a commonly accepted classification of organizations has yet to be developed.

Classification

Classification is a basic procedure of analysis. It is a means of reducing the variation presented by reality and of simplifying understanding of reality, whether for use in everyday life or for more profound investigation. Basically, it is a process of sorting phenomena, things, or actions in terms of their similarities and differences. Those that are perceived to be the same or to resemble each other are classed together, while other things or actions are assigned to other classes. What determines whether things or actions belong together may depend on the interests of the classifier. For some, it may not matter if whales and sharks are classed together as marine animals (or even if both are regarded as fish). This common-sense distinction, however, is rejected by biologists whose classification system distinguishes whales as mammals and sharks as fish. To biologists, for whom evolution is a central concern, it is important to locate animals in the appropriate evolutionary class and, therefore, in their correct evolutionary relationship with other animals. The lesson from biology is that serious analysis in a field of study requires a classification system that is linked to the objectives and the theoretical perspective of the field.

Classification has several objectives. One is to distinguish similarities and differences among the phenomena of interest, allowing the delimitation of a field of study or research. A related objective is to provide a basis for defining the scope of generalizations of findings and conclusions from research. The debate on whether research on animals can be applied to humans arises from distinctions drawn between humans and other animal species as classified by biologists or physiologists. Another objective is to establish classes that provide or lead to fresh insights or understanding.

Classification, then, to be useful for analysis in a field of study, should reflect some theoretical formulation central to that field. The classification system reflected by Everett Hughes' comment (1958, 88) that sociologists who study occupations learn "about doctors by studying plumbers; and about prostitutes by studying psychiatrists" might not be immediately apparent. However, power, authority, and control are basic concerns in sociology, and Hughes goes on to show that a shared characteristic of those employed in these seemingly diverse occupations is their attempts to control evaluations of performance.

In sociology, including the sociology of organizations, it has been easier to recognize the value of a theoretically based classification or way of systematically describing similarities and differences in social phenomena than to develop a classification that is widely accepted in the discipline. In the sociology of organizations, classifications have been developed, but none has been adopted as *the* way to order organizations in terms of selected characteristics. Still, some attempts by sociologists to classify organizations are better known, or judged to be more useful, than others. Examples of two of these, by Blau and Scott (1962) and by Etzioni ([1961] 1975), are described here.

Two Examples of Classifications

Blau and Scott (1962, 42–57) based their classification on a single criterion: who are the *prime beneficiaries* of an organization? They identified four types or classes of organization:

- **business organizations**, such as industrial firms, banks, and wholesale and retail stores, whose prime beneficiaries are the *owners*;
- **service organizations**, such as hospitals, schools, and social agencies, whose prime beneficiaries are the *clients* or *customers*;
- **mutual benefit associations**, such as unions, political parties, and professional associations, whose prime beneficiaries are the *members*; and
- **commonweal organizations**, such as government departments and agencies and fire and police departments, whose prime beneficiary is the *public-at-large*.

The Blau and Scott classification has some useful qualities. It is analytic in the sense that the prime-beneficiary criterion allows organizations that provide the same service or have similar goals to be classified differently. For example, privately owned hospitals (or nursing centres, or schools) may be classed as business concerns while their community-owned counterparts may be classed as service organizations.

Such differences in assignment to a given class may turn out to be important because Blau and Scott propose that each class of organization is characterized by a specific *central problem*. In their view, the central concern of business organizations is to maximize efficiency, whereas that of service organizations is to minimize conflicts between administrative procedures, which regulate the organization, and professional procedures, which regulate the relationship between professionals and their clients. The central problems of mutual benefit associations are to minimize membership apathy and to maximize internal democracy, and the central problem of commonweal organizations is to maintain external procedures of control.

It appears, however, that the distinctions in the types of central problem are not clear.[4] For example, if it is assumed that the maximization of efficiency requires a high level of motivation and appropriate administrative procedures, the difference between business concerns, mutual benefit associations, and service organizations disappears. Even the issue of external control of commonweal organizations may be a matter of motivation, that is, of the commitment of the officers of such organizations to the concept of public control. Indeed, further discussion of this class of organization (Blau and Scott 1962, 55) reveals that motivation is, in fact, a central problem. Although the issues of controlling or regulating authority and power and of motivation are sociological concerns, the difficulty with Blau and Scott lies in a failure to recognize that their central problems—motivation and the control of power—are central to all organizations, indeed, to all collectivities. Despite the introduction of the central problem concept, Blau and Scott used a single criterion to establish their four classes, namely, the prime beneficiary. Given the complexity of organizations, a single criterion is not adequate for this purpose. That this criterion is not overtly sociological is an even more serious limitation. Identifying organizational types on the basis of the prime beneficiaries is as commonsensical as identifying them on the basis of size, activities, and such other characteristics.

In contrast to Blau and Scott, Etzioni's classification ([1961] 1975) is based on criteria that relate directly to the analysis of social relationships: the kinds of power characteristically exercised and the basis of involvement in an organization. On the basis of three kinds of "*means employed to make the subjects comply,*" Etzioni identifies three types of power (Etzioni [1961] 1975, 5):

- **coercive**, which employs physical force;
- **remunerative**, which employs material rewards; and
- **normative**, which uses symbolic rewards.

Similarly, there are three types of involvement (Etzioni [1961] 1975, 10):

- **alienation**, which is characterized by a strong negative orientation to the organization;
- **calculative involvement**, which is based primarily on material reward and may be positive or negative in direction; and
- **moral involvement**, in which duty or a service ethic to the organization and a strong positive orientation are characteristic.

Etzioni argues that there is a tendency toward consistency between types of power and types of involvement, and that a cross-classification of the two variables identifies three main or consistent types of organizations:

those, such as prisons, that employ coercion and in which participants are alienated; those, such as business firms, in which power is remunerative and participants are calculative; and those, such as political or religious organizations, in which power is normative and involvement is moral. Cross-classification also produces six other types of organizations that are characterized by inconsistency between power and involvement. As inconsistency between types of power and involvement results in stress or disturbance in the organization, the tendency is for that stress to produce a change in the type of power or the type of involvement.

It is unlikely that many actual organizations will fit perfectly with any of Etzioni's types. As he observes, "Most organizations employ all three kinds of power" ([1961] 1975, 6). Similarly, a mix of motives for involvement or commitment might be expected of participants. The commitment of prison staff could be motivated by an orientation to material rewards, while prisoners can be expected to be negatively committed or alienated. Similarly, one might expect to find mixed motives for commitment to a political party—some belonging for ideological reasons, others for material gain. Even so, Etzioni's contention that organizations will tend to favour one type of power or involvement is reasonable. Observation is likely to reveal that there are organizations that are primarily coercive, primarily alienative, and so on. The value of Etzioni's classification, as we shall see in Chapter Six, lies in its selection of sociological concepts—control and involvement—to describe the variable features of organizations.[5] Further, he argues that the relations between these features can be hypothesized and the hypotheses tested by observation of actual organizations. Etzioni ([1961] 1975) supports his argument with research, undertaken by others, that provides evidence relevant to these hypotheses.

Although classification is a valuable tool for identifying the variable aspects of phenomena under analysis, it does require, to achieve the highest precision, that the classes in the system be defined in such a way that phenomena can be located unambiguously in the relevant classes of the system. Stated another way, proper classification requires that classes be discrete—that a given phenomenon, whether an organization or some other entity, fits into one and only one class in the system. For organizations, at least, this is a difficult condition to meet. For example, should worker cooperatives be classed in the Blau-Scott system as business concerns or mutual benefit associations? Etzioni recognizes that there are organizations, such as military combat units and some labour unions that must be identified as dual control systems (Etzioni [1961] 1975, 56, 65). Indeed, as already noted, Etzioni asserts that "all patterns of compliance exist in most organizations" but contends that one of the three patterns tends to be dominant (Etzioni [1961] 1975, 23).

Etzioni's statement draws attention to a different procedure for identifying variation, a procedure that may be labelled **dimensionality**. In this procedure, instead of treating the characteristics of phenomena as exclusive to one class or another, it is assumed that all relevant characteristics are possessed by the phenomena but that variation may be identified in terms of different degrees of presence of the characteristic in question. For example, although the identification of human beings as male and female on the basis of biological characteristics is very useful, it may be that the reality of sexual differences is oversimplified. If sexual preference is added as a criterion, it appears that there are at least three categories: heterosexual, bisexual, and homosexual. Moreover, it is possible to conceptualize that all human beings are motivated to seek sexual experience with biological males and females but in varying degrees, with zero motivation for one biological sex or the other being the limiting case or minimum value on a dimension or continuum of measurement.

This dimensional thinking about variation may be useful in classifying variation in organizations. It is promising in contrast to the limited usefulness of other classifications of organizations and is consistent with the approaches taken by the neo-Weberians such as Gouldner ([1954] 1964), by Burns and Stalker (1961), and by those adopting a systems perspective in the study of organizations. It is also consistent with general sociological theory as formulated by Talcott Parsons (see, for example, Parsons and Bales (1953, chap. 3).

SUMMARY

Sociologists study groups or collectivities, and interaction between members of collectivities is a fundamental interest. Collectivities, whether families, friendship groups, or organizations, may be thought of as configurations of social relationships; the fundamental unit for the analysis of any collectivity is the social relationship. Because organizations are a type of collectivity, the sociology of organizations can thus be conceived as the study of social relationships in organizations.

Organizations can vary from one another in three important dimensions—role differentiation, the distribution of authority, and the type and level of commitment. These are essential for the analysis of organizations.

Organizations also differ from other collectivities. Organizations are created to achieve some defined objective, whereas other collectivities evolve. The nature of relationships in organizations may also differ from those in other collectivities—for example, in the intensity and scope of commitments.

The need to classify organizations arises from the great variety of organizations that exist in modern societies. An acceptable classification of organizations is needed in order to establish limits for generalizing research findings on organizations. Although classifications have been developed—and two examples were discussed in this chapter—a universally acceptable classification of organizations has so far eluded sociologists.

ENDNOTES

1   Particularly so, following the publication of Presthus's book, *The Organizational Society* (Presthus [1962] 1978).

2   After 1977, Statistics Canada's *Vital Statistics* reports did not include information about births occurring in hospitals. I am indebted to Professor Karyn Kaufman, School of Nursing, McMaster University, who has a special interest in midwifery, for an expert judgment on the trend in the frequency of home births in the 1980s and 1990s.

3   A statement that an individual is just as much an abstraction as a relationship may be difficult to accept. This may be because, particularly in societies that value individuals and individualism, it is easy to think of the individual as indistinguishable from the human organism. Because an organism has definite boundaries relative to its environment—we know where our bodies stop—we do not confuse someone else's body with our own, or perceive any other material object as part of our body. The concept of *individual*, however, refers to certain aspects of the organism, such as distinctive features or ways of behaving, that set it off from other organisms. The concept of *individual* ignores aspects of the organism, including behaviour, that express interhuman dependency. For further discussion of the "reality" of society and of individuals, see Wolff (1950, 3–21).

4   As various criticisms of this classification have been made elsewhere, see, for example, Richard Hall (1982, 40–48) and Perrow (1986, 140–56). My comments are limited to those necessary to my argument proposing an appropriate strategy for devising a usable classification of organizations.

5   It should be noted that the discussion of the compliance model in Gross and Etzioni (1985) makes no reference to the *three* types of orientation described in earlier statements of the compliance model (Etzioni [1961] 1975). Instead the reference is to the nature of commitment, whether it be negative (alienative) or positive. It would appear that the nine-category scheme, describing variations in compliance, has given way to an emphasis on the means of control as the dominant variable characteristic of organizations.

CHAPTER 2

*B*UREAUCRACY AS AN ORGANIZATIONIONAL FORM

*S*ociological study of organizations began with Max Weber (1864–1920), a German sociologist, whose analysis of bureaucracy provided a model that has endured as an analytical tool.[1]

In his analysis of bureaucracy, Weber proceeded by identifying certain features that he regarded as taking a distinctive form and as being consistent with rationality.[2] Weber held that rationality, a logical process for arriving at decisions or knowledge, is valued in the bureaucracy. That is, rationality is preferred to other possible process or bases, such as intuition, magic, revelation, or reliance on tradition. In this chapter, the focus is on the principal features of Weber's model: authority, technical competence, the division of labour, impersonality, and rules. As well as giving Weber's reasons for regarding each as a critical feature of the bureaucracy, it will be shown that each is consistent with a sociological perspective on organizations.

THE MODEL OF BUREAUCRACY

Authority

Weber focused on power and authority as central elements of bureaucracy. Indeed, his interest in organizations related directly to his study of domination, by which he sought to understand why human beings comply with the commands, directions, and instructions of others. This interest led to his well-known typology of authority and his view that each type of authority is associated with a distinct form of social organization. Since power, authority, dominance, and compliance must all refer to social relationships, his perspective is clearly sociological.

Bureaucracies, like all organizations, are instruments of control, as well as being instruments for defining responsibility, and Weber could not and did not ignore the organizational components of power. He focused on the idea of the legitimate exercise of power, that is, on authority. Although Weber regarded power as an important dimension of social relationships and acknowledged that power could be exercised and maintained by physical force or coercion, he rejected the conclusion that coercion was the sole basis of compliance with commands, directions, and instructions. In his view, a relationship that depended on coercion would be inherently unstable, and other forms of exercising power were required to achieve stability. He saw those who command and those commanded as bound in a relationship in which the issuing of commands and compliance with them are regulated by values and norms shared by those participating in the relationship. By this, Weber meant that the conditions for exercising authority entailed some level of agreement between superiors and subordinates. Such agreement *legitimated* the exercise of power. In his discussion of bureaucratic authority, Weber focused on its **basis** and its **structure** and on the general qualifications required of those occupying positions of authority.

Basis

In pursuing his interest in authority, or more broadly, control, Weber identified variability in the structure of authority. In Weber's view, authority, the legitimate exercise of power, varied according to its base. He proposed three bases of authority.

- **Charismatic authority**, where power is legitimated on the basis of a shared belief that the person giving commands and making decisions possesses unique gifts or characteristics. For example, Christ's followers accepted his authority because they believed him to be the Son of God.

- **Traditional authority**, where the exercise of power is legitimated by longstanding custom. For example, the right of elders, in some societies, to issue commands or make decisions binding on the members.

- **Rational-legal authority**, where commands and decisions are based on a logical relationship to an organization's objectives and have the force of laws.

Weber identified bureaucratic authority as being rational-legal. By this, he meant, first, that the exercise of power in the bureaucracy is legitimated by the demonstrable logical relevance of commands, directions, and instructions to the achievement of the bureaucracy's objectives. In other words, commands must seem rational—they must be justified by their relevance to the tasks of the bureaucracy and ultimately to its objectives. Second, Weber held that authority in the bureaucracy is supported by a shared belief in the "legality of patterns of normative rules" that establish the rights and responsibilities of the members of a collectivity (Weber 1947, 300). In other words, the norms and rules of the bureaucracy are perceived as law-like and the exercise of authority is understood as the rule of law—a rule arrived at rationally, rather than one based on tradition or determined by the personal vision or interests of the incumbent of a bureaucratic position of authority. Commands, directions, and instructions are obeyed because they are legal and are relevant to the task of the bureaucracy and not because they are based on tradition or on loyalty to the person exercising authority.

Structure

The structure of bureaucratic authority, Weber observed, is hierarchical. This is to say that the rights and responsibilities associated with positions of authority are ordered by the range or scope of jurisdiction—those in positions of narrower scope are subordinate to those in positions of wider scope. For example, whereas the chief executive officer of a company has the right to make decisions affecting the entire company, a first-line supervisor may make decisions only relating to his or her unit of the company. Moreover, the incumbent of each position is directly responsible and subordinate to the incumbent of the position at the next higher level. Although authority is unequally distributed in the bureaucracy, Weber also observed that the authority of each position was sacrosanct to its incumbent in the sense that the incumbent was considered the only one with the competence and the legitimate right and responsibility to make decisions appropriate to that position. For example, only the first-line supervisor, assumed to possess the relevant expertise, would have the right to make decisions directly relating to the work of the first line. Neither the chief executive officer nor any incumbent in positions higher than the first-line supervisor should make such decisions. In Weber's view, then, authority in the bureaucracy is structured to support managerial competence and specialization, and can be expected to provide rationally based decisions and instructions that will maximize efficiency and the attainment of the organization's goals.

Technical Competence

Weber pointed out that to qualify for a position in the bureaucracy, an applicant must possess the skills relevant to the position, that is, **technical competence**. Although this may seem obvious, Weber's concern was to contrast this requirement with other practices that allow persons to be appointed or promoted on the basis of attributes such as gender, ethnicity, religious affiliation, family ties, and social class or status. Technical competence is determined rationally and contrasts with qualification on the basis of attributes that may have no demonstrated relevance to performance in a bureaucratic position. Technical competence requires, for example, that a low-level supervisor possess supervisory skills and be knowledgeable about the tasks subordinates are to perform, while a general manager must possess skills relating to planning, the coordination of tasks, and the control of operations. It would be irrational, in most instances, to assume that being male or female, being English or Polish, or being a member of a particular social class, without having had relevant training or experience, would qualify a person for a bureaucratic position.

Although technical competence may not, at first glance, appear to be a sociological concept, it can be regarded as an aspect of the definition of roles, the components of social relationships. Technical competence is a prime influence on definition of organizational roles, but sociologists have shown that neither the qualifications for performing the tasks associated with organization roles nor the attribution of competence are based exclusively on technical requirements. Social definitions based on shared beliefs, which influence people's expectations of roles in a wide range of social relationships, also influence organizational roles. In addition to technical requirements, beliefs relating to age, sex, ethnicity, and religion, for example, may be influential in defining organizational roles. As Hughes has observed (1958, 73), "the division of labour is more than a technical phenomenon; . . . there are infinite social-psychological nuances in it." At one time, for example, the critical qualifications for positions of authority in the British Civil Service were membership in the upper classes, education at a public school, such as Eton, and a Cambridge or Oxford degree (Kingsley 1944, especially chap. 7).

These criteria have changed over time as has the division of labour between physicians and nurses. Hughes (1958, 73, 135) comments that as medical technology has developed, certain tasks have been downgraded and delegated by physicians to nurses. Nurses now routinely take blood pressure, a task formerly restricted to physicians. Indeed, the imbalance in the distribution of males and females in the occupational structure is strongly influenced by social definitions of male and female competence. Although these definitions are changing, women were judged in the recent past to have the skills to be typists, office clerks, salesclerks, nurses, and teachers but not to be managers, engineers, physicians, lawyers, welders, or police officers. Similarly, social definitions of skills and qualifications account for differences in the occupational distribution of members of different ethnic groups or of persons possessing other personal attributes.

Weber's thinking on this issue is consistent with these later developments in the sociology of occupations. His recognition that the shared value of rationality determined technical competence to be the overriding qualification for bureaucratic role incumbency implies that he was aware that role differentiation is a social product.

Division of Labour

The concept of a division of labour is well-established in sociology as an important feature of all collectivities and, therefore, of all social relationships.[3] How the labour is divided, however, varies among collectivities. In some families, there may be a clear distinction in the tasks assigned to women and to men, while in others the distinction may be less specific. Groups of friends may differ from each other in terms of the rights and responsibilities of those in the groups. In both these types of collectivity, the set of tasks tends to be broadly defined. By contrast, as Weber noted, the bureaucracy is characterized by a high degree of differentiation, that is, by a complex division of labour. In effect, all the tasks required for an organization to attain its objectives, for example, to produce automobiles, are divided into limited sets of detailed responsibilities. These responsibilities are allocated to the various positions that make up the organization's structure, according to a rationally conceived plan. Ideally, the tasks and responsibilities of each position in the bureaucracy is unambiguously defined so that each person knows the expectations associated with his or her own position and knows the boundaries of that position relative to other positions in the bureaucracy.

This requirement may be seen to be rational in three ways. First, task specialization means that an incumbent of a position, apart from possessing the relevant competence, regularly performs a limited set of tasks and through practice improves in performance and consequently contributes to efficiency. Second, limiting the number of tasks per person reduces the training time required and facilitates the entry of new members into the organization. Third, a meticulous description of the tasks and responsibilities associated with each position helps to identify who is responsible when things go wrong in the organization.

Impersonality

Human beings are emotional as well as rational animals. They express feelings toward others, toward themselves, and toward objects in their environments. It follows that humans are also the recipients of emotional expression, and they particularly seek to be the objects of positive emotional expression. Normally, because people want to be liked or loved rather than disliked or hated, they tend to act toward others who are significant in their lives in ways that maximize positive and minimize negative responses. Recognizing this fundamental aspect of human action, sociologists have shown a strong interest in the social definition of emotional expression in human relationships. In some relationships, such as among family members, high levels of emotional commitment and exchange are expected. Family members may be expected to love each other, to be loyal to each other, and to express sympathy in times of trouble.[4]

In contrast to such relationships, emotional expression in the bureaucracy is severely constrained. Weber observed that relationships in the bureaucracy are *impersonal* in the sense that the expression of emotion and emotionally based relationships are irrelevant to bureaucratic role performance. Weber did not mean that bureaucrats did not express feelings but that incumbents of bureaucratic positions are expected to give or respond to commands and instructions whether they love, like, dislike, or hate each other. Presumably, Weber regarded action based on feelings as the opposite of rational action and, therefore, as likely to undermine bureaucratic performance. The requirement of impersonality serves to constrain favouritism, for example, and so protects against the neglect of technical competence in decisions concerning task allocation or promotion.

Rules

Rules, whether formalized as laws or informally held as norms or expectations, are recognized by sociologists as characteristic of all collectivities. Rules serve to regulate or control human action and, to the extent of compliance with the rule, ensure predictability of human action.[5]

It can readily be seen that predictability is a fundamental condition of human interaction. Without some reasonable expectation of how others will respond to a given action, social life would be chaotic. In situations where only a few persons interact on a regular basis, explicit rules may not be observed, but action is prescribed nonetheless, and is controlled by non-verbalized understandings. Explicit rules are more prominent and more necessary where members are new to a collectivity or where large numbers of persons form the collectivity. Organizations tend to bring together persons who interact with each other on a partial basis—the organization is not usually the place in which the person expresses her or his complete personality—and who are, in a certain sense, strangers to each other. Moreover, as noted in Chapter One, organizations may involve large numbers of people and this reduces the possibility of frequent interaction among all members of the organization. All these conditions—the large size, the presence of newcomers, and the partial personality involvement—encourage the use of explicit rules to control action and to produce the coordination of action necessary to organizational functioning.

It is not surprising, then, that Weber should be sensitive to the importance of rules in the bureaucracy and to how they were formulated. He observed that written communication was prominent in the bureaucracy, and that decisions, directives, and other matters were written as memoranda and saved in files. These provided the basis for rules intended to regulate bureaucratic activities. In Weber's view, the rules, based on previous experience and rationally formulated decisions, were essential to the achievement of bureaucratic efficiency. In the face of repetitive events requiring decisions, a rule could reduce or eliminate the need to expend time and energy reviewing similar situations by providing a standard and efficient response. For example, illness among employees is a recurrent event in an organization. In the first instance of illness, a decision must be made about whether the employee will be paid for the missing time and for how long a period. As the organization experiences further instances of illness, a rule is formulated. For example, each employee will be credited with one day of sick leave a month, up to a maximum number of days. When any employee is ill, then, it is simply a matter of applying the rule, avoiding the need to determine an individual solution for each case.

Rules also place limits on the actions of those in managerial and supervisory positions. By so doing, the rules may support some other feature of bureaucratic structure. For example, the specification of action to be taken against an employee for some misdemeanour, such as tardiness, may limit managerial discretion concerning punishment. A manager or supervisor may decide not to apply or enforce a rule, but does so at the risk of inviting negative sanctions by superiors and subordinates.

Shared Values

The concept of **shared values** suggests that the nature and control of social relationships are determined by shared conceptions of the desirable. Shared values underlies all the other concepts that identify the critical features of the bureaucracy. This concept of shared values, and specifically the shared value of rationality, is clearly evident in the model of bureaucracy.

The importance Weber attached to shared values as a determinant of human action is most evident in his contributions to the sociology of religion, which focused on the relationship between religious values and secular values and resultant action.[6] In *The Protestant Ethic and the*

Spirit of Capitalism, Weber ([c1904–5] 1930), observed that capitalism originated and developed in the West contemporaneously with the Protestant Reformation—the emergence of various religious groups who expressed dissent against the beliefs and other aspects of Roman Catholicism. In Weber's view, Protestant doctrines expressed values that provided the necessary motivational support for the principal require-ments of modern capitalism, namely, self-interest, individualism, aus-terity, and a shared perception of work as a moral responsibility rather than simply as a means of subsistence. Thus, as Tawney observes in his introduction to the English translation of Weber's work (Weber [c1904–5] 1930, 2), Calvinism, one of the dissenting sects, taught that economic self-interest, far from being "a natural frailty" as it had been defined, was a moral duty. A moral person worked, idlers were immoral. In Tawney's words, "capitalism was the social counterpart of Calvinist theology" (Weber [c1904–5] 1930, 2). Protestants were enjoined to live austerely and to not waste their wealth on ostentatious life styles, but the acquisition of wealth was not seen as a barrier to sal-vation. Under Protestantism, no one, priest or otherwise, could mediate between God and a parishioner. In this way, Protestantism interpreted moral responsibility and salvation as a matter between God and the individual. Hence, individualism emerged as a value.[7]

On the assumption that humans act collectively to realize their val-ues, Weber held that shared values serve as important means of social control and motivation, especially when they are embedded in systems of religious belief. Thus, he argued that Protestantism was an important source of control and motivation in those societies where capitalism was developing. Where work was perceived as a moral responsibility, people would be motivated to work to the highest level of their abilities and to accept the discipline required by capitalistic institutions. Similarly, the moral legitimation of economic self-interest, constrained by the moral prescription to live austerely, would create wealth, and through savings, capital. The value placed on individualism would weaken compliance with kinship and community obligations and so would support the free movement of labour and capital essential to the development and per-sistence of capitalism. Overall, Weber linked Christianity to rationality. Thus, he describes the Roman Catholic Church as "a uniformly rational organization" ([1922] 1963, 181).

Ideal Type Analysis and Reality

Weber's description of the bureaucracy and his claims for its efficiency may strike readers as unreal. In popular opinion, bureaucracies are perceived as the opposite of an efficient form of organization. Bureau-cracies are associated with "red tape," with irritating, time-consuming procedures that appear to divert concern from the applicant's problem, and with tedious forms to be completed. Bureaucracies are perceived as being staffed with a horde of officials who pass the applicant from one to the next without providing the needed service. Bureaucracies are thought to delay making and communicating decisions and possibly to be obstructive in that respect.

Bureaucratic rigidity can be illustrated by a recent case (*The Globe and Mail* 1992) where a suspension order prevented a five-year-old boy from being admitted to kindergarten. The order was issued because the boy failed to comply with an Ontario government regulation requiring a child to be vaccinated against selected infectious diseases on or after its first birthday. The boy had been vaccinated about six hours before his first birthday.

Local health officials informed the parents of three options required to lift the suspension:

1. have the child immunized again;

2. allow blood tests to see if the child had developed the necessary antibodies; or

3. sign a letter agreeing that he would be suspended if anyone attending his school came down with the diseases covered by immunization.

When the parents rejected all of these options—the child's physician apparently advised his mother that there were no medical reasons to support a second immunization—the regional medical officer of health stated that he had no choice but to issue the suspension order. Officials informed the parents of their right to appeal but observed that, on the basis of past cases, a successful appeal was unlikely.

While there can be no denying that these perceptions of bureaucratic inefficiencies can be accurate in relation to specific bureaucratic organizations, it is important to understand that Weber was not attempting to describe how actual bureaucracies worked, but rather to describe the perfect or ideal bureaucracy.

In Weber's terminology, he was constructing an **ideal type**—a model of bureaucracy. Although actual bureaucracies would rarely, if ever, match the model exactly, he believed that a description of the "perfect" bureaucracy would help in the understanding of this form of organization. It may be easy to identify concrete organizations where, for example, males are preferred over females regardless of technical competence, where superiors or subordinates overstep their jurisdictions, where managers or supervisors may "play favorites," or where rules are often breached. However, Weber's analysis implies that focusing on these deviations from the ideal bureaucracy is less useful than trying to understand the bureaucracy as it *should* be.

Stated otherwise, Weber's analysis implies that efficiency would be maximized if all the features of the bureaucracy that he describes were present in an actual organization. If decisions, commands, and instructions adhered precisely to hierarchical requirements; if employment, promotion, and other rewards were allocated on the basis of technical competence; if role definitions were defined properly and adhered to strictly; if relationships were impersonal; and if the rules were formulated on the basis of rationality, efficiency would be maximized. To the extent that specific organizations depart from Weber's ideals in any of these features, there will be a loss of efficiency.

Assuming the validity of Weber's argument concerning the relations between bureaucratic features and efficiency, Weber's model provides a standard for assessing the relative efficiency of bureaucratic organizations. For example, an analyst using Weber's model should be able to predict the efficiency of organizations by ranking them according to how much each organization deviates from the model.

Critical Comments and Further Developments

The Weberian model has had a tremendous impact on the sociology of organizations, and its underlying emphasis on rationality continues to be important in contemporary analysis.[8] Nonetheless, the model has its limitations. At the very least, it is important to ask if Weber's assessment of the bureaucracy as the most efficient form of organization is valid and whether the model can be applied to all organizations.

As observed in the previous section, there are sufficient examples of bureaucratic inefficiency to suggest that the bureaucracy may not be the most efficient type of organization. At the very least, such examples demonstrate that it is reasonable to expect varying efficiency among bureaucracies. However, without careful study of these organizations to assess the extent to which they conform to the Weberian model, it is difficult to say whether any inefficiency is attributable to bureaucracies in general or to deviations from the features Weber identified.

Weber's claim, however, is strongly supported by the fact that most organizations conform in considerable degree to the Weberian model. Most organizations, public and private, have hierarchical authority structures and a complex division of labour, require technical competence, and use rules to regulate employee action. Choice or acceptance of these features, especially in the case of private enterprise organizations whose survival requires that revenues exceed costs, testifies to the efficiency of the bureaucratic model. Certainly, the prevailing view of organizations has been that they should be structured on the basis of rationality.[9]

Structuring an organization rationally means that those responsible for determining organizational structure must accept, and may have good reason to do so, that a hierarchical structure is more likely to produce rational decisions and judgments and better control than any other structure of authority. Similarly, it means that the reduction of large tasks to their smallest subset is preferable to enlarging or expanding task sets and that the person with relevant skills for the job, or a capacity to learn them, will perform more efficiently than one lacking such skills or aptitudes. Again, emotional involvement is better discouraged than encouraged, and the development of rules and of an attitude of respect for the rules are more likely to promote efficiency than a deliberate downplaying of rules.

Efficiency and the Division of Labour

Despite widespread acceptance of the bureaucratic model as the preferred form of organizational structure, the hypotheses implied by Weber's arguments may not be supported by experience. For example, although a division of labour may contribute to efficiency—as a result of practice in the performance of tasks and of facilitating the training and the replacement of workers—it is reasonable to ask if there are limits to the division of tasks. To ask, in other words, if efficiency continues to increase when work is divided into smaller and smaller tasks. It is not unreasonable to suggest that at some point the consequences of increasing differentiation, in the form of communication difficulties, coordination requirements, and loss of interest by participants, may lead to a loss of efficiency or effectiveness. These consequences may fuel the proposals of those who promote a reversal of the division of labour and argue for the enlargement of the number of tasks included in an occupation and for the rotation of members of a workforce through the various tasks of an operation (see Chapter Five). Moreover, as any division between human beings is a potential basis of conflict, the division of labour, necessary as it may be, may generate conflict within the organization—not only between managers and workers but between members of different structural units, such as production and sales departments, and between occupational groupings, such as skilled and unskilled workers. This will be further discussed in Chapter Seven.

Communication Problems

Distortions in information can occur in a hierarchical communication system, the counterpart of hierarchical authority, when human beings are the communication links. Despite the assumption that managers require full information about operations under their control in order to make proper decisions, it is well known that information transmitted upward is, where possible, selective. Subordinates tend to report the good news rather than the bad.[10] Also, insofar as authority is concerned, situational conditions may sometimes make it inexpedient to adhere strictly to hierarchical structure. A need for immediate decisions may mean that not all the required points of the authority line can be consulted.

Compliance with Rules

Although rules are clearly a feature of bureaucratic organizations, as witnessed by the prevalence of company manuals and rules of procedure, they are rarely completely enforced and are invariably broken. Rules may be ignored in certain circumstances, discussed below, without fear of punishment. While impersonality may be important in many organizations insofar as favouritism is discouraged, current thinking (discussed in Chapter Seven) argues for the importance of strong, positive emotional ties between co-workers or co-participants in organizations. Indeed, of the features Weber describes as essential for the bureaucratic model, only technical competence appears to escape criticism.

Weber's emphasis on rules and on the structure and basis of authority may be seen in more general terms as a concern with **compliance**. This represents an interest in the need for ensuring that organization members comply with the rules and the commands of superiors. However, Weber gave greater prominence to **control**, one aspect of compliance, than to the other, **motivation**.

Still, he did not entirely neglect motivation. He identified monetary payments in the form of salaries, and later, of pensions, as the appropriate means of compensation for bureaucratic officials, in contrast to payments in kind. In addition, he observed that officials enjoyed relatively high social esteem, tenure, and an expectation of regular advancement. Weber appears to believe that these rewards operate effectively as motivators, and possibly also, on the basis of his discussion of rational-legal authority, that the existence of a rule guaranteed compliance with it.[11] However, complete compliance with rules is rarely, if ever, achieved, even if rewards are satisfactory. Although the agents that Blau ([1955] 1963, 121–39) studied appeared to be satisfied with the federal agency and to express loyalty to it, a rule prohibiting consultation among agents was widely ignored.

It must be concluded that Weber's discussion of motivation is seriously limited. Indeed, the relationship between rewards and compliance with rules and norms, may be more complex than Weber assumed. For example, it is not enough to establish a "presumed" incentive. If it is to be effective as a motivator, an incentive must be perceived or experienced as rewarding or valued by the recipient. It has been observed that there are class differences in the perception and response to material rewards, such as pay incentives and promotion opportunities (see, for example, Whyte 1955; Davis 1946). Such differences can mean that incentives perceived as rewarding by members of one class, managers for example, may not be perceived as such by those of another class, such as non-managerial employees. Such observations provide support for the view that the perception of rewards is socially defined and not unique to an individual.

THE APPLICATION OF WEBER'S MODEL

During the initial development of the sociology of organizations, Weber's model was accepted as the basic model of organization in modern societies. In effect, the words "bureaucracy" and "organization" were regarded as synonymous. In empirical research the tendency was to analyze organizations in terms of Weberian categories and to describe them by the amount of deviation from the Weberian model. This Weberian orthodoxy gave way in the 1950s when separate studies of organizations were undertaken by Peter Blau, Alvin Gouldner, and Philip Selznick, three students of Robert Merton. In studies of two government agencies, (Blau [1955] 1963), and of a gypsum mine and wallboard plant (Gouldner [1954] 1964), each researcher began with Weber's model but ended by modifying the model on the basis of the observed evidence. Although Selznick did not adopt Weber's model for his research on the Tennessee Valley Authority (Selznick [1949] 1966), his work was also influential in modifying the influence of the Weberian model on the study of organizations.

Gouldner: Bureaucratization

Gouldner's research was based on firsthand evidence obtained by observation and interviews in a plant whose main operations were mining gypsum and manufacturing wallboard. The head office of the company that owned the plant was dissatisfied, in particular, with wallboard productivity and instructed a newly appointed superintendent to increase efficiency of operations.[12] As a result, Gouldner had the opportunity to observe an organization that was undergoing considerable rationalization in the form of the introduction or the reestablishment of various operational rules and greater formality or impersonality in relationships between superiors and subordinates in the plant.

Given this situation, it is not surprising that Gouldner focused on **bureaucratization** and formulated several generalizations about the conditions that might facilitate or inhibit this process or that might determine different bureaucratic outcomes.[13] Stated generally, he concluded that bureaucratization occurred when tensions developed among members of an organization. On the basis of the observed actions of the new superintendent, Gouldner argued that a person who occupies the role of successor ([1954], 1964, part 2), and who is faced with tensions in his [or her] new position, will respond with close supervision of staff and employees, including increased paperwork, with the development and enforcement of rules, and with an emphasis on status and hierarchy. The tensions in this case were generated by head office, which expected increased efficiency, by the existing staff who resented the replacements the superintendent made and the shift away from informality and permissiveness toward formality and strict enforcement of rules, and by worker resistance to productivity pressures. On the basis of this analysis, Gouldner suggested that anyone who succeeds another in an office of authority, or in his words, occupies the role of successor, faces similar tensions and will respond in a similar fashion.[14]

The other main thrust of Gouldner's analysis focused on organizational rules. In fact, he assumed that the rules are the central feature of bureaucracy and apparently assumed that an analysis of the rules is sufficient to provide understanding of an organization. Focusing on the rules, then, he argued that close supervision—strict overseeing of work and enforcement of the operational rules regulating work—is a management's characteristic response to low productivity because it perceives the cause to be low motivation. However, because workers are resistant to close supervision, rules are developed to respond to both managerial and worker tensions.

In his analysis of the functions of rules ([1954] 1964, chap. 9), Gouldner attempted to show how these functions may increase or reduce tensions between management and workers. This led him to an extended analysis of differentiation of rules and the identification of five factors that account for differences among rules ([1954] 1964, chaps. 10–12). Thus, assuming the interaction is between two parties—superiors and subordinates—rules differ:

- in terms of origin: are they initiated by one party or are they negotiated by all affected parties?
- in terms of legitimation: which party's values legitimate the rules?
- in terms of value violation: which party's values are violated by the rules?
- in terms of responses to deviations from the rules: what are the standard explanations for deviations?

- in terms of status effects: what are the consequences for the statuses of the interacting parties?

Since Gouldner held that the rules stand for the bureaucracy, he concluded that as there are differences among rules, there are differences in bureaucracies. He argued, therefore, contrary to Weber who conceived of one bureaucratic form or model, that *three* types of bureaucracy can be identified. He described the three models in terms of the five factors, but they can be described briefly in terms of variations in the origins of the rules:

- **mock bureaucracy**, in which rules are imposed by external forces on both managers and workers;

- **representative bureaucracy**, in which the rules are jointly negotiated by managers and workers; and

- **punishment-centred bureaucracy**, in which either managers or workers impose rules on each other.

The value of Gouldner's analysis for the sociology of organizations lies both in its emphasis on bureaucratization as a process rather than as a static form and on the idea of the variability of organizational structure. His analysis contains the hint that organizational efficiency may depend on the relation between its structure, the type of operation, and its environment (see Gouldner [1954] 1964, part 3).[15]

Blau: Structure and Function

Peter Blau conducted his research in two government agencies, a state employment agency and a federal regulatory agency (Blau [1953] 1963). As these two government organizations could be expected to be organized bureaucratically, Blau approached his analysis with Weber's model. Like Gouldner, he found it necessary to modify Weber's perspective to make sense of his observations.

In the state employment agency, Blau found evidence of a rational perspective: the rules and procedures taught to interviewers were consistent with the agency's goals of finding jobs that would make the best use of clients' skills and of providing an efficient service to employers needing workers. In practice, however, he found that many of the rules and procedures were either distorted or ignored. Non-compliance resulted mainly from competition among the interviewers to achieve high rates of placement, stimulated to a considerable extent by supervisory procedures for measuring performance.[16] In this respect it is important to note that although self-interest may have motivated non-compliance, it appears to be the rules for reporting on performance, which were essentially intended as controls, that allowed self-interest to operate.

In the study of the federal regulatory agency, Blau continued his interest in compliance with rules but also showed strong interest in the **status structure** of the employees and in the evidence of **social solidarity**, or as he termed it, **social cohesion**.[17] He reported that although the agents complied with some of the agency rules, they also transgressed others, including those which were considered to be important rules. For example, although the agency had a rule requiring that an agent needing help on a case should seek help only from the agency supervisor, the agents freely consulted among themselves. In Blau's view, this was not a result of lax supervision but of the recognition by the supervisor and the agents that consultation among the agents increased efficiency of the agency's performance.

As Blau held that any rule or structural element has both positive and negative consequences, he proposed that one element will be replaced by another initially informal element as negative consequences begin to outweigh the positive.[18] Contrary to Weber, whose model did not allow for change, Blau characterized bureaucracies as continually undergoing change. Blau's emphasis on status and cohesion are also important additions to the analysis of the bureaucracy. He observed that the consultation process among agents provided a basis for establishing and maintaining the status structure of the agents.[19] Systematic observation revealed that there were differences in the extent of consultation sought and given and that status in the group was associated with each agent's performance in giving and seeking help. In contrast to a status structure that is essentially divisive, Blau observed that actions that had the effect of developing and maintaining cohesion were also prominent among the agents.

As well as helping each other through consultation, the agents also provided sympathetic audiences for those returning from very stressful inspections and dealings with owners of firms or their representatives. Cohesion was also developed and maintained through social activities during the working day, such as conversing on non-work-related topics and lunching together. It is Blau's position that the cohesiveness of the agents was vital as a means of stress reduction and, therefore, was important to the agency's functioning.

As well as regarding both the status structure, in both its formal and informal aspects, and social cohesion as important elements in agency functioning, Blau argued that there is a dynamic relation between them. The status structure, as an instrument for distributing positive and negative sanctions, and cohesion, as a cushion against stress, have important consequences for motivation. However, both have an optimum level for performing this function. The status structure can promote conflict and reduce cohesion under some conditions, as when it becomes too rigid or elaborate. Similarly, as cohesion tends to reduce status differences, too much cohesion can weaken the status structure. Although Blau did not provide a general formulation for the relations between status and cohesion, he described a situation where a balance appears to have been achieved.

Although Blau started his research with a Weberian perspective and maintained that perspective in his analysis—the rules, the authority structure, and impersonality are prominent concepts—he enriched the perspective by focusing on processes that developed in the interaction of the members of the organizations he studied. Thus, the development and substitution of new rules, the informal status structure, and the process of social cohesion all respond to realities not captured by Weber's model.

Selznick: Another View of Bureaucracy

Although Selznick ([1949] 1966), like Blau and Gouldner, accepted Weber's emphasis on values as an important influence on human action, he did not use Weber's model in his analysis of the Tennessee Valley Authority (TVA), a large agency established by the United States federal government to devise and implement a plan for the development of the Tennessee River Basin.[20] Indeed, Selznick's work derived from that of Robert Michels, a contemporary of Weber, and focused on the barriers to the implementation of TVA's policy of local participation in the development and implementation of its plans.

Selznick's research, like that of Blau and Gouldner, lessened the influence of the Weberian model on the study of organizations. Selznick showed that understanding bureaucracy involves more than studying the relationship of the internal structure of an organization to its objectives—it involves the relations of the internal parts to each other and the relations of the organization to its environment, including other organizations. Thus, he showed that decisions in organizations are not necessarily the outcome of rational consideration but result from the resolution of struggles between powerful interests inside and outside the organization.

Selznick's basic assumption that "[a]ll formal organizations are molded by forces tangential to their rationally ordered structures and goals" led him to conclude that "informal" structures will develop as a means of defence against such forces (Selznick [1949] 1966, 251). It appears that the state of an organization at any one time is determined by the state of the struggle between the tangential forces and the adaptive mechanisms the organizations have evolved.

AN ASSESSMENT OF THE RATIONAL PERSPECTIVE

The work of Blau, Gouldner, and Selznick showed that a fuller under-standing of organizations could not be achieved through a mechanical application of the Weberian model. Their field research made it clear that Weber's model did not sufficiently capture those aspects of reality necessary for an understanding of what goes on in organizations. Blau and Selznick provided evidence to show that organizations tend to change in the face of internal and external conditions rather than to persist as stable structures. Gouldner advanced the related idea that the structure of organizations is variable. Moreover, as he studied an organi-zation undergoing changes aimed at rationalization, Gouldner sug-gested that bureaucratic features were not necessarily present in all organizations but could appear under certain conditions. Indeed, Gouldner conceived of his research as a study of the conditions that facilitated or hindered the bureaucratization of an organization. All of these sociologists accepted the view, introduced by Elton Mayo and dis-cussed at length in Chapter Three, that participants in organizations develop informal structures that may be supportive or destructive of for-mal structure.

Nonetheless, the Weberian model remains an important contribu-tion to the analysis of organizations. It is the basis of an important per-spective on organizations, identified by Scott (1992, chap. 3) as the **rational perspective**, that views organizations as structures wherein decisions are made on the basis of rationality and wherein what takes place is seen as the outcome of rationally based actions.

There can be no doubt that rationality accurately describes and explains some organizational activity. This reality is recognized by the rational perspective in such current concepts as **complexity**, which refers to the division of labour; **centrality**, which refers to the distribu-tion of authority; and **formalization**, which refers to the use of written procedures, rules, and the like (see, for example, Hall 1982, chaps. 4–6). It is also recognized in research by Burns and Stalker (1961) on elec-tronic manufacturing firms in Great Britain that revealed two strikingly different forms of organization—one that closely resembled Weber's model, which they labelled **mechanistic**, and another, its opposite, which they labelled **organic**. On the basis of these findings, Burns and Stalker suggested that analysis might be improved if organizational fea-tures were regarded as forming dimensions or continua. The extremes of these dimensions were the "perfect" mechanistic and organic models, and an actual organization could be described in terms of where its features, such as the division of labour or its characteristic flow of interaction, were located on each dimension. This research (more fully discussed in Chapter Five) and the work of Blau, Gouldner, and Selznick shows that neither Weber's model nor the rational perspective is enough to capture organizational realities completely. Consequently, other perspectives have emerged to explain the inner workings of organizations.

SUMMARY

The model of bureaucracy formulated by Max Weber is the core of the rational perspective. Weber identified the essential features of bureaucracy—its basis in rational-legal authority, its hierarchical structure, its emphasis on technical competence being the primary criterion for membership or employment, its complex division of labour, and its emphasis on rules. In the rational perspective, actions, such as decisions, rule-making, and the division of tasks, are seen as logically derived from organizational objectives. Although later perspectives identified critical features that were ignored in the rational perspective, the main elements of the rational model are persistently found in most organizations.

Weber's model describes the perfect bureaucracy. It can be used to identify the extent to which existing organizations are bureaucratic and to examine the possible consequences of departures from the model. However, Weber's model is not above criticism. His limited treatment of motivation, his assumption that efficiency is a necessary consequence of the complexity of the division of labour, and the problems of communication arising in hierarchical structures are shortcomings of the model. The necessity of modifying Weber's model has been shown by those using it to study organizations.

Even so, the rational perspective continues to be relevant to the study of organizations. Sociological research on organizations has documented the widespread implementation of bureaucratic features in organizations. Despite differences in type, activities, and whether members are volunteers or paid, bureaucratic features are found in most organizations. In some organizations, these bureaucratic features are implemented when the organization is established and in other organizations they emerge in the course of time. Despite sustained criticism of bureaucracy from various quarters, hierarchical authority, rules, the routinization of tasks and procedures, and the emphasis on technical competence and rationality as a basis for exercising authority are commonly found in modern organizations—even those that are regarded as alternatives to bureaucracy. Although many organizational actions may not be rational, judged in relation to manifest organizational objectives, it would be a grave departure from reality to believe that all, or even most, organizational actions are irrational. In the face of such observations it is very useful for analysts to be able to call on a perspective that provides a coherent picture of the model bureaucracy.

EΠDΠOTES

1   Because Weber made contributions to economics and political science as well as to sociology, it is a debatable point whether he should be exclusively described as a sociologist. Nonetheless, he is widely regarded as a founder of the discipline of sociology. As references to his work in this chapter are to English translations published after his death, it should be noted that his analysis of the bureaucracy was written between 1914 and his death in 1920.

2   Weber's analysis of the bureaucracy was confined to the administrative unit, but later scholars used the term to refer to the entire organization.

3   The concept of the division of labour, introduced by Adam Smith (1884), has been appropriated by sociology. The classic work is by Emile Durkheim ([1893] 1933), a French sociologist, contemporary with Weber.

4   There is considerable variation across societies in definitions of the appropriate family members to participate in emotional exchanges as well as in the forms emotional expression should take. Strong emotional commitment and expression appear, however, to be a universal characteristic of family and kin relationships.

5   Although compliance may vary with the importance of a rule, compliance generally appears to be high (Allport 1934).

6   Weber undertook a study of the major religious systems, including ancient Judaism, the religions of China—Confucianism and Taoism—and the religions of India—Buddhism and Hinduism. His death left uncompleted his plan to publish analyses of other religions, including Islam, early Christianity, and medieval Catholicism (Weber [1922] 1963).

7   In some texts the emphasis on individualism was extreme, as Weber ([c1904–5] 1930, 107) showed in his analysis of John Bunyan's *Pilgrim's Progress*.

8   See Perrow (1986, chap. 1) for a strong defence of bureaucracy and of Weber's model.

9   Business leaders were more likely to have been influenced by the rationality of Frederick W. Taylor, the proponent of **scientific management**, than by Max Weber. Taylor (1947) argued that the most efficient way to perform organizational tasks could be identified by objective observation of the performance of workers and, by deduction, relating the purpose of the task to organizational objectives. He also believed that a complex division of labour and technical competence were essential features of efficient organization. Business leaders likely adopted hierarchy and the emphasis on rules from military organizations.

10 See Downs (1967, chap. 10) for a discussion of information distortion in organizations generated by self-interest and other reasons.

[11] In his discussion of basic sociological concepts, Weber refers to "ultimate ends or values toward which experience shows that human action may be oriented" ([c1920] 1978, 5). Weber accepted that material interests as well as values determine human action but rejected Marx's view that human action was determined primarily by material interests.

[12] The new superintendant was appointed on the death of another man whose managerial style had been easy-going and informal.

[13] As Gouldner's observations were based on one case, or two at the most if the mining and the manufacturing operations are treated as two different organizational units, he had limited scope for generalization. It is valid, however, to formulate hypotheses for further testing on the basis of case history findings.

[14] This short summation of an extended argument sacrifices the richness of the observations and the theoretical discussion presented in Gouldner's book.

[15] This assertion is not intended to imply that there are no problems in Gouldner's analysis and generalizations, but a critical review of his research is not relevant to the purpose of this book.

[16] Blau found differences in competitiveness between two sections of interviewers. He attributes the lower competitiveness, yet higher productivity, of one section mainly to its interviewers' shared conception of themselves as professionals and their commitment to professional standards that are characterized by an ethical duty to their clients—employers seeking workers and workers seeking jobs.

[17] Both these concepts were evident but less prominent in the analysis of the state employment agency.

[18] Blau, Gouldner, and Selznick all adopted a structural-functional perspective in their analyses. Blau, for example, uses the terms **functional** and **dysfunctional** rather than **positive** and **negative**.

[19] A formal status structure was established by agency rules and job categories. Although the informal status structure, to which Blau refers, was not necessarily inconsistent with the formal one, it is decided by the interaction and the shared values of the agents.

[20] Selznick's only reference to Weber is in a footnote (Selznick [1949] 1966, 210) and is not directly related to the bureaucratic model.

CHAPTER 3

THE HUMAN RELATIONS PERSPECTIVE

Although some researchers, such as those discussed in the previous chapter, started with Weber's model and discovered that it had to be radically modified, other researchers, working from what came to be known as the **human relations perspective**, found that the Weberian model failed to capture important aspects of organizations. This perspective, in contrast to Weber's structural emphasis, placed its emphasis on aspects of human relationships, such as leadership, informal organization, individual satisfaction, group satisfaction or morale, and group cohesion. From the human relations perspective, these factors are considered critical determinants of organizational performance.

The components of a theoretical perspective or framework can be identified in its research. In this chapter the ground-breaking Western Electric studies and some examples of later research are examined to identify the main components of the human relations perspective. The discussion is followed by a critique of this perspective and a discussion of some issues arising from the design of research undertaken within it.

THE WESTERN ELECTRIC RESEARCH

The story begins with the work of Elton Mayo, an industrial psychologist and faculty member of the Harvard Business School. Mayo's interest was in the problems of industrial societies (Mayo 1933, 1945) and, in particular, the conflicts that arose between factory workers and their managers and owners. Through his own research and his involvement in the Western Electric research, he became an influential proponent of the human relations perspective on organizations.

In 1924 a major manufacturer of telephone equipment, the Western Electric Company, began conducting research on productivity. Although it was well known that productivity varied according to the time of day and the day of the week and also between individual workers, it was not known why such variability occurred. Western Electric's research was directed toward finding an answer to this question. The end result marked an important step in the development of the sociology of organizations, for although a sociological perspective did not inform the investigation initially, it became important as the research progressed and as work guided by other perspectives failed to provide satisfactory explanations for systematic variations in productivity. As it turned out, the course of this research fell into three stages, each marked by different assumptions about the kinds of conditions that influenced productivity. These assumed conditions can be characterized, in turn, as **physical**, **physiological-psychological**, and **sociological**. Each assumption held a distinctive conception of the worker:

- the physical assumed the worker to be an object acted on by environmental forces;
- the physiological-psychological assumed that the worker's actions were determined by personal physiological and psychological characteristics; and
- the sociological assumed the worker to be a social being whose actions are determined in relations with others.

The Illumination Studies

At its inception, the research on productivity at Western Electric was conducted for a period of two and a half years by a group, consisting mainly of engineers, drawn from company managers and from representatives of the National Research Council of the National Academy of Sciences.[1] This group adopted the perspective that productivity variations were determined by the physical aspects of the manufacturing environment. Specifically, the variations in relay-assembling productivity were hypothesized to result from variations in levels of illumination.[2] This hypothesis was tested by systematically varying the lighting in three different departments. The researchers found, however, that the relationship between lighting levels and productivity was essentially random.

The Relay Assembly Test Room Experiments

At the next stage, the researchers, again mainly company managers but with consultants from the Harvard Business School and from the Massachusetts Institute of Technology, took a different position, hypothesizing that variation in productivity was the result of fatigue and monotony. The emphasis was thus transferred from the physical environment to the individual worker. Instead of perceiving workers as objects mechanically reacting to physical aspects of the environment, workers were now perceived as sentient beings with a capacity, at least, for getting tired—a physical and, possibly, psychological condition—and for being bored—mainly a psychological condition—by the routine of assembly work.

For this stage, six women operators were moved from the Relay Assembly Department to what was named the Relay Assembly Test Room. Two of them, known to be friendly with each other, were asked to participate in the experiment and to choose four others to join them. All six presumably met the researchers criteria that participants be "thoroughly experienced in relay assembly work" and be "willing and cooperative" insofar as the research was concerned (Roethlisberger and Dickson [1939] 1947, 21). Five of the women worked as assemblers and the sixth as a layout operator. For slightly more than two years they worked in the Test Room at their regular tasks but in time periods that were varied by introducing rest periods and changing the length of the working day and week. A researcher served as an observer in the Test Room throughout the period.

On the assumption that fatigue and monotony determined productivity levels, it was expected that production would be higher in periods when combinations of rest periods and shorter overall working days or weeks produced shorter working times. The results were strikingly different from what was expected: productivity rose throughout the entire research period. Even when working hours reverted to those in effect in the regular department—no rest periods and a 48-hour week—productivity levels, although lower than those achieved under the experimental conditions, were higher than the levels attained by the workers before transfer to the Test Room.[3] Essentially, the Test Room experiment failed to show that either fatigue or monotony accounted for variations in productivity. The researchers, however, did suggest various reasons for the results they obtained. For example, it was discovered that the women believed that they had been selected for the study because they were high producers, and it was suggested that they worked hard to maintain their reputations.[4] That is, the very fact of being selected for the research was identified as a possible determinant of the persistent rise in productivity.[5] Other suggested explanations were based on the observed actions of the women while at work.[6] For example, as one of the women was observed to give direction to the others, informal leadership was identified as a possible determinant. The fact that the women were asked for their opinions when changes in working-times were considered suggested that participation in decision-making was a possible factor. As observation revealed that the women, who had not known each other well at the outset of the study, developed commitments to each other in and out of the work setting, social cohesion was also suggested as a factor. These suggested reasons for the rise in productivity—leadership, participation in decision-making, and social cohesion—were, as shall be seen, to become key concepts of the human relations perspective on organizations.

Although the Western Electric management was responsible for the design of the Relay Assembly Test Room experiments and Mayo was not directly involved until Period 10 of the research, about a year after it began, it is very likely that he was involved much earlier through his Harvard Business School colleagues, Felix Roethlisberger and T. North Whitehead.[7] In his book on the Relay Assembly Test Room, Whitehead (1938, 1: xi) writes: "A few members of the Harvard School of Business Administration, led by Professor Elton Mayo, have been continuously interested in the Western Electric Studies since their inception, and much of their work has been connected with observation and consideration of these researches," and goes on to state that "many of the ideas have been developed in common between us or as an immediate result of Professor Mayo's teaching and leadership."

The Bank Wiring Observation Room

In this final stage of the Western Electric research, the sociological aspects of the workplace were recognized in a study established to give explicit attention to the social relationships of the workers. The research site, known as the Bank Wiring Observation Room, involved fourteen male employees whose task was to wire equipment for installation in central switchboards.[8] In contrast to the Relay Assembly Test Room there was a slight division of labour in that workers performed different tasks depending on whether they were wiremen, soldermen, or inspectors. No experimentation or planned variability in operations was attempted, but the observer was instructed to record instances of social interaction between workers, especially the frequency and contents of their contacts. Western Electric was interested in the consequences of a group payment incentive for productivity. As payment was based on the production of the entire group, it was expected that each worker would have a vested interest in maintaining the productivity of his fellow workers as well as his own.[9] Observation showed, however, that the workers held a shared concept of a fair day's work that was approximately 10 percent lower than company expectations, and that each worker "was restricting his output" (Roethlisberger and Dickson [1939] 1947, 445). Compliance with the workers' productivity level was maintained by various subtle and not-so-subtle forms of social control, such as directing sarcastic comments or a distinctive form of physical aggression toward any worker perceived to be overproducing.[10] Only one worker produced, on average, more than the shared definition of a fair day's work allowed. Thus, although only three or four workers complied fairly closely with this shared definition, it did appear to be effective in setting a ceiling on production.[11] In interpreting this behaviour, it was held that this shared idea about productivity served as a norm or rule for the workers just as the shared norms of other groups, whether they be religious, political, or family, serve to control the actions of members. The workers complied with the rule because it served as a symbol of the group, just as the rules of a religious group symbolize its religious beliefs. To fail to comply with or to transgress the rule is to deny the group and to suffer any or all of the consequences this may entail. In the Bank Wiring Observation Room, persistent transgression of the productivity norm brought isolation, that is, ejection from the group.

Observation revealed that the Bank Wiring Observation Room workers were, both in terms of pattern and content of social interaction, divided into sub-groups and that there were clear differences in productivity between the two. These differences were interpreted in terms of a sociological concept—**status** (Roethlisberger and Dickson [1939] 1947, 517–22). Group A held itself to be superior in various ways to members of Group B. The latter accepted the lower status but resented it. In consequence, it was argued they held productivity down as a means of expressing their resentment and as a way of evening the score with members of Group A.[12]

Implications of the Research

The Western Electric research was important to the study of organizations because the findings and analysis resulting from the Relay Assembly Test Room, the Bank Wiring Observation Room, and the company's interviewing and counselling program (Roethlisberger and Dickson [1939] 1947, parts 2 and 3) emphasized that aspects of organizations that Weber had ignored were critical. These aspects provided the basis of the human relations conceptual framework for a considerable period of time. This framework implied that much of what takes place in organizations is determined by the social interaction of employees, their level of consensus with respect to employee-generated rules, their level of cohesion, the extent of informal leadership, and their level of individual and group satisfaction, the latter being known as *morale*. The human relations perspective did not ignore the formal aspects of organizations, but the research subsequent to the Western Electric studies certainly gave more prominence to the concepts listed above than to those put forward by Weber.

FURTHER HUMAN RELATIONS RESEARCH

Mayo and Colleagues

The human relations emphasis was clear in research undertaken in the 1940s and 1950s. For example, in a study of differences in labour turnover in three airplane factories, Mayo and Lombard concluded that an increase in management's attention to the "human needs" of their employees and the development of teams among employees "diminished absenteeism and labour turnover" and improved "the quality and quantity of work" (1944, 27). Although "human needs" are not defined, the term appears to refer to employees' concerns and dissatisfactions in the work situation and in their off-work activities. The development of teams is described as "spontaneous," reminiscent of the social relationships that formed in the Relay Assembly Test Room and Bank Wiring Observation Room, and according to Mayo, this development is a result of management action in responding to employee's "human needs." Although teams tend to develop spontaneously, Mayo argued that this occurs when management fosters "a climate of the technical and operating aspects of organizations such that groups can grow" (Mayo and Lombard, 1944, 23). Moreover, it is possible for management, through appropriate action, to promote the formation of teams. Also, although the Relay Assembly Test Room and Bank Wiring Observation Room research revealed that teams or "informal groups" of employees can either facilitate or hinder the realization of management's objectives, Mayo argued that the formation of teams tends to benefit the organization. A similar approach was taken by Fox and Scott, colleagues of Mayo, in a study of absenteeism in the casting departments of three metal industry firms (Fox and Scott 1943). They argued that the lower absenteeism in one of the companies could be explained by differences in its internal organization. The features of this company's internal organization that Fox and Scott perceived as supportive of the formation of informal relationships and cohesion among the workers were:

- procedures that rewarded, rather than penalized, established workers who helped new workers to learn about and to adjust to the work situation;

- a shift rotation scheme that gave the workers experience with different supervisors; and

- a payment scheme that was based on the productivity of all shifts and that supported cooperation rather than competition among shifts.

Fox and Scott also reported (1943, 15, 19) that although shop discipline was strict, management placed strong emphasis on "the systematic handling of human relationships on the job." In keeping with this perspective, they reported that working conditions were better in the shop with the lowest absenteeism than in the other two shops.

Although the Relay Assembly Test Room was quasi-experimental in design, the Bank Wiring Observation Room study and the research that Mayo and his colleagues pursued later tended to be in the field observation tradition. Although statistical data relating to productivity or absenteeism were included in their analyses, data for independent variables were collected largely by interview and observation. In contrast, researchers following the human relations perspective in the 1950s tended to adopt a more structured approach to data collection while retaining the same interest in authority and leadership, satisfaction and morale, and cohesion.

The Michigan Group

A program of research directed by Robert Kahn and Daniel Katz of the Survey Research Center, University of Michigan ([1953] 1960), illustrates this stage of human-relations oriented research. Kahn and Katz collected questionnaire data in an investigation of supervision, morale, and productivity from three firms representing, respectively, heavy industry, light manufacturing, and financial services. In general, they found that supervisors whose roles were more differentiated from their subordinates, who were worker-oriented, and who supervised loosely tended to be found in work units characterized by higher productivity and higher morale.[13] Supervisors whose roles were less differentiated from their subordinates' roles, who emphasized productivity, and who supervised closely tended to be found in work units characterized by lower productivity and lower morale.

These findings stimulated much interest and further research by adherents of the human relations perspective who explored various aspects of supervision. For example, Argyle and his colleagues (1957;

1958), in research undertaken in a number of firms in Great Britain, described five dimensions of supervisory behaviour:[14]

- **general versus close supervision**—the extent to which subordinates were free to work "in their own way" or the extent to which they were given detailed instructions and watched over as they performed their tasks;
- **low versus high pressure** for productivity;
- **employee-centred versus work-centred**—the tendency for supervisors to be helpful and supportive of subordinates or aloof, impersonal, and production-oriented;
- **democratic versus autocratic style** of exercising authority—the willingness of supervisors to consult with subordinates and allow their participation in decisions or to give direct orders; and
- **non-punitive versus punitive** responses to infractions of rules or to mistakes committed by subordinates.

Using several measures to obtain descriptions of supervisors' attitudes and behaviour, they reported that the five dimensions were interrelated such that supervisors who were found to be employee-centred tended to supervise in a general way, to use less pressure for production, to consult with or discuss decisions with subordinates, and to be non-punitive in response to errors and infractions.[15] Work-centred supervisors tended to be described in terms of the opposite extremes of the other four dimensions. Consequently, the contrasting extremes of such dimensions provided a basis for distinguishing supervisors as **supportive** or **autocratic** (see, for example, Filley and House 1969, 393–94). These categories were then used to investigate relationships between the supervisory types and a variety of other variables. In general, although not invariably, this research showed that workers respond more positively to supportive than to autocratic supervisors. Specifically, satisfaction and intra-group cooperation were higher, and intra-group stress, labour turnover, and grievance rates were lower in work units under supportive, as compared to autocratic, supervision (Filley and House 1969, 399–405; Filley, House, and Kerr 1976, 219–22). The fact that similar results were found whether data were obtained by attitudinal measures of satisfaction and stress or by behavioural measures of intra-group cooperation, turnover, and grieving generated greater confidence in the general finding that differences in supervisory attitudes and behaviour make a difference.

Morse and Reimer (1956) undertook an experimental study of the effects that authority structures had on individual satisfaction and productivity. Four clerical divisions in a non-unionized industrial organization provided the subjects of the research. In two divisions, work continued under the existing hierarchical authority structure,[16] while in the other two divisions work was performed under an authority structure that allowed for participation in decision-making by non-management employees.[17] Measures of satisfaction and productivity were obtained for the four divisions before and after the experimental period, which lasted one year. During the experimental period, observation of work activity and measures of the employees' perceptions of the authority structure under which they worked confirmed that each type of structure was both observed and perceived to operate as intended by the experimenters. Comparison of before and after measures indicated that employee satisfaction was generally higher in the participatory and lower in the hierarchical divisions. However, although productivity increased in all divisions, the increases were *greater* in the hierarchical divisions.

Although worker satisfaction or, in its group manifestation, morale, is not an exclusively human relations concept, it is a prominent concept in this perspective. To understand how organizations function, it is mandatory to assess levels of satisfaction or morale, to investigate how satisfaction affects such aspects of organizational behaviour as productivity, and to investigate how other aspects of organizational structure or behaviour, such as the structure or exercise of authority, affect satisfaction. There is a great deal of literature, both research and theoretical, much of it deriving from the human relations perspective, on morale and satisfaction.[18] In the early period being discussed here, the typical interest was in assessing the effect of variations in satisfaction either directly on productivity or as an intervening variable in the relationship of supervisory style and productivity. The relationship between satisfaction and productivity, however, has proven to be more complex than initially supposed (see, for example, Morse 1953, chap. 9), or possibly non-existent (see, for example, Brayfield and Crockett (1955) and Vroom (1964)).

Paterson

Research on morale in an armed service organization provides a good example of the human relations interest in morale (Paterson 1955). In contrast to the usual human relations emphasis on questionnaires for data-gathering, Paterson's action research case study used qualitative methods to provide data on conditions at the research site before and after he introduced changes.[19] These data were then related to statistical data on accidents at the base. During World War II, Paterson, serving as an officer in the Royal Air Force, was assigned to an RAF station located in the north of Great Britain.[20] His task was to find the reasons for the station's bad record of flying accidents, the worst of all RAF stations, and to recommend ways of improving its performance. To gather information he made observations on all operations and activities at the station and interviewed and held conversations with the entire range of personnel.[21] Although runways were in poor condition, and bad weather was characteristic of that part of Great Britain, Paterson diagnosed the flying accidents to be primarily the result of the carelessness of pilots, and he hypothesized that the carelessness was the result of sociological conditions.

Paterson argued, on the basis of his observations and interviews, that social relationships on the station were highly structured in terms of status. The highest status was enjoyed by flying personnel and prevailed even where flying personnel were formally outranked by personnel engaged in non-flying operations, such as aerodrome control, administration, and various staff operations. Paterson observed that pilots failed to show the expected deference and respect to higher-ranking non-flying officers. The high status of flying personnel was reinforced by a physical separation from other personnel. They had their own common rooms and other separate facilities in contrast to non-flying personnel who, despite operational differences, shared working locations. Paterson observed that flying officers kept to themselves when in the officers' mess. As he also observed signs of resentment of the status claims of flying personnel on the part of non-flying personnel, Paterson concluded that status differences and the consequent restriction on interaction between categories of personnel were at the root of the poor flying record—a good flying record required teamwork or cooperation among all personnel. Team spirit, which is dependent on morale (Paterson 1955, 99), was lacking as a consequence of a preoccupation with status.[22]

To rectify the situation, Paterson set out to weaken status barriers. To do so, he redefined the station's primary objective from engaging the German Air Force to combatting the weather. Through group discussions that involved flying and non-flying personnel, such as members of air crews, ground crews, and the meteorology section, Paterson persuaded them to define the weather as the primary enemy and to consider the primary task of the station to be fighting and overcoming the weather. In this way, and with the help of informal leaders he had identified, Paterson persuaded the personnel that successful flying in bad weather could be achieved. The result, shown in a rich presentation of statistical data, was a dramatic reduction in flying accidents. Cooperation, achieved through increased interaction that transcended status boundaries and that developed consensus on an overall objective, solved the station's problem.

Cohesion

The emphasis on informal relationships, raised to prominence by the Bank Wiring Observation Room research, did not receive similar emphasis from those working in the human relations perspective at this time. Instead the emphasis was given to **cohesion**, a characteristic of such relationships.[23] Seashore's (1954) exploration of conditions affecting cohesion among work groups and on the effects of cohesion on productivity is a well-known example of human relations research that focuses on this concept. For his analysis, he used data from a firm that manufactured heavy farm equipment, collected as part of the Kahn and Katz ([1953] 1960, 554–55) program of research on leadership, morale, and productivity. Seashore's data included company productivity records on 228 of its work units and questionnaire data obtained from workers employed in them. Cohesion, defined as the attraction of a group for its members and the resistance of members to leaving the group, was measured by responses to a set of Likert-type questions; the scores were summed to form an index of cohesion.[24] In his analysis, Seashore focused on the relation between cohesion and variations in productivity in the work units. As he had predicted (Seashore 1954, 65), he found that the productivity of individual members varied less from each other in high-cohesive units than in low-cohesive units. He interpreted this finding as indicating that cohesiveness helped the units control individual members' productivity. Furthermore, he found that high-cohesive units, compared with low-cohesive units, varied more from each other, thus showing a greater tendency to either high or low productivity.[25]

As in the case of the Relay Assembly Test Room and the Bank Wiring Observation Room, high work-group cohesion can be associated with higher or lower group productivity. Relevant to this point, Seashore found consistent but not statistically significant evidence that the direction of deviation from the company production standard was associated with a work unit's perception of the extent to which the company provided a supportive setting for its workers.[26] Work groups in which cohesion was low, however, tended to adhere more closely to the company standard and, thus, were associated with more stable productivity. This finding is curious in view of Seashore's finding that the productivity of individual workers varied less in high-cohesive than in low-cohesive groups.[27] Although Seashore's interpretation of this finding—that greater social control in the high-cohesive groups accounted for their systematic deviations from company norms—is reasonable, it is not readily apparent why 59 percent and 29 percent of low-cohesive groups should achieve, respectively, medium (80–94 percent of company standard) and high (95 percent of company standard or higher) productivity. Since there was greater variation in individual productivity in the low-cohesive groups, it would not appear that company expectations exerted a constant effect on individual workers. While the most likely explanation is that variations in individual productivity in low-cohesive groups averaged out at reasonably high levels, the data reported by Seashore do not allow for its testing.

Seashore also sought to account for the differences in levels of cohesion among the various work groups. Although he did not find evidence to support the hypothesis that cohesion is more likely to develop in work groups whose members share personal and social attributes—specifically, age and educational level—he did find that cohesion varied with the size of a group and with the duration of shared membership in a group. On the assumptions that, first, the smaller a group, the greater the probability that all members will interact with each other and, second, the longer the time persons have worked together, the more likely they are to interact, Seashore concluded that cohesion, at least in part, was determined by opportunities for interaction. By implication he saw cohesion as a function of interaction, thus anticipating Homans' (1950, 111) well-known proposition that the more persons interact with each other, the more they will like each other. Seashore also found that occupational prestige was related to cohesion: workers who attributed higher prestige to their jobs tended to belong to the more cohesive groups. Seashore predicted this finding on the assumption that occupational prestige is a basis for attraction among group members. Given the importance of prestige or status to human beings, it may be suggested that because high prestige is more valued than low prestige, those who consider their jobs prestigious will be concerned with protecting their prestige and this concern is likely to be shared with others in the same situation. Thus, a concern for prestige may serve as a basis for cohesion, and cohesion, in turn, is likely to facilitate the development and maintenance of a high concern for prestige.

CRITIQUE OF THE HUMAN RELATIONS PERSPECTIVE

These examples of human relations research undertaken in the late 1940s and through the 1950s clearly illustrate the importance attached to the concepts of informal relations, informal leadership, morale, and satisfaction. The human relations perspective brought ideas to the study of organizations, and evidence to support their relevance, that had been ignored, overlooked, or underemphasized by Weber. Even analysts who focus on the more formal structural aspects of organizations would not reject the idea that informal relationships and their consequent influence on informal authority and norms must be taken into account in understanding organizations. In addition, the human relations perspective emphasized the concept of organizational effectiveness. Much of the research sought data on measures of effectiveness, such as productivity, and investigated relationships between such measures and those of morale, leadership, and cohesion. Some research (for example, Georgopoulos and Tannenbaum 1957) explicitly investigated organizational effectiveness, attempting to refine the concept by including, along with productivity, the concepts of intra-organizational stress and organizational flexibility and by devising measures for these concepts. By emphasizing organizational effectiveness in their research, those working within the human relations perspective implied that effectiveness should be regarded as problematic and was not to be taken for granted, as implied by Weber's view that bureaucracy was the most efficient form of organization.

Despite its contributions to the study of organizations, the human relations perspective is not immune from criticism. Much of the criticism, as Landsberger (1958) observed in the case of Mayo and the Western Electric research, was directed at either theoretical or philosophical writing rather than at the research itself. It has been strongly attacked on ideological grounds for its apparent managerial bias. Certainly, research in this perspective did not explore the possibility that manager-worker conflict could be engendered by formal structures and procedures and by ideological differences between management and workers. Some critics argued that the emphasis on satisfaction and morale were attempts to substitute attitudinal rewards, such as satisfaction and self-actualization, for material rewards, such as pay and promotion. The emphasis on organizational effectiveness and its relation to cohesion, morale, and satisfaction is certainly consistent with managerial interests.

Although the fear that human relations research and its perspective would be used to protect or advance managerial interests to the disadvantage of non-managerial employees is realistic—certainly as long as management-employee relationships are adversarial—there seems nothing intrinsically contrary to worker interests in undertaking research using these concepts. Organizational effectiveness can, as we shall see, be as important for workers' cooperatives as for conventionally owned firms. What is important is whether a perspective neglects other important aspects of organizations. On such grounds, despite the contributions of the human relations perspective, charges of managerial bias are justified because the research did not focus on the advantages or disadvantages of formal authority structures, on employee concerns about safety or other undesirable working conditions, or on the role of unions in organizational functioning.

Apart from bias, ideological or otherwise, in the human relations perspective, criticism can be legitimately directed to the research methods adopted in human relations studies. Criticism of the Western Electric research, focused mainly on the Relay Assembly Test Room (RATR), began early and has continued.[28] The main concern of this criticism was whether the data and analysis supported the conclusions drawn by the original researchers. An early critic, Argyle (1953) held that the RATR data failed to support the researchers' conclusion that social factors were responsible for the gains in productivity. He claimed that a change in the pay incentive system, the replacement of two workers whose productivity was below average by two above-average producers, and the Hawthorne Effect accounted for the 30 percent increase in output (1953; 1972, 106; Argyle, Gardner, and Cioffi 1958, 29). Carey (1967), who took a similar position, also called attention to weaknesses in the design and analysis of the RATR project. Carey's detailed criticism extended to the second Relay Assembly Group study and to the Mica Splitting Test Room study, which were conducted to test hypotheses derived from the first RATR study. He argued that the Hawthorne researchers' claim—that "friendly" supervision and the strengthened social relationships of the women accounted for the observed increases in productivity—was based on evidence flawed by the research design and by events that occurred during the research. Furthermore, he alleged that the researchers ignored strong evidence that pay incentives accounted for substantial increases in productivity.

In the late 1970s, a group of researchers, which included Richard Franke, assembled and organized the Western Electric research data (Bramel and Friend 1981, 809) in a form that allowed rigorous quantitative analysis of the RATR data. The resulting re-analysis has led to opposing conclusions about the effect of actions representing human relations concepts. Franke and Kaul (1978) and Franke (1980) found no support for concluding that variations in productivity resulted from humane treatment of workers, that is, from actions consistent with human relations concepts such as friendly supervision and actions to promote morale. Instead they show that most of the variation in productivity resulted from the imposition of managerial discipline, such as strictness and productivity-orientation; from the scheduled time changes, these being the rest pauses and the changes in length of the workday and workweek; and from the onset of the economic depression. Schlaifer (1980), however, had a different interpretation of shifts in productivity rates—shifts that were treated by Franke and Kaul as the result of introducing managerial discipline and of the onset of the depression. His analysis reveals that scheduled time changes and a variable, representing a continuous but decreasing rate of growth in productivity over the duration of the research, have strong explanatory significance. Schlaifer interpreted the latter variable as a proxy for unmeasured variables that likely include those representing human relations concepts. Consequently, he concluded that his findings "are in all respects consistent with conclusions reached by the original researchers" (Schlaifer 1980, 1005). Stephen Jones (1990), whose re-analysis of the same RATR data provides evidence that the RATR operators influenced each other's productivity, also saw his research as supporting the conclusions of Roethlisberger and Dickson and of Whitehead, the original researchers.

If the enduring interest in the Western Electric research surprised Carey in 1967, how much more surprising to find that interest surviving into the 1990s. The re-analysis, however, does allow the application of statistical procedures that were not readily available to the original researchers.[29] Moreover, there is no reason why data collected some sixty years ago should not be analyzed. On the other hand, whether or not re-analysis upholds the original researchers' conclusions, there are severe limits on the generalizations that can be drawn from findings based on data obtained from five workers, even where the unit of analysis is weekly productivity rates.[30]

SOME ISSUES IN HUMAN RELATIONS RESEARCH

Of the questions that can be raised about post-Mayo human relations research, those discussed here concern data-gathering strategy, analysis, and theoretical assumptions.

Data

Since the studies by Mayo, human relations research has centred primarily at the University of Michigan, where researchers adopted a different data-gathering strategy. In contrast to the observational and interview techniques used by Mayo and his colleagues, questionnaires figured prominently in Michigan research. As a consequence, the Michigan data consisted mainly of expressions of attitudes or perceptions of situations rather than accounts of actual actions. For those who have doubts about the reliability or validity of questionnaire data, their use constitutes a weakness. However, it is doubtful that the validity and reliability problems of questionnaire procedures are any greater than those of observational procedures.

Although an account of a supervisor's actual exercise of authority may, to some, be more "real" than a report of workers' perceptions of supervisory style, the two procedures simply produce different kinds of data. A purist might object, pointing out that observation consists of the observer's *perceptions* of a situation. Although the data obtained by one procedure are not necessarily more reliable or valid than the other, it should be noted that these two types of data may, for good reason, either coincide or diverge. Although use of such data is acceptable, observational data relevant to human relations concepts might have strengthened the research. It can be worth knowing, for example, if a supervisor who is perceived as supportive actually acts supportively.

Bivariate Analysis

In much of the post-Mayo research, such as that on supervision and on morale described above, analysis was limited to two variables, such as supervisory style and productivity. Reviews of this research (for example, Dubin et al 1965; Vroom 1964) on the association of either supervisory style or morale and productivity revealed that there was considerable inconsistency in findings from individual studies. Stated briefly, both strong and weak associations in both directions, positive and negative, were reported. At best, such inconsistent findings suggest that the effects of conditional variables should be taken into account, and at worse, that the association could be random. Although the researchers may have been aware of the possible effects of intervening variables, they may have wished to keep the analysis simple and to attempt to achieve more easily interpretable results. However, as two-variable models are rarely adequate to capture reality, it is necessary to test the conditioning influence of other variables on the specific relationship under investigation. Thus, when unemployment is high, workers under production-oriented supervisors may be more likely to maintain high productivity levels than when unemployment is low.

Causal Assumptions

The strong tendency in such research was to assume that variables such as leadership and satisfaction influenced productivity. However, it can be difficult to identify the *direction* of a relationship when data are collected for only one period of time. Even if the effects of intervening variables are shown to be negligible, a correlation coefficient indicating a strong association between, for example, production and a worker-oriented style of supervision, allows only the possibility that supervisory style *causes* changes in productivity. It is also possible that productivity causes changes in supervisory style. For example, when productivity is high, supervisors may adopt a worker-oriented style.

The possibility that satisfaction may be a *consequence* rather than a *cause* of changes in productivity was tested on the basis of a theoretical model (Lawler and Porter 1967, 23) in which rewards, which are assumed to cause satisfaction, are seen as outcomes of job performance. The authors also argued that the causal status of satisfaction will be indicated if its relation to performance is stronger than its relation to effort (Lawler and Porter 1967, 26).[31] Their findings, based on measures of satisfaction obtained from 148 middle and lower level managers, and performance and effort ratings obtained from superiors and peers, support their prediction.[32] These results led the authors to conclude that satisfaction was a *consequence* of productivity rather than the other way around. However, since the research did not eliminate the possibility that the satisfaction to be gained from the available rewards did motivate both higher effort and performance, it failed to determine the direction of causality. Although an analysis of data collected in the same time period supporting a hypothesis grounded in systematic theory may enhance the plausibility of a causal relationship, it is clearly necessary to collect data for independent variables for time periods prior to those for dependent variables to attain a more convincing test of causal hypotheses.

PERSISTENCE OF THE HUMAN RELATIONS PERSPECTIVE

Although the criticism of the human relations perspective, whether focused on its bias toward management's interests or on its data-gathering and analytical techniques, undoubtedly reveals weaknesses in this perspective, it must be recognized that it is a perspective that claimed, and continues to claim, a great deal of attention from students of organizations. Many leading texts (for example, Gross and Etzioni 1985; Perrow 1986; Scott 1992, chap. 4; [1981] 1987) describe and comment on it. Perrow, for example, was severely critical on the general ground that human relations research, because of its focus on individuals, fails to yield useful information on organizations.[33] On more specific grounds Perrow argued that the human relations perspective has been unable to provide support for the hypothesized association between its main concepts: productivity or organizational effectiveness and either leadership or morale. Nonetheless, he admitted that current perspectives, such as structuralism, might not have a better record of achievement if they had as long a history of research as the human relations perspective. As we have seen, the research conducted within this perspective has been attracting criticism for about fifty years. While such interest could be sustained by the challenge to prove it wrong, there may be other reasons for its endurance.

The perspective may have earned its standing by its emphasis on empirical research and on observations of the workplace that Weber had ignored or neglected. Certainly, the emphasis on the group, particularly on workers' commitments to their groups and to group norms, and on leadership as a form of authority are relevant to the interests of sociologists. For sociologists whose interests are not limited to accounting for varying productivity but are directed toward understanding a wide range of social behaviour in organizations, such concepts are important and find a place in other perspectives on the sociology of organizations.[34]

Although the 1940s to the 1960s were the glory years for the human relations perspective and work that adheres to the early formulations continues, the ideas were carried forward to newer perspectives by various researchers: by Seashore and Yuchtman (1967) to organizational goals, by Katz and Kahn ([1966] 1978) to open systems, and by Tannenbaum (1968) to control in organizations. Some of these further contributions to the study of organizations will be discussed in the chapters that follow.

SUMMARY

The human relations perspective drew attention to the possible significance of the affective aspects of social relationships in the workplace, of leadership, and of motivation. All three continue to be relevant. It is commonplace for members of organizations and experts alike to observe that friendships and enmities are developed and maintained in organizations. Although the effects of these friendships and enmities may be differently assessed, they are undeniable realities of organizations.

It is also commonplace to observe individuals who, without occupying formally established authority, give direction to their peers. Individuals who "take charge," who give direction and formulate objectives for co-workers or co-members, can be found in all manner of organizations.

Those working in the human relations perspective formulated the concept of leadership to recognize this reality. This expanded the conceptualization of organizational authority by treating leadership not only as informal authority, but as a variable aspect of formally defined authority roles.

Motivation, focused on individual satisfaction and on morale, was recognized in the human relations model as important for understanding action in organizations. However, the theoretical and methodological problems associated with these concepts are grounds for questioning their adequacy for the analysis of motivation. The importance of motivation as a concept for understanding organizations is firmly established, but a broader range of concepts and their indicators is required.

ENDNOTES

1   See Franke and Kaul (1978, 623–27) and Franke (1979, footnote 2) for brief accounts of those involved in the research.

2   At the time of research, a relay was a piece of telephone equipment assembled by fitting thirty-five parts in an "assembly fixture" (Roethlisberger and Dickson [1939] 1947, 20).

3   The details of the research design, the variations in working time and the various tests the women underwent, are difficult to include in a brief description but can be obtained from various publications by the researchers (for example, Roethlisberger and Dickson [1939] 1947).

4   In fact, selection criteria, as specified by the researchers, were thorough experience in relay assembly and a willingness to cooperate in the research (Roethlisberger and Dickson [1939] 1947, 21).

5   This idea became well known as the Hawthorne Effect, a variant of the idea that the behaviour of objects of observation, human or otherwise, are affected by the techniques and measures of observation used in research. Although there is evidence that supports this idea, it is ultimately untestable since it is impossible to know how the objects of research would behave when not under observation.

6   Systematic observation was not included in the research strategy, but the observer kept a record of events that appeared to be important.

7   It is difficult to get a consistent description, from published accounts, of Mayo's involvement in the Western Electric research. Although Whyte (1972, 82–83) referred to him as "the director of the program," his statement is at odds with Wrege's account of the origins of the research (1976), which is consistent with Baritz (1960, 91). Baritz concluded that although Mayo had some involvement in the interpretation of the Relay Assembly Test Room findings, his more direct involvement was in the counselling and interview program and in the Bank Wiring Observation Room study.

8   Roethlisberger and Dickson ([1939], 1947) provided a detailed account of this study. A very readable account plus a theoretical interpretation can be found in Homans (1950).

9   Payment was distributed on the basis of the hourly rates of the individual workers. According to Roethlisberger and Dickson ([1939] 1947, 409), the hourly rates depended "largely upon differences in efficiency."

10 Physical aggression took the form of *binging*, a rap by a fist on the arm or other body part. Binging varied in meaning—it could express affection or varying degrees of aggression. In relation to work, it signified that the recipient should slow down or stop working.

   Various physical tests of the workers failed to provide evidence that their work efforts represented the top of their energy potential. Moreover, it was customary in the Bank Wiring Observation Room for the workers to work steadily throughout the morning and early afternoon and then in the later afternoon until quitting time to spend their energy on various non-work activities.

11 The workers regarded 6600 connections per day or 825 connections per hour as a fair day's work. The overproducer, W2, achieved an average of 35 connections per hour more than the worker-sanctioned amount. The three wiremen, W3, W6, and W5, who complied most closely with the agreed-upon production levels underproduced by 2, 3, and 21 connections per hour, respectively. A fourth wireman, W4, reported by the authors to be among those who "managed to approximate the standard fairly closely" (Roethlisberger and Dickson [1939] 1947, 446), underproduced by an average of 68 connections per hour (see Roethlisberger and Dickson [1939] 1947, 434–36, fig. 36).

12 Since earnings were directly related to the total productivity of all workers, it may appear that Group B members were behaving irrationally. However, although they earned less than they would have if they had matched Group A's productivity, they penalized Group A members by reducing their earnings while at the same time gaining more than their own productivity entitled them to through Group A's higher productivity. Group B members also buffered their losses by overreporting their productivity and by above-average daywork allowance claims (payments based on a set hourly rate when production was suspended for various reasons). Both overreporting and daywork claims had the effect of inflating Group B members' productivity rates and inflating their share of group payments.

13 The more time spent on supervisory activities, the more supervisors were considered differentiated from their subordinates.

14 Each dimension is described by the labels of the opposing ends of the dimension, for example, general versus close supervision.

15 The rank order correlations between dimensions, ranging between .30 and .42, were not high but were statistically significant.

16 The researchers noted that in the planning period, higher line officials in these divisions were authorized to increase their role in running the divisions and to initiate changes in them. In addition, supervisors were trained to act in a manner consistent with a hierarchical structure.

17 The idea of participation in decision-making may be seen as an attempt to exploit the informal leadership qualities of employees. The idea also relates

to another human relations perspective stream manifest in Lippitt's widely known research on leadership types (White and Lippitt [1953] 1962).

[18] Gruneberg (1979, 1) cited Locke (1976) as reporting that over three thousand articles and dissertations had been written.

[19] **Action research** was the term used to refer to projects whose aim was both to determine the reasons for problems and to implement testable remedies for their solution.

[20] Prior to and after his war service, Paterson was a member of the Tavistock Institute, which undertook research on organizational behaviour from the human relations perspective. In 1947, Tavistock joined with the Institute of Behavioral Research at the University of Michigan to establish the journal *Human Relations*.

[21] This combination of participant observation and formal and informal interviews was more like the data-gathering strategy of the Mayo group than the more structured methods of the Michigan group.

[22] Paterson (1955, 99) defined **morale** as "obedience to an internal, personal authority" that is based on "an ideal or value common to the group." In his usage, morale refers to value consensus rather than to group satisfaction. **Team spirit**, which he defines as "common appreciation by [team] members of [their] unity of purpose," that is, commitment to the team's goal, could be interpreted as reflecting group satisfaction.

[23] Although cohesion is an important characteristic of any social relationship, whether formally or informally structured, the human relations perspective focused on cohesion as an important property of informal relationships among workers. A related concept, **consensus**, the degree of agreement on norms and values among participants in a relationship, was not explicitly included in the human relations perspective although it was implied by an interest in worker homogeneity of attitudes.

[24] Workers were asked to respond to such questions as:

> "Do you feel that you are really part of your group?"

> "If you had a chance to do the same kind of work for the same pay in another work group, how would you feel about moving?"

> "How does your work group compare with other work groups at Midwest on each of the following points?
> - the way the men get together
> - the way the men stick together
> - the way the men help each other on the job"

[25] Most low-cohesive units (59 percent) achieved medium productivity levels relative to the company standard. While most high-cohesive units (46 percent) achieved high productivity levels, a reasonably high proportion (41 percent) achieved medium levels. Relatively small proportions of high- and low-cohesive units achieved low productivity levels.

[26] Note that this finding relates to the distinction in supervisory styles, supportive versus autocratic, which is part of the human relations conceptual framework.

²⁷ High-cohesive groups were those that had average cohesion scale scores of five through seven on a seven-point scale.

²⁸ At the time of writing, the most recent article is Stephen Jones' further re-analysis of the RATR data (1992).

²⁹ It should be noted that at the time these research projects were conducted, social scientists had to rely on punchcard processing to conduct their analyses. This technology imposed limits on both the numbers of records and the number of variables that could be analyzed. For those social scientists who did not have access to this technology, and there were many in the 1940s and 1950s, the limitations on analysis were all the greater. More sophisticated statistical analysis of both numerical and categorical data had to await the spread of computers as commonplace tools in social science analysis.

³⁰ Where N = 270.

³¹ The authors adopted Maslow's hierarchical concept of needs and need satisfaction (1954) and related it to the distinction between extrinsic rewards such as pay and promotion, which are controlled by others, and intrinsic rewards, which derive from the job or work itself. Their model includes the assumption that satisfaction is more clearly related to intrinsic than extrinsic rewards. They claimed modest empirical support for this assumption (Lawler and Porter 1967, 27, table 1).

³² Performance and satisfaction, .32 and .30, respectively for superiors and peers, compared with .23 and .20 for effort and satisfaction. No significance tests between correlation coefficients were reported.

³³ Even its interests in groups is directed toward the interaction of individuals.

³⁴ It is worth keeping in mind that some sociologists thought that the Western Electric research led to the rediscovery of the **primary group**, a concept proposed by sociologist Charles H. Cooley to identify groups or relationships that were perceived as a prime source of satisfaction in themselves. Groups or relationships entered into as a means for realizing some other interest Cooley categorized as secondary. The effort to identify different kinds of groups has a long history, beginning with Toennies, a German sociologist, who used the terms **Geschellschaft** and **Gemeinschaft** to draw a similar distinction. The terms **instrumental** and **expressive**, emphasized by Talcott Parsons in some of his work, are currently used by many sociologists to draw a basic distinction between social relationships.

CHAPTER 4

ORGANIZATIONS AS SOCIAL SYSTEMS

Despite the criticisms that can be sustained against the rational and human relations perspectives, they did shape the early development of the sociology of organizations and provided concepts that identified sociologically important elements of organizations. The emphasis Weber gave to the structure of formal elements, such as the prescribed division of labour and the formal distribution of authority complemented the human relations emphasis on motivation and on the informal structuring of interpersonal relations and of authority. It is not surprising, then, that a perspective incorporating elements from both of these early perspectives should emerge. The complementarity of the rational and the human relations perspectives did not require that organizations should be perceived as **social systems**, nor did the social system perspective require the merging of the earlier perspectives. However, the application of the social system perspective did allow the inclusion of concepts from the rational and human relations perspectives.

In this chapter, attention is focused on the idea of social systems as it developed sociology and in social psychology and as it applies to the study of organizations. The discussion begins with a short statement of the system perspective as it concerns the study of all living phenomena, whether it be at the level of individual cells, organisms, or societies. This is followed by a brief account of early approaches in anthropology and sociology that were precursors of the general conception of social systems. The discussion then turns to the application of the social system perspective to the study of organizations. The discussion draws largely on the work of Talcott Parsons and of Daniel Katz and Robert Kahn and is focused on the ideas of the system perspective rather than on the associated empirical work, which is discussed in subsequent chapters.[1] The chapter ends with a consideration of the strengths and weaknesses of this perspective for the understanding of organizations.

THE SYSTEM CONCEPT IN GENERAL

The emphasis on **system** in sociology, although not easily traced,[2] may have been influenced by a growing agreement on the value of the idea of system, as a broad conceptual orientation, for responding to questions raised in a variety of academic disciplines. The general system perspective as a mode of inquiry is largely a twentieth-century development. Miller (1978, xiii) identified A.N. Whitehead, in work published in 1925, as an early proponent of the system concept as applicable to all reality. However, Ludwig von Bertalanffy, a theoretical biologist, is the scientist whose name is most closely associated with the system perspective, whose formulations were basic to the work of scientists representing a variety of disciplines, and who formed the Society for General Systems Research.[3] Bertalanffy began to formulate the system perspective in the 1930s and continued to do so for several decades (Bertalanffy 1933; 1975).[4] The system perspective gathered impetus in the late 1940s and 1950s as a result of work in cybernetics and information theory.

In system theory a system is conceived as consisting of a set of **structured components** designed to meet the conditions required for the survival of the system. The degree of specialization and structural organization of these components may differ in relation to the level of phenomena under analysis. The conditions of survival may be referred to as **functional requirements** and the actions in response to them as **processes** or as **functions** of the structures involved.[5] It is a fundamental assumption of this perspective that the structures of a system are interdependent or interrelated. The structures, that is, are *systematically* rather than *randomly* associated. The processes associated with these structures are similarly interdependent. Although the degree of interdependence may vary, this assumption means that the actions of structures and processes serving a particular functional requirement can be expected to have consequences for other structures and processes of the system.

The system, whatever its level, is viewed as existing in an **environment** and as being separated from its environment by a **boundary**.

The maintenance of the boundary between a system and its environment is tantamount to system survival. The disappearance of the boundary is the loss of organization or the demise of the system. The overall functional requirement, then, of the system is **boundary maintenance**.

This basic functional requirement is typically divided into various sub-categories of functional requirements. For example, defensive action may be required to ward off external threats. System persistence will also require the acquisition of resources, generally referred to as **inputs** of energy; various transformations of such energy, called **throughput**; and **output**, which relates to the objectives or purpose of the organism. For example, analysis at the level of the organism may identify various structures and processes that provide inputs of oxygen, water, and food that will transform these resources to meet organic requirements and that will provide for waste disposal. As well, the organism must be able to distinguish between benign and noxious resources. These various structures and their related processes are usually identified as a subsystem.

The system perspective also includes the concept of **feedback**, that is, a self-regulating process that monitors the level of system pressures and that, as necessary, sets subsystems in motion to respond to pressures that threaten system equilibrium. For example, a subsystem of the human organism must respond to the changes in ambient temperatures, which threaten a stable internal temperature. Another must provide for the coordination of all subsystems in order to maintain a balance, usually referred to as equilibrium or a steady state.

To sum up, the general system perspective postulates a more or less differentiated system consisting of structured components and processes arranged to meet the system's functional requirements. The objective of the system is to maintain boundaries and, therefore, to ensure system survival. These general concepts, however, must be interpreted as required for the level of system under analysis.[6] The discussion, then, turns to a description of the principal interpretations of the system perspective in sociology.

THE SOCIAL SYSTEM CONCEPT

The idea that the elements or parts of any entity are interdependent was very attractive to those trying to make sense of social action or behaviour. This perspective, as it related to total societies and to other social forms, was implied in the work of early sociologists such as Durkheim, Marx, and Weber (see, for example, Merton 1949, chap. 1). The concept of social system, as applied to organizations, had already appeared in

Mayo's Western Electric research. Moreover, a general perspective identified as **functionalism** or **structural-functionalism**, which dominated British social anthropology in the 1930s and 1940s, may be seen as a forerunner of the system perspective in sociology.[7] It was a basic assumption of this school that elements of culture or social structure endured because they performed one or more functions for the society or one of its subsystems.

From the functional perspective, for example, religious beliefs, ceremonies, and practices, which are found in all human societies, are not explained in metaphysical terms (proclaimed, for example, by a god or gods who control the universe) but in terms of functions that serve either individuals or society as a whole, including its subsystems. From this perspective, religion is seen as providing answers to questions that appear unanswerable on the basis of factual evidence but are directed toward determining the meaning of existence. Religious answers to questions that concern ultimate reality, on the other hand, provide explanations of the nature, the origins, the continued existence, and the meaning of the universe, and of the place of the individual in that universe. Religious answers may offer assurances that the universe has a creator, that there was a purpose in its creation, and that each person's life has meaning and is not an event that happened by chance.

In the functional perspective, religion also functions to provide support for the individual in times of personal crisis or tragedy. Such events call up questions about the meaning of life, to which religion responds with assurances—for example, that even tragic events fulfil a creator's purpose. Such explanations assume that people cannot tolerate the idea that life is meaningless and is the result of a chance combination of events.

An Example of a Functionalist Interpretation

The work of Bronislaw Malinowski provides a good example of the functional perspective.[8] In a series of investigations of so-called primitive societies, Malinowski, as a functionalist, assumed that any persistent element of human behaviour, such as the use of magic, of religious ceremonies, and so on, must meet either an individual or a social need, or both.[9] This assumption guided the analysis of his observations of magical and religious practices in the Trobrianders daily round of activities, including such instrumental activities as the production of food as well as expressive activities that celebrate a birth or a marriage. For example, Malinowski concluded that although the Trobrianders possessed the technical knowledge necessary for growing yams—they knew, for example, that yams had to be planted at a specific time of the year, that they had to be watered, and that they required cultivation—and they also knew that the presence of bush pigs and locusts, and various uncontrollable environmental elements, such as the weather, could endanger their crops of yams. To protect the yams from such hazards, the Trobrianders participated in rites conducted by a garden magician "in rigorous sequence and order" (Malinowski [1948] 1981, 28). In performing these rites, the magician used everyday substances, which were given special protective powers by the magician's incantations.[10]

Where fishing was concerned, Malinowski again concluded on the basis of his observations that although the Trobrianders were technically competent fishermen, they also used magical practices in fishing. However, Malinowski made the important observation that magic was used only in relation to deep-sea fishing and not to fishing that was confined to the lagoon. He concluded that magic was used as a means of warding off or controlling the dangers, such as heavy storms or being lost at sea, to which fishermen were exposed on the open sea but that were unlikely to occur in the calm, familiar conditions of the lagoon.

In Malinowski's view, then, magic and religion served to reduce the stress individuals suffered as a result of events that were beyond their control, that is, beyond the limits of their technology. A *function* of magic in these activities, therefore, was to reduce individual stress.

Although Malinowski's perspective emphasized the functions of cultural and social elements for the individual, he, like others working in the functional or structural-functional perspective, also regarded cultural and social elements as having *societal* functions. Social and cultural elements that reduce stress for the individual may, of course, be societally relevant but the term **societal function** is used here to refer to those cultural and social elements that are directly relevant to the functioning, maintenance or survival of social relationships or societal structures. In this perspective, religious ceremonies that dramatize social values or generate social consensus in the course of bringing people together are seen as primarily functional for society even though they may serve functions in maintaining personal stability for individuals. For example, the mourning customs and ceremonies associated with death in many societies serve a function for the bereaved by allowing a public expression of grief and by providing for public expression of support from relatives and friends. But these customs also serve an important social function by defining, for the bereaved, the limits on grieving and the priority of the bereaved's commitments to ongoing social relationships and to the community or society over commitments to the dead.

Although Malinowski's functional interpretation of the use of magic, and the presence of religious ceremonies and structures has been used to illustrate the functional perspective, it is important to recognize that in this perspective, as used by social anthropologists and sociologists of the time, any cultural or social element was seen to serve a function or functions.[11] Parsons (1951, 436), for example, interpreted the authority of a physician to decide whether or not someone was ill as serving a social function. According to Parsons, the decision legitimated deviance, that is, it justified a person's failure to meet role expectations defined by the various social systems in which the person participated.

MAIN IDEAS IN THE CONCEPT OF SOCIAL SYSTEMS

Interdependence, Boundaries, and Boundary Maintenance

Consistent with the general system perspective, the functionalists and structural-functionalists did not assume that the effects of cultural and social elements on the social units, or their individual members, were random. To the contrary, they argued that these cultural or social elements either caused a certain condition or set limits on the variability of some condition in the individual or the social unit. Thus, to say that religious belief reduces stress for an individual or promotes solidarity between community members is to say that such beliefs determine, to some degree, the reactions of humans as individuals (that is, as personalities) or in their roles as community members.[12] To hold that some event causes another or that two or more events occur either simultaneously or in sequence links the functionalist argument to the general system assumption that **interdependence** is a fundamental condition of all components of activities or situations. The system perspective, therefore, assumes that when change is introduced in a structure or process of a social system, changes will occur in the system's other structures and processes.

Another basic system concept that applies to social systems is the concept of boundaries. Social systems are assumed to exist separately from their environments. As organisms, human beings recognize that their bodies are separate from but not independent of their environments. In simple terms, we see our skins as the boundary between ourselves and the environment. Even though the differentiation between organism and environment may vary in distinctness according to the level of observation—under natural observation, for example, unicellular organisms are less distinguishable from their environments than are higher orders of organism—the general idea is not difficult to understand or to illustrate.

However, social systems do not have "skins," and it is more difficult to establish system boundaries empirically than to do so for biological organisms.[13] The legal boundaries of communities, for example, do not necessarily coincide with the ideas of community membership held by those who live inside or outside the communities.[14] And although marriage and birth are the building blocks of families, the boundaries between families, except in the case of the immediate nuclear family, may appear to be established arbitrarily. For example, where a household includes people who are not related by birth or by marriage, immediate family members will have no difficulty identifying who belongs to their family, whereas an outsider may have difficulty doing so.[15]

The difficulties in establishing the boundaries of kinship units larger than the immediate family are greater. Although it is conceivable that everyone in a society is related to everyone else, lines are drawn in virtually all societies. This is perhaps most clearly evident in societies where lineages and clans are important units of kinship structure and where rules of descent define rights and responsibilities of members and, hence, lineage or clan boundaries. Rules of marriage may also identify boundaries. Even in societies such as ours where kinship rules are minimal and where formal structures of extended families are not explicitly defined, recognition is given to a larger unit, to a "greater family"—distinctions must be drawn between relatives and non-relatives, and decisions made about which aunts, uncles, nieces, nephews, and cousins are to be acknowledged.[16] Although such relationships may be traced biologically, they are not necessarily recognized or even perceived. Instead, mutual recognition of rights and responsibilities or the frequency of interaction among persons related by marriage or birth may serve as bases for setting the boundaries of kin relationships.[17]

Although families may be easily distinguished from work organizations, from political parties and government organizations, and from religious and community organizations, the boundaries of these collectivities may be blurred, because the same individuals may assume roles in several of these different subsystems. Moreover, the energy contributed to one subsystem may affect another subsystem. For example, a person may work hard to earn more income or to earn a promotion, thus contributing to a company's objectives, but as a father or mother, may do so to fulfil family expectations relating to lifestyle or social status. Since the person is responding to both organizational and familial role expectations, the exact boundaries between the two social systems can be difficult to identify.

The idea of boundaries as a means of distinguishing systems, including social systems, from their environments implies that the integrity or persistence of a system depends on its capacity to manage these boundaries in the face of environmental pressures.[18] In his work, Parsons regarded the management of boundaries, or in his terminology, boundary maintenance, as the dominant priority of social systems.[19] For organizations, then, this assumption differs considerably both from Weber's view that goal-achievement is the overriding concern and from an early human relations emphasis on productivity as the measure of organizational effectiveness.[20] In the system perspective, as we shall see, goal attainment is important to boundary maintenance but may, depending on the relations between a system and its environments, be subordinated to the management of other boundary concerns.

To understand this emphasis on boundary management, it is necessary to understand how, in the system perspective, the boundary concerns are formulated. To do so requires an introduction to the idea of structural differentiation and the idea that the survival of all systems, including social systems, ultimately depends on maintaining a sufficient supply of energy.

Structural Differentiation

Social systems are **structurally differentiated**: participants act in different roles and in larger units to serve specialized functions. The degree of differentiation may vary from system to system and will be related to the functional requirements of the system, as the general system perspective suggests. For example, treating societies as social systems, Parsons (1966; 1971) argued that structural differentiation, which increases from primitive to modern societies, is positively associated with adaptive capacity.[21] Although any social system, to maintain its boundaries, must defend itself from environmental threats, obtain necessary resources, and transform these resources into products that benefit the system, Parsons (1977, chap. 11) regarded adaptive capacity as variable. A society's adaptive capacity may be sufficient for survival but not high enough to exploit the environment at a level that brings greater benefits to the system. Parsons held that structural differentiation is the engine that produces increased adaptive capacity, but it is possible that these two processes are interdependent.

Although Parsons associated modernity with increasing structural differentiation and adaptive capacity and invoked history to support his argument, it cannot be readily assumed that greater differentiation in organizations means greater modernity. It is, however, reasonable to expect a similar relationship between an organization and its environment—one organization may survive by operating in an environmental niche while another, by improving technology (throughput resources) and marketing (output resources), and by making structural changes (coordination resources) may increase its adaptive capacity and accrue higher benefits to the organization. A furniture manufacturing firm whose market consists of affluent customers could more safely adopt a craft technology with its low division of labour than could a firm whose market is moderate to low income-earners.

As will be seen, structural differentiation in an organization can take various forms: the division of labour or role differentiation, the levels and forms of authority, and the division of the organization into sub-units, such as production and marketing. All of these are concrete manifestations of a division of rights and responsibilities.[22] The importance of structural differentiation is not simply theoretical. It is related not just to the general idea of adaptive capacity but to more specific functional requirements of the organization. A statement of those functional requirements is, therefore, essential to an understanding of the system perspective.

Functional Requirements

The term "functional requirements" is straightforward in meaning: it refers to the conditions that must be achieved for a social system to cope with external and internal pressures and, ultimately, to maintain its boundaries. Although those who adopt a system perspective provide different specifications of the functional requirements of social systems, it is generally agreed that there are ever-present forces inside and outside any system that can disrupt system functioning. These forces are usually referred to as system or functional problems.[23] To survive, then, a social system has to deal effectively both with conditions *external* to it, for example, competition from other organizations, and with *internal* conditions, such as achieving and maintaining required levels of coordination of action and motivation among system participants.

Although there is widespread acceptance of the theoretical distinction between functional problems whose source is in the environment and those whose source is within the social system itself, distinguishing *empirically* between external and internal pressures can be less straightforward. For example, absenteeism, which may seem to be an internal problem, may, on investigation, turn out to be a consequence of a participant's role in another system, as when a parent misses work to tend a sick child.[24] Moreover, the external-internal dichotomy, like many dichotomies, is too great a simplification of reality to be very useful for analysis. Consequently, more detailed classifications have emerged, which preserve, for the most part, the distinction between those requirements relating to the environment and those internal to the organization.

The functional requirements described below are based on categorizations proposed by Talcott Parsons and by Daniel Katz and Robert Kahn. Parsons identified four functional requirements, calling them "dimensions of social action" (1966, 7; see also Parsons 1967, 196–97;

Parsons and Bales 1953, chap. 3; and Toby's introduction in Parsons 1977). Two of these relate to the external environment: **adaptation**, which includes providing for input resources and protecting the system; and **goal attainment**, which refers to the definition of goals, their prioritization, and maintenance. The other two dimensions relate to the internal environments of social systems: **integration**, which concerns the exercise of authority, coordination, and participants' solidarity; and **pattern maintenance**, which concerns the maintenance of values and norms and the provision of incentives appropriate to their compliance. Katz and Kahn, who acknowledge their intellectual debt to Parsons (Katz and Kahn 1966, 13, 96–99), provide a five-category scheme, reflecting a familiar division of organizational operations. In their scheme, each functional requirement is related to a specific subsystem, shown here in tabular form in Table 4.1 (Katz and Kahn [1966] 1978, 52–57).

TABLE 4.1   Organizational Subsystems

Functional Requirement	Subsystem	Source of Pressure
Organizational throughput or Main productive process	Production or Technical	Internal
Procuring input, disposing of output	Supportive	Environment
Attraction-retention of personnel; Rewards and sanctions	Maintenance	Internal and Environment
Structural and process change in response to environment	Adaptive	Environment
Control, coordination	Managerial and Directing	Internal and Environment

To clarify the concept of functional requirements, the number of categories discussed below is increased to eight by establishing separate categories for certain requirements included in the Parsons and Katz-Kahn classifications. The first five requirements—the need to remind members of the organization's purpose, to secure the resources needed by the organization, to maintain the organization's clientele, to defend the system against external pressures, and to define who is and who is not a member of the organization—relate to external environmental pressures. The system, however, must cope with pressures whose sources are within the system. The latter three requirements—the need to coordinate the activities of members, to ensure members comply with role definitions and rules, and to provide for communication within the organization—relate to pressures from within the organization. Although the requirements will be described here with reference to organizations, it should be borne in mind that the general requirements, while differing in their concrete details, apply to any social system.

Organizational Purpose

Given that an organization is a type of social system deliberately established to realize some purpose, one requirement for the organization is to maintain the priority of that task over other competing demands. Just as societies seem to require reaffirmation of their principal values, often done in the context of ceremonial occasions, as in Canada Day ceremonies, organizations appear to require periodic statements from someone in authority reminding members and outsiders of the nature of the central task. University presidents, perhaps using a ceremonial occasion, such as convocation, remind faculty, staff, students, and the public that the central tasks of the university are teaching and research, thereby giving unspoken lower priority to service, business, and government. Chief executive officers of corporations remind employees, shareholders, and the public that "the bottom line" is the most important basis for corporate decisions. Such reaffirmations, presumably, are required because of the realistic possibility that people, in the heat of daily activities, tend to forget the purpose of their activities. As Merton (1949, chap. 6) has written, there is a tendency for people to become preoccupied with means, neglecting ends.

Securing Resources

Obviously, each organization must develop procedures directly concerned with performing its main task, that is, the operations required to produce goods or services.[25] Whether the organization is a firm manufacturing television sets, a psychiatric hospital, a military unit, or a family services agency, its operations must be organized so that the relevant tasks are assigned, work schedules are established, and so on. In sociological terms, a division of labour directly related to throughput operations must be established and ancillary roles defined. Although this requirement seems obvious, it must be stated, not only because it is a basic requirement of organizations, but also because observation reveals that people may be prevented from performing assigned line or throughput operations by other non-line responsibilities. In a study of training in Canadian army units (F.E. Jones 1954), training officers complained that administrative tasks, "desk work" as they called it, prevented them from taking a direct part in the training of recruits.

Whether the purpose be to manufacture material goods or to provide a service, organizations must secure the necessary resources,

.human and non-human, to do so.[26] A hospital, for example, must be able to attract and retain employees with the various skills required to provide contemporary medical care and treatment. Indeed, the need for organizations to obtain and retain personnel sometimes leads to attempts by organizations to monopolize the energies or loyalties of their members. Such organizations are labelled *greedy* institutions by Coser (1974). Organizations must also acquire various supplies and services provided by other organizations. For example, ambulance services are required to transport some patients to hospitals. An organization that functions in a competitive environment may also have to prevent competitors from obtaining knowledge of its technology, production, and marketing plans.

Maintenance of Clientele

Because organizations without customers, clients, or a constituency are unlikely to survive, action is required to develop and maintain a demand for their goods or services. A company whose product is in stable or declining demand may add a new product to its line. A social agency may stay in operation or expand its services by discovering "new" social problems, such as spouse assault, child abuse, and sexual harassment, and so identify new categories of clients.[27] In other instances, direct attempts to promote customer or client loyalty is undertaken.

Defending the System

Organizations must also ensure that throughput and other operations are not disrupted by the actions of "outsiders." A responsibility of receptionists and secretaries is to screen telephone calls or visitors in order to minimize disturbances of the organization's work. Service representatives are employed by various firms, and although they are helpful to customers, they may also provide a first-line defence against complaints that might otherwise require action and interfere with company routines. The saying, attributed to anonymous school teachers, that "the best pupil is an orphan," similarly reflects the perception of parents as intruders who pose a threat to established teaching curricula and procedures.

Definition of Membership

As participation or membership in a social system entails rights and responsibilities, it is essential, as Parsons (1971, 7) has pointed out, for all social systems to define who their members (or potential members) are and to establish criteria that distinguish between members and non-members. For example, religious organizations may use naming ceremonies, such as baptism, and initiation ceremonies, such as confirmation, for this purpose. A political organization may require its members to adhere strictly to a specific ideological position. For many organizations, technical competence, the possession of explicitly defined skills, is a criterion, especially for those whose products, whether goods or services, entail payment by the recipient. It is also important for members to know what rights and responsibilities they may claim from others and what others may claim in return.

Human societies utilize a variety of membership criteria but these may be grouped under such categories as:

- **achieved characteristics**—these are defined skills or abilities relevant to a person's organizational responsibilities that members must possess or develop.

- **ideological criteria**—these require members to be committed to specified political, religious, or other beliefs.

- **ascribed characteristics**—these are personal attributes such as age, gender, and ethnicity, which define levels or territories of rights and responsibilities. In some instances ascribed characteristics are claimed to be associated with the possession of characteristic skills and to imply technical competence. For example, members of an ethnic group may claim rug-making skills to be a component of their traditions and so may justify their being given priority in hiring for rug-making jobs.

Although Weber's bureaucratic model of organizations may prescribe universalistic criteria that apply to all members of a society regardless of differences in ascribed characteristics, not all organizations limit themselves to these criteria.[28] On the assumption that homogeneity in characteristics will support cooperation and reduce conflict, some organizations may adopt hiring criteria that will help them establish exclusiveness in terms of an ascribed characteristic, such as age, gender, ethnicity, or in terms of an achieved characteristic such as status. Rothschild-Whitt (1979, 513–16, 519, table 1) observes that *collectivistic* organizations, as illustrated by an underground newspaper, a free medical clinic, a legal collective, a food cooperative, and a free school, aim for a homogeneity of characteristics in their memberships. For example, an underground newspaper included in her research selected members of the same social class for its staff.

The question of who is and is not a member can also be ambiguous and may become an issue. As there are no clear rules for deciding who is a member, drawing the line between insider and outsider may be arbitrary. Should hospital patients or students in schools be regarded as members of these organizations or as outsiders?

The answer may depend on how it is sought. The researcher may try to find out how the unambiguous members define the ambiguous—are the latter included or excluded? Alternatively, a researcher may investigate the boundary between ambiguous and unambiguous members by taking into account such variables as duration of contact and extent of influence on organizational activities. Students spend years in schools and other educational institutions and may exercise significant influence on policies through home and school associations and through students' organizations. Although patient stays vary in duration, a trend in health care is to give the patient, as consumer, greater say in treatment as well as other hospital activities.

The type of organization may also be a consideration. Students, patients, and clients of professionals are all supposed to be the prime beneficiaries in these relationships. Although business organizations may say "the customer is always right" and though consumers' associations exercise varying degrees of influence on manufacturers and on retail firms, the "bottom line" is frequently voiced as the prime consideration of business organizations. Customers of manufacturers and of retail business organizations do not, for the most part, interact intensively or for long duration with representatives of these organizations. Customers do not exercise as much formal influence as seems to be the case for schools and hospitals.

Time and influence, then, may be helpful in deciding membership boundaries: Do the rights of the apparent outsiders compare favourably with those of the established insiders? Perhaps the most important consideration is the significance of the boundary location—will an observer learn more about an organization by regarding boundary straddlers as insiders or outsiders?

Coordination

Organizations must also have some means of coordinating the actions of their participants. In some collectivities, such as families, or even non-familial groups whose members have associated with each other for a long period of time, coordination may be achieved through unspoken understandings and without a formal structure. Although coordination may also be achieved informally in organizations where members have worked together for a considerable period of time and know their jobs well, coordination characteristically requires a structure that formally defines the rights and responsibilities of its participants. Such definitions tend toward specificity, that is, toward precise, explicit, limited descriptions of rights and responsibilities, and incorporate rules relating to role performance, such as those that define working hours or the consequences for failing to fulfil responsibilities. In many instances, the structure is given physical form in a manual of procedures, which may take on a quasi-sacred character.

Compliance

In addition to a structure of roles and of higher units, an organization must provide some means of ensuring that members do what is expected of them. There must be some means of ensuring a participant's compliance with role definitions and associated rules. While a measure of compliance may result from the nature of a participant's commitment to the organization or be encouraged by exploiting the participant's work and moral standards, participants, in many instances, must be induced or compelled to comply.[29] Compulsion or inducement in organizations is customarily achieved through a formal authority structure.[30] In addition, as the human relations perspective has revealed, compliance may result from the actions of superiors or peers. However, such compliance may not meet the standards set by those in the formal authority structure. Finally, as participants may also comply with role expectations to obtain rewards or avoid punishment, organizations must provide appropriate sanctions and criteria for applying them.

Communication

As social relationships are the basic units of collectivities, conditions must be provided to allow them to develop and persist as appropriate to the requirements of the organization.[31] As the human participants in social relationships must communicate, that is, exchange information, structural provision must exist to allow it. Basically, communication in social relationships concerns both the culture of the social system—its ideas, values, norms, symbols, and social perceptions—and the nature and intensity of emotional ties between participants. The first concern results in varying levels of *consensus* and *dissensus*, the second, in varying levels of *cohesion* and *conflict*.[32] The functional requirements are to maintain levels of consensus/dissensus and cohesion/conflict that are consistent with boundary maintenance.

It is an assumption of system theory that these processes of consensus/dissensus and cohesion/conflict are interdependent with those of other subsystems. For example, these processes, depending on their strength, are assumed to influence productivity. Alternatively, an emphasis on productivity may generate higher or lower levels of consensus/dissensus or cohesion/conflict. The direction and strength of these relations are seen as being significant for boundary maintenance.

THE RELATION BETWEEN STRUCTURE AND FUNCTIONAL REQUIREMENTS

In systems analysis, a system has identifiable requirements to which its components are structured to respond by a series of operations.[33]

Although social and organic systems contain the same elements—a set of functional requirements that are met by the activities of components within the system—the empirical identification of these elements in social systems is more difficult than it is in an analysis of biological systems. Organisms, analyzed as biological systems, have an anatomy and a physiology; the structure of the organism is still "there" whether the structure is active or not. The components of the circulatory or the nervous system can be identified whether the organism is alive or dead. When the organism is active, the components can not only be identified, but may also be observed to meet some organismic function, such as the maintenance of body temperature or the provision of nutriment to the organism.

In contrast to biological systems, personality and social systems are "a structuring of events rather than of physical parts" (Katz and Kahn [1966] 1978, 36–37) and structural and functional requirements are not observably separate—both are observable only in action. Personality structure is not observable as is anatomy, but only as resulting individual acts. Similarly, an authority structure in an organization can be "seen" only by observing interactions between people. This difference between systems that are event structures and those that can be observed as anatomies makes studying the former more difficult than the latter.

For biological systems, given correct anatomical observations, the functional requirements may be identified by deduction and by observation, and the relation between structure and functional requirements may be established. Although biological or physiological structures may serve more than one subsystem, it is less difficult to identify a structure's functions at the level of the organism than at the level of social system. For social systems, since the structure can only be identified when it is serving a particular function, it is difficult to determine whether a structure may serve other functions and, therefore, to identify the degree of a structure's functional specificity. Thus while a given structure in an organization may be perceived as having one major function, it may also have less frequent or less noticeable consequences for other structures and subsystems. On the whole, it seems prudent to proceed on the assumption that identifiable actions and structures of social systems, even where they appear to respond to a specific functional requirement, may have consequences, often unanticipated, for other functional requirements.

The Allocation of Energy

A social system depends on the *energy* of its members. It is they who must act as required by the system. A health organization, for example, depends on its staff to carry out various duties—seeing patients, maintaining records, up-dating skills, etc. However, the allocation of energy for performing these various duties must be responsive to priorities of the health organization's functional requirements.

Although an organization may be able to increase its total energy by recruiting new members or by motivating greater effort by current personnel, its supply of energy at any point in time is finite. Consequently, the allocation of energy to meet any one functional requirement—production, for example—means that portion of total energy is not available to meet other functional requirements, such as the development and maintenance of cohesion. The various functional requirements need not necessarily exert equal pressures on an organization—production pressure is often stronger than other functional requirements in a manufacturing firm, while pressure for consensus on social norms may be stronger in religious or political organizations. To function optimally, though, the organization must achieve a balance in its allocation of energy to functional requirements that corresponds to the differing pressures of these requirements. This correspondence in the allocation or structure of action (energy) with the pressures of the different functional requirements is referred to as **equilibrium** or **steady state** in the system perspective.

Maintaining equilibrium may be difficult because the relative strength of these pressures may not be constant. If, for example, the pressure to achieve agreement on organizational goals is stronger, at a given time, than pressure for production, more energy should be allocated to achieving consensus. If procedures controlling organizational participants arouse opposition, directing more energy toward compliance or coordinative requirements will reduce the energy available for responding to other functional requirements, such as productivity or relations with other social systems.[34] Generally, therefore, directing energy to reduce pressure of one functional requirement draws energy away from the others and causes pressures on those other requirements to increase. Consequently, a persisting social system is in a state of dynamic equilibrium. In the social system perspective, the normal situation is for equilibrium to be temporarily achieved as energy is directed toward reducing the pressure of a specific requirement, but for the system to move to disequilibrium as the pressure of other requirements increases, then back to another equilibrium, and so on. As this equilibrium-disequilibrium cycle does not require the restoration of the previous balanced allocation of energy, it is referred to as a **moving equilibrium**.[35]

The Concept of Dysfunction

Although it may seem obvious from the discussion of the dynamics of a moving equilibrium that concrete structures and actions can have *negative* as well as *positive* consequences for functional requirements, this was not always recognized. The idea that every cultural or social element has only a positive or adaptive function dominated the functionalist perspective until Robert Merton introduced, in his penetrating critique of the structural-functional perspective (1949), the idea of **dysfunction** to account for the contra-adaptive or destructive effects of such elements. In Merton's view, a cultural or social element could be both functional and dysfunctional, that is, it could have both positive and negative consequences for the system to which it belonged. The balance between these functional and dysfunctional consequences determines whether or not the element persists as part of the system. For example, in the government agency Blau ([1955] 1963) studied, a rule that proved to be impractical, such as one requiring agents not to consult with each other, gave way to more practical informal practices. In general, when an element, such as a rule, is more dysfunctional than functional, there is a tendency for it to be replaced by an informal practice or informal structure that is more functional than dysfunctional. It is likely that such informal elements will eventually be formalized.

In stating that organizational elements are simultaneously positive and negative, or functional and dysfunctional, Blau does not mean that a given element, such as a rule, is necessarily equally functional and dysfunctional. He means that it will exert consequences in both directions, even if the force of one direction is stronger than the other. In his view, this functional-dysfunctional balance is subject to change and can be affected by the internal and external environments of the organization.

The idea that organizational structures and actions can have both positive and negative effects is particularly important for analysis when combined with the system perspective's emphasis on interdependence. The result of this combination is a broad conception of what is required for optimal organizational performance. The basis for system persistence is the achievement of an appropriate balance of action—ultimately, of energy—in response to system requirements.

Consistent with the general system perspective, social systems are assumed to have monitoring processes that provide feedback on subsystem functioning. Feedback monitoring evaluates the functional pressures and the positive and negative effects of responses to them. The effects may be indicated by the presence or absence of *stress*, which signals disturbance in the system. Some indicators of stress are conflict among participants, absenteeism, high participant turnover, low motivation, and low productivity. The more adequately system components respond to functional pressures, the lower the level of stress in the system.

In the rational perspective, these responses would be interpreted in terms of their logical fit with organizational goals. In the system perspective, although an action or structure that is intended to fulfil a purpose can be interpreted in terms of that specific functional requirement, analysis is also directed to other consequences, some possibly unanticipated and unintended.[36]

For example, determining the division of labour and deploying people in jobs is clearly an attempt to mobilize the organization's human and technological resources to achieve organizational, production, or service goals. However, these efforts may also be seen as having consequences for consensus and cohesion since the division of people in terms of occupational roles, or work groups, carries the potential for, and may result in, conflict. Similarly, a hierarchical authority structure, though intended to achieve a necessary level of coordination and compliance, may in certain circumstances, such as the presence of a highly educated staff or an emphasis on democratic values in the surrounding political culture, increase the pressure of motivational problems in the system. An emphasis on efficiency in the gypsum plant studied by Gouldner ([1954] 1964), perceived by management as a positive response to goal-achievement, led to a breakdown in management-employee relations in the form of a wildcat strike, which can be interpreted as an increase in both cohesive and motivational pressures.

The system perspective, because of its emphasis on functional requirements as well as on goal-achievement, also helps to make sense of actions taken by organizations that, in terms of goal-rationality, appear to be irrational. For example, whereas an outsider may regard concerns over office furnishings as trivial, members of organizations may be keenly interested in the sizes of their desks, whether their offices are carpeted, the size of the carpet they can claim, and, apart from gender differences, which washroom they are entitled to use. In the system perspective these organizational artifacts are seen to symbolize the status structure. To the extent that the status structure and its symbolic expression is accepted by a majority of participants as "right" or appropriate, and is therefore legitimate, it contributes to the coordination requirement by ordering relationships.

Even though the degree of interdependence may vary, what happens in one part of an organization will have positive and negative consequences for its other parts. Thus, procedures to motivate participants in an organization may be expected to have repercussions for productive behaviour (resulting in higher or lower productivity), for cohesion (e.g., by increasing or decreasing conflict among different salary groups), for compliance (e.g., by increasing or decreasing the need for a formal exercise of authority), and for goals (e.g., by maintaining or distorting system goals).[37] Although it may seem simple-minded to suggest that procedures designed to improve motivation may affect productivity—since that is presumably the reason for introducing them—it is less widely recognized that procedures and other substructures may have unanticipated as well as anticipated effects. Blau's account ([1955]

1963, chaps. 3 and 4) of a procedural change in the state employment agency that he studied illustrates this point. A division manager introduced changes in the manner of reporting statistics on the performance of interviewers. These statistics, posted monthly in the division offices, reported each interviewer's rate of successful placements rather than, as in the past, counts of the number of interviews that had taken place. The changes in the way of reporting the statistical information were introduced as a means of providing the division manager with more useful information on the interviewers' productivity. The information would allow identification of differences in this respect among the interviewers and provide a possible basis for motivating improvements in productivity. However, the interviewers in one section responded by adopting a variety of practices to inflate their placement rates. This had the effect of reducing the quality of service to employers and job-seekers alike and distorted the goals or objectives of the agency.

It is important, then, to recognize that the system perspective and the assumption of interdependence means more than the simple notion that "everything affects everything else" but requires identification of the degree and direction of interdependence of the various system elements.

CRITIQUE OF THE SYSTEM PERSPECTIVE

By merging the concepts of the rational and human relations perspectives, the system perspective provides a richer organizational model. More important, it provides a radically different conception of the relationships among components of organization and organizational performance. The system perspective allows for analysis of organizations in terms of structures and processes. Processes are the essential requirements that are satisfied by structures directed toward boundary maintenance. The system perspective also differs from its predecessors by its emphasis on the interdependence of system requirements and by its stipulation that the minimal objective of organizations is survival, that is, maintaining the boundary between the organization and its environment.

Although the evolution of the system perspective has led to different conceptions of the relationships between organizations and their environments—characterized, for example, by the terms natural systems and open systems—the environment has been a key concept throughout the history of the system perspective. In addition to the emphasis on the interdependence of system requirements, they are seen as variable, depending on both the internal and external pressures on the organization as well as on the type of organization. System interdependence itself is seen as variable: components may be loosely or tightly tied. System requirements, although seen as essential, may be more or less significant for the system depending on its type or the time at which the evaluation is made. The structures may vary in relation to the system's process: more than one structure may meet system requirements, and a structure may meet more than one system requirement. The system perspective, then, provides a very different conception of organizations than its predecessors, one that provides a basis for developing dynamic models.

The system perspective provides a different way of thinking about organizations. Instead of interpreting or assessing organizational performance by comparing actual organizational structure with the rational bureaucratic model or, as in the human relations perspective, by analyzing goal-achievement or organizational effectiveness, the emphasis is on the survival of the organization. To survive, an organization must respond to the pressures from its environments. These conditions are seen as differentiated in their sources and their significance to the organization. At the least complicated level, the source of these pressures is located in an organization's external or internal environments. More complex levels of differentiation, such as those by Parsons and by Katz and Kahn, have been developed.

What happens to a social system is seen as the result of the interplay between pressures from the system's external and internal environments and its responses to such pressures. The condition of the system is always determined at any instant by that interplay of forces. It is also assumed that system responses differ in relation to system requirements, taking the form, for example, of action directed toward coordination, compliance, consensus and cohesion, and toward maintaining goal-orientation. On the assumption that the supply of energy necessary to meet functional requirements is finite at any point in time, the response to one class of functional requirement results in an increased pressure from other functional requirements. Moreover, it is recognized that the interdependence of structural components and processes means that structural changes in relation to any one functional requirement can have positive and negative implications for other structural components and processes. Such assumptions support a conception of a system undergoing continual change.

It is, however, one thing to identify the assumptions of the system perspective and another to show that these are valid. This requires more than illustrative examples. It requires research conducted in a system perspective documenting that the functioning, good or bad, of organizations results from the interplay between a system and its environments. Before such validation can be achieved, there are problems to be solved.

At the theoretical level, there is no clear consensus on the fundamental dimensions or system requirements of organizations conceived as social systems. Parsons' model—adaptation, goal-attainment, integration, latency[38] (AGIL)—provides a very general set of dimensions, while

Katz and Kahn provide a set that reflects customary divisions of the main activities carried out in organizations. Parsons' model is a high level theoretical formulation that needs elaboration to specify empirical indicators. Katz and Kahn's set, though partially derived from Parsons' system, consists of indicators that lack a theoretical rationale. Although both these formulations provide a starting point, further attempts to refine the categorization of functional requirements are necessary for the perspective to be used more effectively in empirical research. Just as the external-internal categorization is inadequate to cope with the realities of organizational structure and action, so Parsons' AGIL model of system dimensions requires refinement for research purposes. For example, although communication structures and communicative actions could fit into any of Parsons' four dimensions, their importance for organizations suggests that they should be given equal standing as a dimension.

A classification that will capture the complexity of functional requirements should focus on lower levels of analysis than that proposed by Parsons. For example, adaptation, which refers to a system's relations to its external environment, can be refined by identifying processes for getting and transmitting information about the environment, for evaluating such information, and for determining and ensuring that the information is utilized. The integration requirement can certainly be elaborated to incorporate such processes as decision-making and rule-making as well as those that respond to the pressures of cohesion or conflict. Structures of decision-making, for example, may be based on effectiveness criteria, such as the time required to reach a decision and the knowledge required by those engaged in the process, but it may also be necessary to consider the significance for cohesion of the decision-making structure. Indeed, an elaboration of concepts of functional requirements is necessary for the development of hypotheses concerning the relations of structures and processes in the face of functional pressures.

Although the concept of interdependence is essential to the system perspective, it also needs refinement. Moore (1965, chap. 5), for example, recognized that it is not realistic to assume that all social system elements have the same degree of interdependence. In a university, changes in the organization of the registrar's office or in the business office are not likely to have a great impact on the organization of the curriculum or on research. In fact, the degree and nature of interdependence of organizational elements is a matter both for hypothesizing and for empirical investigation.

The five-category system that Kahn and Katz propose is more concrete. The labels given to the five functional requirements and their subsystem counterparts (described earlier in this chapter) are recognizable organizational operations. There are, however, two main difficulties. First, there is the problem of functional specificity. Analysis suggests that structures and processes, as shown earlier in the discussion of the division of labour, are not uniquely related to single functional requirements. A possible solution is to expand the categorizations beyond those proposed by Parsons or Katz and Kahn, or to abandon the idea of one-to-one relations between subsystems and functional requirements. Second, apart from the question of whether the categories proposed by Parsons or Katz and Kahn are exhaustive or whether the subsystems, as conceptualized, can satisfactorily capture the reality of organizational operations, it is doubtful that these schemes fully capture *sociological* reality. For example, cohesion and conflict, shown in Chapter Seven to be persistent interests in sociological analysis, may require greater prominence in analytical schemes rather than being absorbed into broader categories, such as Parsons' integration dimension or Katz and Kahn's managerial subsystem.

At an empirical level, a set of indicators is required to measure or assess organizational performance relative to system requirements. Solutions to this problem must focus on the system consequences of organizational features, but this is only a first step. Just as a structural component, such as a task or occupational-based division of labour, may have positive or negative consequences for goal-achievement and for cohesion or conflict, such multiple consequences must have unambiguous measures. However, finding indicators, as in the case of goal-achievement (discussed in Chapter Eight), is an extremely difficult problem.

It is also necessary to formulate models of the relationships of the system requirements. If it is assumed that equality of system requirements is empirically unlikely, a model should state the likely values or priorities for organizations of a given type. The model could then be tested against indicators of actual organizations. A further important step would require the formulation of dynamic models that would test hypotheses concerning temporal change in pressures from system requirements.

The system perspective has been criticized as inadequate for the analysis of change. Winship and Rosen (1988, S9), for example, assert that functionalism, which they associate with Parsons' system approach, may be useful in explaining the existence of institutions[39] in terms of their societal functions but has not been successful in relating institutional change to functional change. Winship and Rosen are correct in identifying such analyses as post hoc explanations and are realistic in arguing that functional explanations are difficult to test. Their criticism, however, does not allow the conclusion that hypotheses concerning future change cannot be formulated and tested. Their comments appear to be directed to earlier versions of functionalism rather than to Parsons' conceptualization of the dimensions of social action (see, for example, Parsons, Bales, and Shils 1953, chap. 3), which includes the concept of a dynamic or moving equilibrium, consistent with a general systems perspective (Miller 1978, chap. 2). Parsons' analysis of social change in *The*

Evolution of Societies (1977) is directed toward the problems of social systems in maintaining stability and in adapting to environmental pressures through changes in cultural and structural components.

Theory and research in the system perspective continued into the 1980s and 1990s. For example, it is prominent in discussions of organizational theory by Evan (1993) and Scott (1992, chap. 5). Recognizing systems theory as an "epochal paradigm" but challenged by postmodernist critics, Hassard (1993) argues that a plurality of perspectives is required for the understanding of organizations. Mayhew (1983) provides a research example that uses a system perspective to analyze the structural consequences of exchanges between organizations and environmental elements. Kuhn and Beam (1982) bring together work in several social science disciplines to describe a system perspective on organizations that they see as a field of study in its own right. A system perspective is certainly consistent with the formulation developed by Ahrne (1994) for studying organizations.[40] The system perspective also persists among those who identify organizational behaviour as their discipline (see, for example, Donaldson 1985), one that has its roots in the human relations perspective.

The rich variety of perspectives and emphases found in recent studies of organizations makes it difficult to identify any one as dominant. However, there are concepts whose importance to the understanding of organizations is recognized in a variety of perspectives, including the system perspective. Consequently, in the discussion to follow, each chapter will be organized about one of these concepts, namely, the environments of organizations (Chapter Five), authority and power (Chapter Six), consensus and cohesion and their opposites (Chapter Seven), and the goals of organizations (Chapter Eight). Research relevant to each concept will be reported and related to the system perspective and to other perspectives.

ENDNOTES

[1]   Parsons, who may be identified to a considerable degree with Max Weber, made his principal contributions to the system perspective from 1950 through the 1970s. Katz and Kahn ([1966] 1978, 6) who declared an intellectual debt to Parsons, worked initially within the human relations perspective.

[2]   Parsons' work was undoubtedly influenced by L.J. Henderson, a biochemist, who used an early form of system perspective in his work. Henderson and Parsons translated part of Weber's work (Weber [1925] 1947).

[3]   The Society was affiliated with the American Association for the Advancement of Science. See Bertalanffy (1968, 14–17) for a brief account of the formation of the Society.

⁴ Bertalanffy died in 1972 but his last book was published posthumously.

⁵ Terms vary among authors. Miller (1978), for example, uses the term **subsystem** to refer to functional requirements and **process** to describe the required actions. Sociologists use functional requirements but also **functional prerequisites** or **requisites** as alternatives. They use function to refer to the consequences of action for the system.

⁶ The level of analysis defines the system and its subsystems. If the human organism is the level of analysis, its subsystems could include the circulatory system, the digestive system, and so on. When a subsystem of an organism is the focus of analysis, and the total organism is not referred to, the subsystem is regarded as the system and its components as subsystems.

⁷ Whether the term functionalism or structural-functionalism is applicable depends on the emphasis given to social structure. For those, such as Malinowski ([1948] 1984) who emphasized culture and the functional consequences of cultural elements for the individual, functionalism is the appropriate label. For others, such as Radcliffe-Browne (1933; 1935) and sociologists who emphasized social structure—Merton's (1949, 27) "standardized activities"—and its functional and dysfunctional consequences for society, structural-functionalism is more fitting.

   Among these British social anthropologists were Evans-Pritchard (1962), Radcliffe-Browne (1935), Firth ([1951] 1961, chap. 1), and Malinowski ([1948] 1984).

⁸ It is likely that Malinowski, who taught at the London School of Economics when Parsons studied there, influenced Parsons' sociological perspective.

⁹ Malinowski's principal fieldwork was conducted on the Trobriand Islands, belonging to the Micronesian group located in the South Pacific Ocean (see, for example, [1929] 1932; [1922] 1961). More general interpretations of human social behaviour are to be found in his books on specific topics, such as the practices of magic and religion ([1948] 1984).

¹⁰ Malinowski does not describe the substances used in garden magic, but those used in rites associated with building and using canoes included dried banana leaf, stale potatoes, and birdnests ([1922] 1961, 452–53).

¹¹ Examples include Durkheim ([1912] 1947), Radcliffe-Browne (1935), Evans-Pritchard (1962, chap. 3), Cohen (1955), and Kluckhohn ([1944] 1967).

¹² Such assumptions may be more acceptably stated in probabilistic terms. For example, it may be hypothesized that stress reduction is a probable outcome of an individual's participation in a religious ceremony, with probability values from empirical research attached to the proposition.

¹³ Although the concept of social relationship is no more abstract than that of the individual, the latter, as a highly valued element in Western ideology, enjoys a considerable measure of concreteness in everyday thinking—the tendency is to equate the individual with the human organism.

¹⁴ Researchers use a variety of indicators, such as newspaper circulation and frequency of trips by peripheral residents to the community's central area, to define community boundaries.

[15] The Census of Canada partially recognizes these different perceptions of family by reporting information on, for example, "economic" families, "census" families, family size, living arrangements, and relationships of members in households (Statistics Canada 1992).

[16] Even in our society, the rules of marriage, which forbid marriage between certain categories of kin, serve to define boundaries.

[17] George Homans' procedure (1950, 82–86) was to define the boundaries of a group by the ratio of the frequency of interaction between members of a group to the frequency of their interaction with non-members.

[18] Death, in the case of biological systems, has been defined as the dissolution of an organism's boundaries vis-à-vis its environment.

[19] For a brief readable statement of Parsons' action theory, see chapter 1 of *The Evolution of Societies* (Parsons 1977), which was edited by Jackson Toby.

[20] In early human relations research, organizational effectiveness tended to be measured by productivity but was later expanded to include measures of organizational flexibility and intra-group tension (see, for example, Georgopoulus and Tannenbaum 1957). With this conceptual expansion, organizational effectiveness could be regarded as a synonym for boundary maintenance.

[21] Adaptive capacity appears to be an aspect of boundary maintenance.

[22] In research, it is essential to establish empirical indicators of these structures. As we shall see, many researchers use the concept of **complexity** to refer to the degree of structural differentiation in organizations.

[23] The term *functional requirement* refers to an action or condition necessary for system persistence, and the term *functional problem* refers to a pressure that is potentially disruptive of the system.

[24] Talcott Parsons, who distinguished four levels of system (organism, personality, social, and culture) in his general theory of action, would interpret a disruption in an organization that arises from the personalities of the participants as environmental. Even so, the external-internal distinction could be preserved by distinguishing between external and internal environments.

[25] These operations are often referred to as *line*, in contrast to *staff*, activities and are also referred to as *throughput* activities.

[26] Examples of service organizations are government departments and agencies, public and private welfare agencies, business services, courts of law, unions, and professional associations.

[27] The classic example is the agency that ran the March of Dimes campaign to provide funds for research for a cure for poliomyelitis and for services to those suffering from the disease. Although the discovery of the Salk vaccine meant that the first objective had been realized and the second was being realized by a dwindling demand for services, the agency survived by expanding its objectives to include raising funds for research and services for other disabling diseases (Sills 1957).

[28] Although specialized skills may be possessed by persons of given ethnicity or other ascribed characteristics, technical competence exemplifies a universalistic criterion.

29 Etzioni's typology of organizations, discussed in Chapter One, recognized differences in the degree of self-motivation of organizational participants. In particular, he proposed that in religious and political organizations, the compliance of some members relates to the intensity of their commitment to the organization's ideology. In organizations that depend on participants who are paid for their services, the collective interest and organizational ideology is subordinated to self-interest.

30 One legitimized by technical competence or on some other basis.

31 Social relationships may, of course, be analyzed as social systems, but here attention is focused on the larger system, on the organization, of which they are components.

32 Here I regard alienation—the distancing of an individual by others—as a form of conflict.

33 To Miller (1978, 369), a subsystem includes (1) the name of the functional requirement, (2) the structure of components responding to the requirement, and (3) the process, that is, the action of the components. Thus, in the human organism, Miller names the subsystem that processes matter and energy the *distributor* subsystem. The structure would include the blood vascular system (heart, arteries, veins, etc.) and the process would include the actions of the gastrointestinal tract, lungs, the blood vascular system, etc. In Miller's analytical scheme, a component or a structure of components may serve more than one functional requirement.

34 If additional energy could be obtained, for example, by increasing the number of participants or by inducing existing participants to commit additional time to the organization, the allocative problem would be eased. However, since securing resources is also a functional requirement, the organization may, under the finite energy assumption, respond to this requirement only by a further reduction of energy for other requirements.

35 Although it has frequently been asserted that the structural-functional model is inadequate for the analysis of social change, this particular model, developed by Parsons, interprets change as disequilibrating but as allowing for change as the system moves to a *new* state of equilibrium rather than a return necessarily to a former state. The conditions that lead to a new equilibrium rather than a restoration, however, require formulation.

36 Merton (1957, chap. 1) refers to intended and unintended consequences, respectively, as *manifest* and *latent* functions.

37 Evidence of these various effects will be provided in later discussion.

38 This last dimension is also named **Latent Pattern Maintenance** (Parsons, Bales, and Shils 1953, 189) or just Pattern Maintenance (Parsons 1960, 164).

39 The authors refer to organizations and to economic institutions without offering explicit definitions. In their discussion, the terms appear to be synonymous.

40 Ahrne extends the term *organizations* to all collectivities.

CHAPTER 5

THE ENVIRONMENTS OF ORGANIZATIONS: PRESSURES AND RESPONSES

An understanding of organizations requires analysis of their relationships to their environments. To understand these relationships, sociologists identify different aspects of organizations. The major distinctions are technology, size, and culture. Technology refers to the tools, skills, and production processes used to provide goods and services. Size refers to the number of participants—employees, volunteers, members—in an organization. Culture refers to the beliefs, values, rules, and norms of both the organization's external environment—the society to which the organization belongs—as well the organization's internal environment—its own culture. As the sociological analysis of organizations' environmental relationships is a complex topic, an exhaustive discussion is not attempted in this text. Instead, the discussion is focused on technology, size, and values. The evident importance of these components of the environments of organizations justifies their selection as the main topics of this chapter.

Although sociologists have always been aware of the importance of environmental forces in understanding social action, the system perspective strongly enhanced this awareness by providing, as we have seen, a statement of the relationship between the dimensions of organizations and their environments. In the system perspective, the organization relates to the environment both actively and reactively. Organizations must actively exploit their environments to obtain necessary resources, such as materials, technology, skilled personnel, and clients.[1] As well, organizations must react or respond defensively against environmental pressures that threaten its structures and performance. Such reactions may serve to deflect specific environmental pressures—as when a customer service unit keeps complaints from reaching the part of the organization that could most effectively deal with them. On the other hand, the organization's reaction may be to require modification of organizational structures, such as its division of labour, communication patterns, or its structure and processes of decision-making.

As research and theoretical discussions of the organization-environment relationship have proceeded, the conception of the environment has narrowed. Whereas the definition of the environment had included any element that was not part of an organization, a more specific formulation of environmental dimensions or components emerged. Thus, Scott ([1981] 1987, 125–34; further elaborated in 1992, chaps. 8 & 10) distinguished between **technical** and **institutional** components of the environment, which are seen as polarities or extremes of an environmental dimension. He drew further distinctions within these polarities. For example, technical components include "sources of inputs, markets for outputs, competitors and regulators" (Scott 1987, 127). The institutional components include other organizations and historical and cultural features, such as the values, norms, and customs of the surrounding society and its subsystems.

This change toward thinking of the environment as a collection of differentiated components arises from the recognition that different environmental components may have different effects on organizations. Carroll and Huo (1986, 838, 867), for example, found support for this possibility in research showing that task components of newspapers' technical environments, compared to their institutional environments, were more closely associated with newspaper circulation rates, whereas institutional components had a stronger effect on the "births and deaths" of newspapers. It is possible that task components tend to affect performance while institutional components tend to influence organizational structure. It is premature, however, to conclude that what has been accomplished so far in empirical research and theoretical discussion is the last word on organization-environment relationships. It is possible, nonetheless, to discuss how specific environmental components, such as technology, size, and values, exert influence on organizations.

TECHNOLOGY

In a limited view, organizations may be thought of as a complex of objectives and tasks. As an example, for Revenue Canada to achieve its objective of collecting the money required to pay the costs of government, its staff must recommend policies for taxes, duties, and other forms of revenue. In addition, they must provide the means for collecting these various levies, for checking that individuals, corporations, and others do meet these levies, for recording their operation, and so on. Hospitals, to achieve their goals of providing treatment and care for those who are ill, must have appropriate equipment, expert staff, and other employees to meet a variety of service demands. Social service organizations must similarly obtain resources that allow them to perform the required procedures to meet their various objectives, whether these be to provide advice and consultation for family problems, to help the young deal with their problems, to provide havens for victims of domestic violence, or some other objective. In short, all organizations must perform throughput operations that transform various kinds of input resources into organizational output as defined by their objectives. For many organizations, input primarily takes the form of material resources that are to be transformed into a higher stage of material output, for example, automobiles made from steel, plastic, rubber, etc. For other organizations, such as banks and other financial organizations that provide a service, money is both input and output, with throughput taking the form of processing customers' accounts, providing and monitoring loans, etc. Some organizations, such as manufacturing firms, mining companies, and power companies, process materials; others, such as banks, stockbrokers, and insurance companies, process paper; and still others, such as schools, hospitals, social agencies, and prisons, process people. It is important to recognize that all of these organizations utilize technology in the form of tools and machines, and in the form of skills and knowledge appropriate to their throughput tasks. The technologies may differ: some may be machine-intensive as is the automated or robotic factory, while others may be people-intensive, as are hospitals, schools, and prisons.

It is reasonable to assume that technology and technological change will have an impact on organizations. Obviously, different technologies will require differences in the mix of occupations, emphasizing some occupations over others, and possibly requiring different managerial arrangements. A system perspective anticipates that technology, as an element of the environment, will have an impact on organizations. In general terms, such effects are experienced through their effect on the organization's various functional requirements. However, this perspective anticipates neither the various effects of different technologies nor the specific effects of a technology on any functional requirement. Two early studies undertaken by Burns and Stalker (1961) and by Woodward ([1965] 1980) have been very influential.

The research by Burns and Stalker (1961) provides an example of the effects of demand on organizational structure. In a study of a number of electronic manufacturing firms, they found that one or the other of two organizational models could be used to characterize the firms.

The features of one model, which they called mechanistic,[2] are much like those of Weber's bureaucratic model and include:

- an emphasis on a specialized and precisely defined division of labour;
- responsibility limited to the rights and obligations of each occupational role;
- hierarchical authority and communication structures;
- interaction that is characteristically vertical;
- work operations and behaviour that are governed by the instructions and decisions of a superior; and
- an insistence on obedience to superiors and on loyalty to the firm.

The features of the other model, called organic, are in direct contrast to those of the mechanistic model. The organic model includes:

- an emphasis on the firm's common task, with each employee contributing special knowledge and skill to its completion;
- a rejection of the concept of limited responsibility—problems cannot be transferred as someone else's responsibility;
- communication and control emphasizing responsiveness to colleagues and a commitment to a working community, rather than to a contractual relationship with a corporation represented by a superior;
- interaction that is characteristically lateral, with vertical interaction tending to take the form of consultation;
- communication that tends to consist of information and advice rather than instructions and decisions; and
- commitment to the firm's overall task, to a technical ethos of material progress, and to expansion rather than to obedience and loyalty.

The influence of the environment was revealed by the finding that organizations with a mechanistic structure tended to operate in a stable environment—one in which the demand was for products that were not subject to a high degree of change in design—whereas organic structures tended to be found in environments marked by customer demand for products that were subject to rapid change. This generalization suggests that a stable environment supports the establishment and maintenance of routine procedures and the discipline and control necessary to maintain compliance. By contrast, an organic structure supports demands for creativity and the ability to solve new problems that persistently develop and that require a pooling of talent and a collectively supported innovative approach.

Although Burns and Stalker discussed organizational structure in what appear to be two types—mechanistic and organic—they insisted that it is more productive to think of variations in structure in terms of a continuum than in terms of a typology. Thus, mechanistic and organic refer to the extremes of the continuum. In reality, an organization's structure is likely to combine characteristics of both these extremes. Depending on the balance, an organization can be placed somewhere between the end points of the continuum.

Among the important implications of this conception is the realistic assumption that there are viable modern structural types that must be considered as such, rather than as deviant forms of bureaucracy. Moreover, it may be more useful to think of *bureaucratization* rather than *bureaucracy* when analyzing organizational structure—that is, to consider the process rather than the structural type.[3] The idea of a continuum between bureaucracy and its opposite also supports the assumption that some elements of bureaucracy may be present in most if not all organizations.

Although Burns and Stalker provided evidence of technology influencing organizational structure, they also proposed other influential variables. Basically, they held that without the intervention of other variables, organizational structure should tend toward compatibility with the environmental conditions.[4] As these structural changes may not occur in actual organizations, Burns and Stalker suggested, presumably on the basis of their data, three variables that may act to enhance or weaken this "natural" tendency:

- status and/or power concerns—organizational change will be supported or resisted depending on whether it is perceived to maintain (or improve) or threaten a person's status and/or power position;

- commitment to organizational improvement—the degree of individual and/or collective support for improving organizational performance will affect how the organization changes; and

- the chief executive officer's influence—this person's capacity to interpret the environment accurately and to motivate employees to support organizational improvement can encourage or discourage change.

By drawing attention to these variables, which are seen to interfere with a "natural process," it is clear that Burns and Stalker are not technological determinists even though they regard technology as the strongest influence on organizational structure.

Woodward's ground-breaking research on 110 manufacturing firms in southern England provides an example of the effect of production technology on organizational structure. Briefly stated, her research revealed that differences in technology were associated with differences in organizational structure. Although all the firms included in the survey processed materials, they used different technologies to do so. Some produced one-of-a-kind items or were engaged in small volume production and characteristically employed craft or relatively high-skilled employees. Some engaged in mass or large volume production using assembly lines. Others used a production technology that merged various manufacturing operations to form a continuous process. For example, in a brewery included in the survey, after bottles were hand-fed into the production line, bottling was a continuous process that included sterilizing, filling, stoppering, labelling, counting, and crating. With this technology, the workforce is primarily engaged in monitoring and servicing the process, checking dials and other instruments, and performing maintenance and repair tasks rather than directly transforming input materials.

Woodward found variation in the organizational structures of the firms, as measured, for example, by the number of management levels, the number of employees per supervisor (called the *span of control*), and other ratios such as supervisory to non-supervisory staff, and industrial workers per staff worker. Although Woodward explored the possibility that such variables as company size, amount of profit or loss, and type of product might account for the observed variation in organizational structure, only technology showed a clear relation to structure.

In most instances, she found that variations in structural measures were related systematically to variations in technology. For example, she found that continuous-process firms had the most levels of management, craft firms, the fewest, with the assembly line firms being in between (Woodward [1965] 1980, 52). She found a similar pattern for the ratio of supervisory staff to non-supervisory staff and for the ratio of staff to industrial workers (Woodward [1965] 1980, 56, 60). If the technologies were assumed to increase in complexity from craft to continuous process, the dominant pattern of association between these various measures of organizational structure and technology could be described as being linear in form.[5] In other words, the magnitudes of the ratios of these measures of structure, such as supervisory to non-supervisory, increased from low to high technical complexity. The association of these measures of structure and of technology supported Woodward's conclusion that technology was a prominent influence on structural variation. Woodward's conclusion received further support from Zwerman (1970), who used her production technology categories in a study of organizational structure in manufacturing firms in the U.S.A.

In addition to what Woodward and others have reported on the association between production technology and authority, there is evidence that structural changes occur with the adoption of automation or continuous-production technology. On the basis of their survey of findings on the effects of high-technology production, Hodson and Parker (1988) observed that the demand for middle managers declines when many functions of this management level are automated. Moreover, they

cited studies that either found or concluded that high technology is associated with severe modifications of hierarchy in organizations.

However, other research, such as undertaken in Britain (for example, Hickson, Pugh, and Pheysey [1969] 1980; Child and Mansfield
1972;) and in Canada, Britain, and the United States (Hickson et al.
1974) has failed to find support for an association between production
technology and organizational structure, finding instead that the *size* of
a firm was more closely related to variations in organizational structure. Blau et al. (1976) also found organization size to have a strong
effect on organizational structure—as identified by various measures of
the authority structure and the division of labour—but also found a U-
shaped relationship between technical complexity, as measured by
Woodward's scale, and certain aspects of the division of labour and the
span of control of front-line supervisors.[6] In terms of Woodward's categories, batch production would have lower ratios for these structural
features than either craft or continuous technology. That is, the relationship between technical complexity and organizational structure is
curvilinear rather than linear.

Although much research has focused on the effects of technology
on organizational structure, the effects of technology on other dimensions of organizations, such as on conflict and on workers' attitudes,
have also been investigated. Sayles (1958) provides, indirectly, an example of the effects of manufacturing technology on the expression of grievances. On the basis of a study of three hundred work groups in thirty
plants and the grievances of workers employed in various manufacturing occupations, Sayles identified four patterns of grievance expression,
which he called **strategic, conservative, erratic**, and **apathetic** based
on the frequency and level of planning of the grievance activity.

Sayles found a high frequency of grieving to be associated with a
low division of labour, high-density employment, middle-level status
occupations, and occupations where a worker had some control over
operations.[7] Low frequency is associated with a relatively high division
of labour, low-density or long assembly lines, and either high- or low-
status occupations. However, although Sayles identified clear differences in grievance strategy, it is not apparent that effective grievance
planning is associated with production technology. While the internal
disunity observed among apathetic groups could result from a high division of labour, the production technologies of the other groups do not
appear to account for differences in emphasis that the groups give to
planning grievance activity.[8]

Blauner (1964) used attitudinal data obtained from employees of
firms representing craft, machine-tending, and continuous-process
technologies to investigate the relationship between production technology and alienation.[9] He characterized this relationship in terms
of four dimensions: powerlessness, meaninglessness, social alienation,

and self-estrangement. On the basis of their content, Blauner classified attitude questions in terms of these four dimensions.[10] In general, results for each dimension of alienation showed that workers in the printing (craft) and chemical (continuous-process) industries showed markedly less alienation than those employed in automobile or textile manufacturing (machine-tending).[11]

Shepard (1971) provided further support for the hypothesis that alienation varies with production technology. He used first-hand data— responses to questionnaire items constructed to represent dimensions of alienation similar to but not identical to Blauner's—from samples of blue-collar and white-collar employees representing three production technologies: "non-mechanized, mechanized, and automated" (Shepard 1971, 10).[12] Consistent with Blauner, he found that blue-collar employees in non-mechanized and continual-process production to be less alienated than those engaged in mass production. The pattern for white-collar employees was very similar, but there were differences between white- and blue-collar employees (Shepard 1971, 91).

When Shepard compared alienation levels of white- and blue-collar employees working in the same technology, he found that white-collar employees tend to express less alienation than blue-collar employees. However, levels of alienation within a production technology could vary between these two kinds of employees. For example, crafts-people reported less powerlessness than their white-collar counterparts in both non-mechanized technology and the other two technologies. A summary of the five scales reveals five instances where white-collar employees expressed less alienation than blue-collar, two instances where blue-collar employees expressed less, and eight where there were only small differences between the two categories of employees (Shepard 1971, 98–99).

In summary, there is much research evidence to support common-sense and theoretical expectations that technology will affect organizational structure and processes. However, that evidence conflicts with other findings, especially those resulting from research on the effects of size on structure and process. Hodson and Parker's conclusion (1988, 24ff.) that research on the effects of high technology reveals "all too few consistent, undisputed findings" also applies to research on the effects of technology in general.

SIZE

Anyone who has been involved in both small and large organizations serving similar purposes, whether they be schools, hospitals, or companies, or who has been in an organization during a period of growth, is likely to have observed differences between small and large organizations. Typically an increase in the size of an organization coincides with a greater use of rules and with a move toward impersonal relationships among people at different levels of authority. From at least the time of Simmel who, in the late nineteenth century and the beginning of the twentieth, theorized about the effects of numbers of members on group processes, sociologists have been aware that differences in the number of participants may alter aspects of the social relationships and social interaction in a collectivity or an organization. This sensitivity to numbers is markedly evident in the sociological study of organizations. Sociologists have given a great deal of attention to the effects of size or, at least, to the co-variation of size and other features of organizations. Indeed, Baron (1984, 41) observes that organization researchers "have probably devoted more attention to the link between organization size and work arrangements than to any other topic."

There are various reasons for this interest in the effects of size on organizations. For example, size is expected to affect a collectivity or an organization because each additional member is seen to add to the number of possible relationships.[13] For example, if a third person is added to a collectivity that consists of two persons, the number of possible dyadic (i.e., two-person) relationships increases from one to three. If seven more persons are added, the number of possible dyadic relationships increases to forty-five.[14] Moreover, the greater the number of members in a collectivity, the greater the possible number of relationships involving more than two people. The term **density** is used to refer to the state of the relationship structure as revealed by differences in the numbers of dyads and higher-order relationships. In this sense, size increases the density of the relationship structure. Simply as a consequence of the increasing density of the relationship structure, it may be anticipated that maintaining required levels of communication, coordination, consensus/dissensus, and cohesion/conflict—all sociological conditions—will become increasingly problematic. Indeed, it may also be anticipated that problems associated with these conditions are likely to induce various structural changes in an organization. For example, a pattern of sub-units, such as sections and departments, may be established, or changed if one already exists, or changes may be made to the authority structure.

"Small" collectivities are thought to differ in various respects from "large" collectivities. Simmel (Wolff 1950, 114–15) observed that in societies where extended families are the norm, households tend to a maximum of thirty members. As numbers increase beyond thirty, new households tend to be established. This suggests that increases in size beyond this limit exert negative effects on conditions required for the functioning of the household. Research on small groups reveals that as the number of participants increases, interaction patterns shift from relatively equal to markedly unequal participation (Parsons, Bales, and Shils 1953, 130–32). Granovetter (1984, 333) suggested one hundred employees as a sociologically significant cutting point for economic organizations. In his view, it is easy for employees of establishments of one hundred or fewer to know each other and for supervisors to know their subordinates in "a detailed and intimate way."

Interaction may be differently regulated in small and large collectivities. In collectivities, including organizations, where the number of participants is small, as in families, street corner gangs (Leibow 1967; Whyte [1955, 1966] 1981), and in work teams and crews, interaction is governed more by understandings, often implicit, of what is expected and what the consequences of non-compliance will be rather than by written rules and company manuals. However, as organizations increase in size, unless participants are drawn from a very homogeneous population, an underlying consensus reflected by implicit understandings or expectations will be difficult to achieve. Rules, which tend to emerge where dissensus or conflict exist, may be expected to become more prominent as a means of regulating members' actions. This is implied by Tepperman's finding that the standardization of decision-making in Massachusetts juvenile courts was associated with court size (1973). Increased court size meant an increase in the density of relationships among court personnel *and* increased heterogeneity based on occupational specialization. Tepperman argued that the greater standardization observed for large as compared with small courts was a response to both the greater density and to the potential conflict based on differences in occupational ideologies. The Aston Group[15] (Hickson, Pugh, and Pheysey [1969] 1980) also provided evidence that as organizations increase in size, **formality**, as revealed by a proliferation of rules and formal written documents, becomes more prominent as a means of controlling employees.

As organizations grow in size, either the number of supervisors will increase or the number of employees under each supervisor will increase. In the latter case, the possibility of close personal relations between supervisor and supervised is reduced. If an emphasis on rules as a substitute for direct supervision is introduced at the same time as interaction between supervisor and supervised is reduced, the relationships between those in superior and inferior positions are likely to become more formal.

Size has also been found to be associated with structural differentiation or complexity in organizations as assessed by the division of labour or the occupational or role structure of the organization and by the presence of specialized sub-units such as divisions, departments, and sections. Functional or task specialization is clearly more easily achieved when an organization increases the number of its members—

a manager of a small firm, for example, may be responsible for a variety of functions, such as production, maintenance, marketing, and personnel, that in a larger firm could be assigned to four specialized managers. Moreover, as noted above, as an increase in the number of members in an organization is likely to increase the complexity of its relationship structure, communication difficulties are likely to increase, with consequent problems for organizational functioning—especially for the development and maintenance of consensus and cohesion.

A possible response to problems caused by increasing membership is to introduce a more complex organizational structure—to divide the organization into units, such as divisions, departments, and work units, and to organize roles on the basis of task specialization. The anticipated effect of such complex restructuring, apart from the gains that result from specialization, is a limitation of required interaction to a smaller number of participants, those involved in the specialized function, and a limitation of those who occupy roles requiring them to represent the organization in its external relations. Contradictory as it may seem, a more complex *organizational* structure is seen as a means of coping with the problems generated by a complex *relationship* structure.

An organization's size may also relate to its centrality: the restriction of decision-making to a limited number of roles in an organization. For example, Hickson, Pugh, and Pheysey ([1969] 1980, 218, table 8) found a moderate, statistically significant negative association between size and the centralization of authority in a sample of manufacturing firms—the greater the number of employees, the less authority was centralized or the more authority was delegated. It is not immediately apparent why size should affect the *formal* distribution of authority, although it may, as Simmel argued, affect its *actual* distribution. The effect of size on the distribution of authority may, in fact, be indirect. It is reasonable to assume that as increases in size lead to increased organizational complexity, authority must be assigned to those who are responsible for specialized tasks or functions. In other words, as organizational complexity increases, so should decentralization of authority.

For those who adopt a system perspective, new members of an organization, or of any social system, may be thought of as elements of its environment that must be absorbed with the least disruption to system functioning. Indeed, Parsons (1966, 8) takes this argument further by proposing that the personality systems of *all* members of a social system should be treated as components of its environment. In other words, the needs (*need-dispositions* in Parsons' terminology) of the members of a collectivity constitute an environmental force or pressure with which an organization must cope to protect its boundaries. This may require a measure of accommodation wherein the collectivity recognizes and responds positively to the personality requirements of its members. It also may require measures, such as the resocialization of members, intended to ensure the dominance of the collectivity's values and norms as regulators of action. In the case of new members, a period of intense socialization may be required to ensure compliance with the collectivity's values and norms.[16] Here, however, the issue is the possible effects on an organization of increasing the number of members or on differences in characteristics between organizations that differ in size.

Although research has been conducted on the relationship of size to various aspects of organization, the main thrust has been on the relationship of size and such dimensions of organizational structure as complexity or vertical and horizontal differentiation and of centrality of decision-making. As an example of this research, the work of Peter Blau and his associates, widely acknowledged for its contributions in this area, will be discussed. On the basis of his research on U.S. employment security agencies, Blau (1970) developed a set of propositions that identifies size as directly influencing certain dimensions of organizational structure, such as the division of labour and the structure of authority,[17] and as indirectly affecting others, such as the administrative component, which are conceived as direct effects of differentiation. Briefly stated, Blau's reasoning is that size increases structural differentiation, which increases problems of coordination and communication. The administrative component must be expanded to cope with these problems. In relation to these problems, he observes that size, through its effect on differentiation, increases the overall heterogeneity of interests among members of the organization who represent different sub-units and occupations, but this is offset by increased homogeneity within those sub-units.

As Blau's propositions were based on his research, he was able to provide empirical support for them, although admittedly after the fact. However, as Blau has argued that size exerts a greater influence than technology on differentiation, he and his associates conducted further research (1976) to determine the effects of size and technology on the structure of a sample of manufacturing firms located in New Jersey.[18] On the whole, structural dimensions of the factories were found to be independent of technology. Although the pattern of association between technology and various measures of structure took the form of a curve, as Woodward had found, Blau et al. found that size had a stronger relationship to some structural measures. This finding, similar to those of other studies, led Blau et al. to conclude "that the structure of factories, like that of other organizations, depends greatly on their size" (1976, 26). Nonetheless, if the magnitudes of differences in the structural measures are ignored, the pattern of association shows several measures to have U-shaped (curvilinear) associations with technology (Blau et al. 1976, 24, 28).[19] Blau et al. identified two of these measures—the proportion of direct production workers in the labour force of a firm and the spans of control at various supervisory and management levels—to support their conclusion that "advances in production technology . . . do have curvilinear relationships with various aspects of plant structure" (Blau et al. 1976, 30). By contrast, size, with and without controls, was shown to be relatively strongly associated with measures of differentiation, occupational structure, and even spans of control.

Along with the widely held view that size exerts an influence on, or is at least associated with, variations in the structure and other characteristics of collectivities, including organizations, Blau's findings for manufacturing firms and similar findings by Blau and others for government agencies, department stores, universities, and colleges (Blau et al. 1976) are very convincing. Armandi and Mills (1982) tested a model that incorporated Blau's proposition that size causes structural differentiation and several propositions formulated by Jarrald Hage (1965) on data obtained from 104 New York State savings and loans associations.[20] Basically, the findings from this research supported Blau by showing strong associations between size and complexity, hierarchy of authority, and stratification. Although some Hage propositions, or those derived from them, were supported, on the whole most were rejected (Armandi and Mills 1982, table 5). Even so, the authors optimistically concluded that a generalized model for all types of organization is feasible.

Despite the important contributions of Blau and others to research on the effects of size, the claim that size is the principal determinant of structural differentiation has not gone unchallenged by other researchers and critics. Hall (1982, 58) found the evidence of Blau et al. and the Aston Group, relating size to organizational structure, to be inconsistent or in conflict with evidence from other research. Although Hall, Haas, and Johnson (1967), in their research on seventy-five organizations of different types, found some relationships between size and complexity and formalization, their analysis resulted in only a few significant values for measures of association and also revealed a significant number of deviant cases, leading them to conclude that "size may be rather irrelevant as a factor in determining organizational structure" (Hall, Haas, and Johnson 1967, 912).

As most studies on the effects of changes in size on organizational structure have been based on cross-sectional data, it is possible that findings do not take into account possible different effects of growth and decline in size.[21] In response to this concern, Freeman and Hannan (1975) used longitudinal data to investigate the effects of size on administrative intensity—the relative size of the administrative or supportive units and the units whose work is directly related to achieving the objectives of the organization.[22] In a study of school districts in California, they show that estimates of the effects of enrolments, as an indicator of size, on the size of support staff differ substantially, depending on whether the numbers of students increased or decreased during the selected time periods. A study of periods of growth and decline in enrolments at the University of Toronto also provides evidence that changes in size have differing growth effects for both **direct** (numbers of faculty and student services staff) and **supportive** (numbers of university and academic administrative staffs) components of the university (Goh and Evans 1985). Analysis of enrolments, used as a measure of size, for the period 1924 to 1944, revealed that although both direct and supportive components tended to grow proportionately in periods of increasing and decreasing enrolments, growth was lower for direct than for supportive components in periods of declining enrolments. Hummon, Doreian, and Teuter (1975) developed a model that, consistent with a system perspective, allowed for either structural differentiation or size to be interpreted as causal. A test of the model with longitudinal data on the size and structure of city, county, and state finance departments in the United States revealed that size does generate differentiation, confirming Blau, but also that increasing differentiation generates increasing size.

Valuable contributions to the debate have also been made by those who direct their criticism to theoretical and methodological issues. For example, Kimberly (1976) focused on both issues in his review of eighty research projects on the relationship between size and structural differentiation. He was generally concerned about the atheoretical nature of much of the research in this area, suggesting that the decision to study the relationship between size and structure frequently appears to be related to the availability of the relevant data. Among more specific theoretical issues, he noted that "conceptual definitions of size are lacking" (1976, 574), that generalization is hampered by the absence of an accepted typology of organizations (1976, 575–78), and that there are few unambiguous answers to questions concerning the role of size in its relationship to structural variation or concerning the conditions that may cause that role to vary (1976, 593). He doubted that the assumption that size is a cause of structural differentiation, made by many researchers, including Blau, is firmly established. Consistent with a system perspective, Kimberly suggested we consider the assumption that differentiation may cause or require increases or decreases in size (1976, 579-581).

Kimberly also identified a number of problematic methodological practices. Although size is frequently equated with the number of personnel, there are other possible indicators, such as production volume, sales volume, and number of clients, each of which could produce different results. He noted that there has been little discussion of the theoretical significance of transforming the size variable, for example, through the often-used log transformation, even when it is justifiable on mathematical and statistical grounds. Following Freeman and

Kronenfeld (1973), he identified **definitional dependence**—"where an independent variable is also a component of the dependent variable" (Kimberly 1976, 584)—as another common problem. For example, if the administrative component is measured as a ratio of the number of administrative personnel to total personnel and is used in an investigation of the relationship of size and the administrative component, a correlation may be found even when the variables are randomly distributed (Freeman 1973).

Slater (1985), who was also concerned about the absence of theory in research on the relationship between size and structural differentiation, argued that a clearer understanding of the relationship requires analysis of the assumptions and concepts, such as size and social organization, that underlie such research. On the basis of an analysis of a number of contributors in the area, Slater held that much of the inconsistency in findings relates to whether the organizations under investigation are assumed to be **natural systems** (**crescive** organizations), which are composed initially of undifferentiated individuals but which become differentiated as their numbers increase, or **rational systems** (**enacted** organizations), in which roles, and role-sets, and organizational units are defined prior to the entry of members. It is appropriate, he argued, to investigate the effects of size on differentiation in crescive but not in enacted organizations. In the latter, he suggested, attention should be focused on an organization's structural components, such as its administrative and production components, since the problem is to understand both the effects of the already differentiated components on each other and the effects of environmental forces on structure.

A COMMENT ON THE EFFECTS OF TECHNOLOGY AND SIZE

Research into the effects of size and of technology on structural differentiation and other characteristics of organizations has produced ambiguous results. While research suggests that size is more influential than technology, there remains good reason for caution in assessing the findings for both variables. There seems to be more to discover about their effects than is presently known. The problems previously identified with using size as an independent variable—the lack of a developed theory, the limits on generalization in the absence of an accepted typology of organizations, the differences in operational definitions of variables, etc.—may also be applied to studies wherein technology is regarded as the major independent variable.

At an intuitive level, the possibility that both technology and size may affect structure and process in organizations is plausible. However, investigation of this relationship has, as Kimberly (1976) and Slater (1985) noted, been underanalyzed. Much of the research in this area is focused on readily available data and ignores other aspects of organizational functioning that may be related to both variables. That, in brief, is the problem identified by those who emphasize a need for theoretical development. If a social system perspective is adopted, the analysis should focus on the interdependence between technology or size, on the one hand, and structure and process, on the other, as it bears on system survival. In such an approach, attention should be given to the relationships of both technology and size, as environmental variables to system functioning—categorized, for example, as goal-achievement, coordination, consensus, and cohesion. Although these concepts are not totally ignored, little research that has been undertaken includes them.[23] A model is needed that relates the technical features of production and changes in numbers of members to dimensions of both social interaction and social systems. Some of the research cited allows interpretation in these terms. Sayles' research on technology, for example, which reveals an association of teams, short assembly lines, and a low division of labour with a high frequency of grieving, suggests the possibility that the workers concerned were able to reach a collective decision to grieve because they interacted frequently and, because they performed similar tasks, had similar interests. In other words, the technical characteristics of the workplace facilitated the development of consensus about working conditions.[24]

Woodward expressed some ideas on the way technology affects organizational structure that are relevant to a system perspective. She proposed that organizational structure serves two broad functions: a *technical* function, which provides for the coordination of work in terms of planning, execution, and control; and a *social* function, which establishes status, communication, and interpersonal relations structures. Technology, in her view, exerts an influence on both these functions, but the effects could be opposite in direction. For example, an organizational structure that might maximize efficiency in planning, execution, and control might also alter the status structure or any of the other constituents of the social function and consequently impair cooperation or motivation. Her research, however, gave far more emphasis to the effects of technology on the technical than on the social function.

Although size and technology are not sociological concepts, they are important variables in organizational analysis and have sociological significance. Sociological analysis requires that the emphasis should be placed on understanding that significance. As organizations, like other collectivities, are systems of interaction, the important questions ask how size and technology influence both individual interactions and interaction systems as well as how interaction systems influence size and technology. As noted in the preceding discussion, some of the research can be interpreted as asking such questions. Tepperman followed this line of thought by suggesting that bureaucratization is not a direct result of increases in size but is an outcome of the direct effects of size on systems of interaction.[25] Tepperman's idea can be expanded to suggest that *all* organizational structures and processes are the outcomes of the direct effects of size, technology, and values on systems of interaction. The problem, however, is to determine how these and other possible variables result in differences in systems of interaction. In a system perspective, the possible interdependence of these variables and those describing systems of interaction must also be investigated.

VALUES

Social structure is concerned with the forms of social relationship, and culture with the shared ideas, values, symbols, norms, and rules upheld by the participants in social relationship.[26] Although the concept of structure tends to dominate sociological analysis, culture is also an important concept. **Values** was a key concept in Weber's sociology, Durkheim introduced the term **collective representations**, which included "common ideal norms" (Parsons 1949, 389–90), and other sociologists have included similar concepts in their theories.

Culture and social structure are interdependent—cultural elements serve to bind the members of a collectivity and influence its structure, that is, the forms of its relationships. Social structure, on the other hand, may be seen both as maintaining a culture and as influencing cultural change.

This section begins with a brief account of perspectives and related research that take account of culture. The main focus, however, is on the relation between shared societal values and the structures of organizations. Several models of organizations are described and discussed as possible consequences of the cultural environments of organizations.

There has been considerable interest in cross-societal comparative research on organizations.[27] Such research is focused on the similarities and differences of the organizations studied, but also, in varying degree, on the relation between the structural characteristics of these organizations and the cultural and societal characteristics of the societies to which they belong. In many studies, the main interest is to compare the relative influence of technology and cultural and societal characteristics. The results provide some support for the hypothesis that technology is dominant and is associated with similarities in organizations among societies. However, other studies provide evidence that cultural and social influences are associated with distinctive features in organizational structures (see, for example, Form 1979 and Lincoln and McBride 1987).

On the basis of a review of research on organizations in several societies, Lammers and Hickson (1979, 420ff) constructed a typology to summarize organizational differences in terms of such structural dimensions as degree of centralization, rigidity of stratification, degree of complexity, and such cultural components as variations in the type and application of rules. On the basis of survey data, Hofstede (1980) relates variations in structure and processes in subsidiaries of a multinational corporation located in thirty-nine countries to differences in values in their respective societal environments. Mercier (1985, 46) found that a Quebec public service organization resembled its Ontario counterpart in several respects, but he also found differences. For example, employees in the Quebec organization revealed a higher preference for face-to-face interaction and communication by telephone rather than by memos or in formal meetings. The Quebec employees were more accepting of rules and regulations than those in Ontario (1985, 43–44). While some differences could be attributed to occupational status and gender, others could be attributed to cultural differences between English and French.[28] Some of these differences, as reported by Quebec respondents, corresponded to those reported by Crozier in his pioneer study of cultural influences on bureaucracy in France. Indeed, the studies reported here may be regarded as delayed responses to Crozier's argument (1964, 237) that the "processes by which bureaucratic organizations control their members and employees" are related to the basic personalities, social values, and patterns of social relationships that exist in their surrounding societies. From a system perspective, it is important to recognize that these various contributions locate, explicitly or implicitly, socio-cultural components in the environments of organizations.

In more recent work, the culture of organizations and the influence of societal institutions on organizations, defined as complexes of norms, rules, and laws, have emerged as specialized areas of study. For example, Ouchi and Wilkins (1985) and Zucker (1987) are concerned with the analysis of symbols, myths, and other cultural components of organizational cultures. Scott (1992, 132–41), who provides an example of the *institutional* approach, identifies norms and other cultural elements as the core of institutional environments, one of his categories of organizational environments.

Apart from the increased research interest in socio-cultural influences on organizations, the long tradition of the conceptual importance of such elements as well as research findings in general sociology support an expectation that organizations will tend to conform to relevant values in their cultural environments. In societies where authoritarianism is valued, that is, where the decisions of those in authority tend to be unchallenged and where deference and respect are expected responses to incumbents of positions of authority, hierarchical authority is likely to be a prominent and stable feature of organizations. In societies where equality and individual rights are valued and where, consequently, deference and respect for authority are tempered by social support for dissent, there will be less emphasis on hierarchy in organizations. These expectations will be explored in the discussion to follow.

At first sight, there would appear to be little support for the theoretical expectations proposed in the preceding paragraph. In general, as has been discussed in earlier chapters, the prevalent structure of organizations in Canada and elsewhere conforms to the bureaucratic model and includes hierarchical authority structures. Moreover, changes in the authority structure of existing organizations can be explained without reference to cultural or value imperatives. Such changes are seen as attempts by management to weaken employees' loyalties to unions, as responses to employee dissatisfaction, and as efforts to achieve other goals that will benefit management. Rinehart (1986), for example, regards the popularity of **Quality of Working Life** (QWL), another term for the socio-technical perspective (described below), as the result of an interaction between both environmental forces, such as technological change and increased uncertainty in consumer demand for products and services, and managerial commitment to enduring objectives, such as maximization of profits and maintaining control over employees. Nevertheless, over the last thirty-odd years, there have been important developments in organizational structure that provide some support for the socio-cultural hypothesis. These developments, based on theory and implemented in actual organizations, all concern the structure and exercise of authority, but vary in important respects. They are described here in terms of a rough continuum of the restructuring of conventional hierarchical authority.

The Socio-technical Perspective

The **socio-technical perspective** was developed by several scholars working in the human relations tradition associated with the Tavistock Institute in Great Britain and the University of Michigan in the United States.[29] This perspective focuses on two aspects of organization: the division of labour, and the allocation and exercise of authority.

In terms of the division of labour, this perspective advocates **job enrichment**, an expansion of the task content of jobs. Achieving this goal will necessarily mean reducing the complexity of the division of labour characteristic of the bureaucracy. The socio-technical perspective also advocates rotating workers among jobs as another means of enriching the work experience and thereby of improving the quality of working life. As for authority, certain responsibilities, such as ordering supplies and deciding on and maintaining the pace and quality of work, are delegated to the workers or work teams.

A well-known example of the application of this perspective is the Swedish automotive manufacturer, Volvo, which in the 1970s built an assembly plant in Kalmar specifically designed to implement a work organization consistent with the QWL approach.[30] Instead of installing a conventional assembly line, which controls the progress of the automobiles in the assembly process, the Volvo approach moves the automobiles on carriers whose movements are controlled by the workers. The members of the team at any station in the assembly process are trained to carry out all the required tasks performed at their station, such as installing electrical systems or steering controls. This training enables workers to exchange jobs if they wish. Two patterns of work have emerged: in one, each member performs a different task; in the other and the one most frequently adopted, team members divide into sub-groups of two or three members and carry out all the required tasks in a buffer, that is, a holding zone for automobiles temporarily removed from the moving assembly line. The teams are also responsible for ordering supplies and for quality control inspections. Because this experiment proved successful, Volvo adopted the approach in some of its other factories. The other main Swedish automotive manufacturer, Saab, also adopted the approach in some of its operations. When the conventional assembly line was changed to an automated line, rank and file workers made shop-floor decisions relating to materials supply, quality control, job assignments, and others relating to some dozen or more distinct operations.

QWL has proved popular in the United States where many companies, including large corporations, have adopted forms of the QWL approach.[31] Although QWL has been less popular with management and union leaders in Canada,[32] the approach was promoted by the federal government and has been adopted or tried by several firms.[33] QWL can be viewed as an alternative to bureaucracy because it runs counter to an emphasis on specialization of task and allows more decision-making by rank and file workers.[34] However, these changes are focused on the actual workplace and the lower levels of management and they have only a limited impact on hierarchical structures.

Co-determination

A prominent form of change in the structure of authority, known as **co-determination**, is required by law in many European countries and can be found in West Germany, Denmark, the Netherlands, Norway, and Sweden. This system requires owners and managers to share some responsibility for decision-making with employees. Although the specific co-determination requirements may differ between countries, they are variants of a model established in West Germany.[35] That model, as reflected by 1976 legislation, is described here.[36]

Basically, three structures are required for co-determination in West German firms:

- a supervisory board on which blue-collar, white-collar, and management employees fill half of its places, and which is responsible for setting company policy and for overseeing the management board;

- a management board responsible for day-to-day operations, with workers appointed to one-third of its positions; and

- a workers' council that has three levels of rights and responsibilities:[37]
    i) joint decision-making—matters such as working conditions and wage procedures are decided with management;
    ii) consultation—the council must be consulted on matters such as vocational training;
    iii) access to information—the council must be informed about certain matters, such as lay-offs and organizational or technological changes planned for the company.

The co-determination model is focused at the top-level of company decision-making—policy decisions and the overall supervision of operations management. The workers' councils that function at the plant level allow worker participation in lower-level decisions, but only in specifically defined areas of responsibility.[38]

Workers' Control

Workers' control, also called **self-management**, is another important development in organizational change. It was pioneered in Yugoslavia and has spread to a number of countries, including Israel (Rosner 1973; Tannenbaum et al. 1974) and Poland (Kolaja [1960] 1973).[39] Under the Yugoslav model, all enterprises were required by law to establish Workers' Councils consisting of elected representatives of employees (see Pusic and Supek in Pusic 1972, 1:5). These councils exercise decision-making responsibilities on all matters of policy, for example, those relating to production, marketing, personnel, capital investment, and the distribution of surplus. The council appoints and supervises the managing director of the enterprise, who serves as its chief executive officer.

The main thrust of the model is to give power to the workers. Conditions that have an impact on worker well-being are not ignored, but do not have the primacy they are given in the QWL approach. The Yugoslav model allows workers direct or representative decision-making, depending on establishment size. Participatory structures are located at all levels and in all important divisions of an enterprise. For example, in a textile factory studied by Adizes (1971), workers' councils exist at the level of departments or production units, and there is a central workers' council for the total enterprise. There is a wide scope of authority: decisions range from those that concern the immediate workplace to those, such as the allocation of surplus value, that affect the entire enterprise.

Employee Ownership

The extent of restructuring of hierarchical authority in models of worker ownership is variable. Generally, ownership through stock purchases is associated with far less structural change than is the case when ownership is through cooperatives.

Stock Ownership

Various degrees of employee ownership are possible and exist in firms that allow stock purchases by their employees. There are variations in the categories of personnel, such as managerial, professional, and non-managerial, who may purchase or be given shares. Whether or not voting rights are attributed to shares and consequently the degree to which shareholders may influence policy and introduce and maintain structural changes in a firm and its workplaces also varies. Democratic employee stock ownership plans (ESOPs) have been established in the United States (Rothschild and Russell 1986, 317) and elsewhere. On the whole employees tend to be minority shareholders under stock ownership. In the United States in 1984, employees were majority shareholders in only 8 percent of the firms that had established ESOPs under government legislation (Rothschild and Russell 1986, 309).

Although Nightingale observed (1982, 155) that neither stock ownership nor profit sharing is popular in Canada, there are exceptions. Dofasco, a Canadian steel manufacturing company, established a profit-sharing fund in 1937 with contributions from employees and the company. Membership in the fund was voluntary. Storey's description (1987, 373–74) suggests that the fund served as a savings or pension fund. Byers Transport, a Canadian trucking company, was purchased by its employees, whose stock gave them voting rights and a share of profits.[40] This model combined worker ownership and worker participation in decision-making (Long 1978). Nightingale (1982, 171) identified Superior Aluminum Industries, Tembec Forest Products, Lincoln Electric (Canada), and Canadian Tire as examples of Canadian companies that combine profit-sharing, employee ownership, and democratic decision-making structures and that meet his criteria of "a fully democratic workplace."

Producers' Cooperatives

Although producers' cooperatives have a history dating back to the late nineteenth century when the cooperative movement was established in Great Britain, a resurgence of interest in this organizational form justifies its inclusion here.[41]

Because producers' cooperatives are based on the idea that those who produce should control policy and the management of the firm, the purest (or simplest) cooperative is one that requires all its employees to purchase a share in the firm and restricts share ownership to employees. In such cooperatives, control is said to be linked to employment. There are, however, cooperatives that permit share ownership by non-workers or that employ non-owner workers. For example, some cooperative plywood mills in the Northwest United States employ both worker-owners and non-owners (Bellas 1972; Bernstein 1976). In such cooperatives, control is said to be linked to ownership.[42] In Great Britain and in France, control tends to be linked to ownership, whereas in Spain control is linked to employment (Oakeshott 1978, 31). This distinction between control by share ownership and by employment may be important in understanding variations in the organizational structures of cooperatives, especially in the degree of bureaucracy and the structure and distribution of authority in a firm. Whether a cooperative is share or employment controlled may not be significant in determining whether modifications, such as QWL, are introduced, but non-worker owners are less likely than worker-owners to support exclusive worker control over policy and the right to hire and fire managers. Some support for this proposition comes from Nightingale's observations that "in North America, relatively few [producer cooperatives] offer a high degree of rank and file participation in decision-making" and that "the classic producer co-operative is rarely found in North America" (Nightingale 1982, 226–27).[43]

Cooperatives exist in most European countries, most notably in Spain where the very successful Mondragon multi-enterprise cooperative is located. In their comments on the proliferation of "alternatives to bureaucracy," Rothschild and Russell (1986, 308, citing Case and Taylor 1979) observe that "thousands of worker cooperatives and collectives have been created in communities all around the United States." Canada also has a long history of producers' cooperatives formed mainly by farm-owners and boat-owners for marketing purposes. Still, Mungall (1986, 1) estimated that there were 350 operating worker cooperatives in Canada in 1986 and reported that their number has doubled since 1981.[44]

INFLUENCES ON THE DEVELOPMENT OF PARTICIPATORY ORGANIZATIONS

As most of these changes in authority and decision-making structures have occurred in democratic societies such as Canada, Great Britain, Israel, West Germany, Sweden, and the United States, there is reason to suggest that the democratic values that are part of the institutional environment of these countries influence the changes that reduce hierarchy in organizations. However, that conclusion could be too hasty. There may be other reasons for such changes. For example, the increase in cooperatives could also be motivated by a commitment to entrepreneurship, an acceptance of risk, or could be attributed to the ideal of ownership of small businesses, which thrive in capitalist and, apparently, socialist societies.

Workers' control, which was firmly established in East European countries whose governments were autocratic, also presents a challenge to the cultural hypothesis. It is notable, nonetheless, that this form of organization was not prominent in the former USSR but in Yugoslavia, which resisted Soviet domination. Other societies in the then-Soviet zone of influence, such as Poland and Hungary, also adopted forms of workers' control and were resistant to Soviet control and to indigenous autocracy. These societies also established democratic governments following the collapse of the USSR. On this evidence, it might be argued that a latent support for democracy facilitated the establishment of workers' control in Eastern Europe.

However, such a conclusion must be modified in the face of other evidence of gaps between the models of workers' control and their empirical manifestations. For example, several Yugoslav sociologists, on the basis of their research, have observed that the control exerted by the State and the Central Committee of the Communist Party over the Yugoslav economy and its constituent organizations was inconsistent with the philosophy of worker control. These sociologists have expressed doubts about the actual degree of control transferred to workers. In short, while workers' control may have been a welcome expression of democratic tendencies in these societies, it may also have been an attempt by autocratic governments to manipulate their workers.

There is also some scepticism about the degree of control that is surrendered in organizations in Western democracies. Various scholars have suggested that the changes in the structure and exercise of authority in capitalist societies, particularly changes related to QWL, are a means of responding to worker dissatisfaction, which is believed to reduce motivation. In other words, by relinquishing some authority and perhaps not a significant amount, owners and managers expect to increase productivity through greater worker compliance to organizational rules, procedures, and objectives.[45] Researchers such as Batstone (1976) questioned whether worker-directors exert much power; Batstone suggested that they are co-opted by the more experienced non-employee directors whose greater experience at the board level give them correspondingly greater influence on decisions.

While the stubborn fact that hierarchical authority is predominant in most organizations in democratic societies suggests that societal values may not exert a strong force on organizational structure, most of the changes described here are fairly recent and may foreshadow a strengthening trend toward a reduction of hierarchy and of other bureaucratic characteristics. Although the effect of societal values on organizational structure and process is not easily separated from other environmental influences, the hypothesis that societal values exert an influence on organizations requires further investigation.

A NOTE ON THE ECOLOGICAL PERSPECTIVE

During the last decade and a half, an ecological perspective on organizations has developed whose central focus is on the environment. The concepts that constitute this perspective are drawn from the biological discipline of ecology—the study of the spatial distribution of organisms and the processes determining growth and decline of the great variety of species that inhabit the earth. Ecological concepts were introduced to sociology in the 1920s by Robert E. Park and E.W. Burgess to provide the basis of the sub-field of human ecology. These two sociologists used an ecological approach to analyze the dynamics of patterns of urban land use by various institutions and groups (see, for example, Park, Burgess, and McKenzie 1925). This approach was championed and further developed by Amos Hawley (see, for example, Hawley 1950).

Although ecological concepts have been primarily of interest to sociologists who study urban problems, several sociologists whose work centres on organizations (for example, Aldrich 1979; Hannan and Freeman 1977a; Carroll 1984) have used these concepts to generate a considerable amount of theoretical work and research since the mid-1970s.

In the ecological approach, the environment is seen as the major determinant of the emergence of organizations, of their ongoing activities or performance, and of the change and the "death" of organizations. While the ecological perspective allows that organizations may adapt, or "learn" from experience, and that participants may deliberately decide goals and courses of action to realize such goals, such action is unambiguously seen as having far less influence on organizations than the environment does (for example, see Aldrich 1979, 55).

In the ecological perspective, the units of analysis are *populations* of organizations rather than individual organizations. These populations may be categorized in terms of principal activity (Aldrich 1979, 109), such as manufacturing or health care, or in terms of structural features, such as complexity or centrality.[46] The focus of analysis is on the relationship between these organizational populations and their environments. These latter are seen as a complex of resources (Aldrich 1979, 111) and as "the central force of change" in organizational populations (Aldrich 1979, 55). Competition for resources occurs both within and between populations and the competitive process determines the structural features of the organizations composing these populations as well as their emergence, growth, decline, and ultimately, their survival or death.

Research undertaken within the ecological perspective reveals what is of most interest about organizations to its adherents. Carroll's review (1984, 81–85) indicates that such research is mostly concerned with what he terms "organizational demography," that is, the births, growth, decline, and deaths in populations of organizations. Such research yields information about the populations of organizations. Much less research using an ecological perspective has been undertaken on organizational forms or on the structures of organizational populations (Carroll 1984, 87–90). However, although the ecological perspective has primarily increased knowledge about populations of organizations, it has the potential to contribute knowledge of change and stability of organizational structure.[47] Furthermore, an ecological perspective can contribute to a system perspective by identifying specific resources relevant to organizations and by identifying variable conditions of the environment, such as those described by Aldrich (1979, 63–74).[48]

While the analysis of populations of organizations is undoubtedly a legitimate way of studying organizations, it is important to recognize that other perspectives and levels of analysis are also necessary to the sociological understanding of organizations. Just as the demographic analysis of human populations yields valuable general information, such as average life expectancy, but cannot provide for specific predictions, such as an individual's age at death, let alone the reasons for such deaths, the ecological perspective on organizations cannot yield information specific to individual organizations or other collectivities. Although demographic findings are important for understanding society and social action, other kinds of analysis and other methods are necessary for the study of social systems.

For example, where the focus is on sociological variables and the units of analysis are social relationships, the data required for analysis may not be easily obtained within a perspective, such as the ecological, that requires data for long time periods and that focuses, mainly, on macro-level variables. It may not be impossible to obtain data, as suggested by Hannan and Freeman (1977a, 934–35), on organizational activities and the normative order over a period of twenty-five years or more, but it would certainly be difficult to do so. While such data might be obtained from documents and, retrospectively, from interviews, they certainly cannot be obtained through direct observation.

In the present state of knowledge, it is prudent to continue to assess, through research, various perspectives as bases for understanding organizations. Even if it is reasonable to expect, as system and ecological perspectives do, the environment to exert a strong influence, it is too soon to reject rationality, intra-organization conflict, and leadership as important influences on organizational structure and performance. For sociologists whose interests focus on issues such as changing normative structures, decision-making structures, and levels of consensus and cohesion, and on the relationships between these features of organizations, perspectives such as those discussed in Chapters One through Four may be more useful than the ecological perspective at its present state of development.[49]

SUMMARY

In sociological analysis, the environment of organizations is identified in terms of three major components: size, technology, and culture. Size and technology have been intensively and extensively studied and the results show that both components exert an influence on organizational structure. Despite the compelling findings reported in this chapter, it cannot be said that either technology or size is always dominant or always influential. The case for either component remains open. Cultural components, studied for over thirty years, have also been shown to be influential. There remains, however, a lively debate over the relative strengths of technology and culture. Like the other components, the case for cultural influences is open to further developments in theory and research.

This chapter also provided a description of actual organizational structures, which differ from bureaucracy by allowing greater participation in decision-making. These models are examined further in Chapter Six, which centres on authority and compliance in organizations.

ENDNOTES

1   In Parsons' theory (1977, 7) the procurement of resources is categorized as adaptive action. See Aldrich (1979, 61–63) for a discussion of different kinds of resources and the problem of classifying them.

2   The features of the two models are selected and rephrased from Burns and Stalker (1961, 120–21).

3   This implication is consistent with Gouldner's emphasis on bureaucratization rather than bureaucracy. In fact, Gouldner states that the objective of his study of the gypsum factory "is to identify some of the variables relating to bureaucratization" ([1954] 1964, 17).

4   The environmental variations recognized by Burns and Stalker are currently referred to as levels of *certainty* or *uncertainty* of the environment.

5   There were some exceptions—the number of workers per first-line supervisor was lowest in assembly line firms, while the number was about the same in craft and continuous-process technologies (Woodward [1965] 1980, 60–67).

6   Among the U-shaped, or **curvilinear**, aspects of the division of labour are the ratios of supervisors to non-supervisors, and staff positions to direct production workers. In the latter, the curve is an inverted U.

7   In some of the manufacturing firms studied by Sayles, workers assigned to such operations could slow or completely shut down operations.

8   It should be noted that low grievance frequency does not mean absence of discontent. Members of apathetic groups were known to have complaints, but they did not respond by collective formal or informal grieving.

9   These data were drawn from previously collected data on job and work satisfaction obtained from three thousand workers employed in sixteen industries. The different technologies were represented by printing, automobile manufacturing, textile manufacturing, and chemical production.

10 For example, Blauner interpreted a question that asked workers to assess the pace of work to be a measure of *powerlessness*; and a question on the level of interest of their work to be a measure of *meaninglessness*. For a detailed description of the questions and their classification, see Blauner (1964, chap. 2, appendix C).

[11] For example, 12 and 10 percent, respectively, of chemical and printing workers felt that "their jobs made them work too fast" compared to 33 and 32 percent of automobile and textile workers.

[12] The three categories parallel Woodward's craft, batch, and continual-process categories and Blauner's craft, mass production, and continual-process categories. Shepard also recognized that the three types of production technology could co-exist in a firm. The blue-collar sample was obtained from an oil refining firm and an automobile manufacturing firm. The white-collar sample from a "large bank, a large insurance company and four small insurance company" (Shepard 1971, 17).

[13] The number of participants—employees, members, patients, faculty, students, etc.—is the most commonly used indicator of size. Other indicators are possible, for example, the value of resources or assets or the volume of activities (transactions, operations, degrees granted, etc.). Different indicators of size may show different effects.

[14] The number of possible dyadic relationships is determined by $n(n-1)/2$ where n is the number of persons in the collectivity.

[15] A research group located at the University of Aston in Birmingham, England, that included, among others, D.J. Hickson, C.R. Hinings, and D.S. Pouch.

[16] The armed services provide an example of organizations that strive explicitly to impose, through rigorous recruit training, the values and norms of the organization on its members (see, for example, Jones 1954).

[17] The division of labour was measured by, for example, the number of subunits, such as sections and departments, and the number of distinct occupational positions in the organization. Measures of the authority structure included the number of levels of authority and the span of control of the different levels of authority.

[18] Blau focused primarily on Woodward's findings on the effects of technology and used her measures and categories of production technology.

[19] That these relationships were curvilinear means that structural dimensions associated with craft production and continuous-process production, the low and high ends of production technology, were more alike structurally than they were to mass production firms. A *linear* association would mean that an increase in size would result in a proportionate increase or decrease in complexity.

[20] Propositions, for example, that treat formalization as a consequence of centralization, and efficiency as a consequence of formalization.

[21] Cross-sectional data are those that are collected for one point in time but for different units or sources of information representing different points in time. Longitudinal data are those that are collected for two or more points in time for the same units or sources of information. For example, a cross-sectional study of changing life habits may be based on a one-time sample of respondents representative of different age cohorts, whereas a longitudinal study would follow a sample, drawn from the same cohort, over succeeding time

periods. A cross-sectional study of organizational growth might select organizations representative of different establishment dates, whereas a longitudinal study would follow a sample of organizations, established at the same time, over some finite period of time. A problem arises if a researcher using cross-sectional data assumes that differences in variables, for example, size and a measure of structure, reflect a developmental or historical process. While it is possible that such data may accurately reflect process, longitudinal data entail less risk in relation to validity. The risk, of course, is a function of the appropriateness of the variables and the completeness of the time series.

22 Research on the effects of size on administrative intensity has yielded different findings. Freeman reported (1973, 751) that most cross-sectional studies report negative association between size and administrative intensity and findings from longitudinal studies are inconsistent. He suggested that a use of a ratio of administrative personnel to total personnel may result in either type of study. However, he argued that the inconsistency of findings between the two types lies with the modes of data collection and further argued for the superiority of longitudinal over cross-sectional data.

23 Armandi and Mills (1982), for example, claimed to be the first to include efficiency—that is, organizational goal-achievement effectiveness—as a variable in the size model. Kimberley (1975) studied the effects of external constraints on the goals of rehabilitation organizations.

24 For further discussion, see Jones (1968; 1956).

25 In Tepperman's words, "We may finally discover that bureaucracy is merely an epiphenomenon of large-scale interactional systems (1973, 365).

26 There are many definitions of culture, some of which involve material objects such as tools and other artifacts. References to culture here are to non-material phenomena such as ideas, values, and symbol systems. Under this definition it is permissible to include the ideas underlying material technology.

27 Examples are Form's study (1976) of automobile factories in four societies, Dore's (1973) comparison of British and Japanese electronics factories, Marsh and Mannari's study (1976) of various Japanese manufacturing firms, and Cole's study (1979) of a Japanese automobile manufacturing firm.

28 Proportions of employees who were Francophone in the Quebec organization and Anglophone in the Ontario organization were virtually identical (95 percent or higher).

29 The socio-technical perspective is also known as the QWL—the Quality of Working Life. For detailed descriptions and discussion of this perspective, see Bolweg (1976); Emery and Thorsrud ([1964] 1969; 1976); and Mansell (1987).

30 For a succinct description of the plant and the underlying philosophy of its design, see Gyllenhammar (1977).

31 About a third of Fortune's five hundred most successful companies have been reported as having adopted this approach (Rothschild and Russell 1986, 308, quoting Walton 1979).

[32] A Labour Canada survey (Sept. 1991) of 1248 collective agreements covering almost 2.5 million employees showed only 21 agreements, less than 2 percent, with a provision for a QWL committee, and 22 with a provision for job rotation.

[33] The province of Ontario promoted this approach until 1989 when it closed down its Quality of Work unit. The federal government also closed down its QWL program during the 1980s. See Mansell (1987) and Nightingale (1982) for names of companies and government units who have adopted or tried QWL. Rankin (1990) provides a detailed study of the implementation and operation of a QWL program in a chemical plant located in Sarnia, Ontario.

[34] As some applications result in the elimination of first-line supervisors, resistance to QWL is strong among middle and lower managers.

[35] Although co-determination became prominent in Western Germany in the 1970s, the first attempt to establish this kind of authority structure was made in the late nineteenth century by Prince Otto Bismarck, Chancellor of the German Empire. However, co-determination was abandoned during the period of the Weimar Republic because of lack of support among both industrialists and workers. At the end of World War II, it was revived by the British occupation authorities, who imposed co-determination on the iron and coal companies of the Ruhr Valley. Since the reunion of East and West Germany, the legislation presumably applies to what was formerly the jurisdiction of East Germany.

[36] My principal references are Adams and Rummel (1976) and Kühne (1980). The Co-Determination Act of 1976 applied to all joint stock and limited liability companies with two thousand or more employees and to all political, religious, educational, artistic, and charitable organizations and news media. Coal and iron and steel companies are under the 1951 co-determination law and its 1956 amendment. Firms with fewer than two thousand employees are covered by the Works Constitution Act, 1952 (Kühne 1980, 36).

[37] A requirement, under the 1952 Works Constitution Act, of every private company (Kühne 1980, 35–36).

[38] In multi-plant firms, there is likely to be a central council as well.

[39] The description of the Yugoslav model is based, in part, on Jones (1984). As civil war was in progress in Yugoslavia at the time of writing, the future of workers' control legislation and its implementation were uncertain.

[40] Stock-holding was restricted to employees and over 70 percent were share owners. The board of directors included representatives of management and rank-and-file employees. The company has since been sold to private interests.

[41] Robert Oakeshott (1978) provided a valuable general account of cooperatives in Great Britain and various Western European countries.

[42] Mungall (1986, chap. 1) drew a distinction similar to Bernstein's between worker-cooperatives and producer-cooperatives.

[43] The classic producer cooperative includes, among its five attributes, formal provision "for direct and indirect participation in decision-making by worker-members at all levels" (Nightingale 1982, 225).

[44] See Nightingale (1982) and Mungall (1986) for names of some of these cooperatives.

[45] The relationship between worker satisfaction and productivity is discussed in Chapter Six.

[46] Classification of organizations is as much a matter of debate among organizational ecologists as it is among other organizational sociologists. For example, in discussions of the classification of structure, the essential issue is whether to establish categories in the course of research or to develop a classifications system based on theory, analogous to that used in biology. In his summary of the debate, Carroll (1984, 78–79) identified McKelvey (1982) and Warriner (1977) as proponents of a theory-based classification system and Hannan and Freeman (1977a) as taking the more pragmatic approach. The latter approach, also evident in Aldrich's work (1979), allows the classification to emerge from the specific research project. However, Hannan and Freeman proposd (1977a, 934–35) that three features of organizations—the formal structure, the patterns of activity, and the normative order—could be used to define populations and communities of organizations. This approach, analogous to biology's definition of species, could be used as a basis for an a priori classification as well as for more pragmatically determined classifications.

[47] Students of structural change, whatever their perspectives, cannot ignore the hypothesis, basic to the ecological approach, that populations of organizations are constrained in the direction of structural homogeneity by environmental forces.

[48] Aldrich (1979, 61–63) discussed attempts to identify specific resources relevant to organizations. Aldrich also identifies six variable conditions of the environment: environmental capacity (rich/lean), environmental homogeneity/heterogeneity, environmental stability/instability, environmental concentration/dispersion, environmental consensus/dissensus, and environmental turbulence.

[49] Young (1988) is severely critical of the concepts and methods of the ecological perspective and concludes that "it has not contributed to the understanding of organizations."

CHAPTER 6

ORDER IN ORGANIZATIONS

All social systems, to persist, require some level of order or, to use Parsons' term, integration. If interacting people responded randomly to each other's actions, and actions had no predictable pattern, relationships would be completely disintegrated or maximally disordered. Such an interaction situation could not be identified as a social system. This chapter begins with the identification of the basic requirements for the achievement of order—the expectations of required action and compliance with these expectations. The two sections that follow constitute the main body of the chapter. The first provides a discussion of the sources that generate compliance and describes some compliance models. The second is focused primarily on authority in organizations as a source of such expectations and on differences in authority structures and their consequences for organizations.

In contrast to other social animals whose social relationships are integrated primarily through instinctive mechanisms, integration of human social relationships or systems depends on discretionary human action. Consider a simple model of a two-person relationship as a means to understand the process of achieving order or integration. Under the model, it is assumed that both persons agree about their expectations of each other. If each complies with the other's expectations, integration is perfect. This simple model generates questions about the sources of shared expectations, about what determines compliance, and about the consequences of non-compliance.

To be shared, expectations must be legitimated by some source. Although legitimacy may result from a simple agreement of participants as their interaction evolves, other sources of legitimacy may be more influential. One such source is the authority that flows from the beliefs and values shared by the participants. Values, such as honesty and equality, shared by participants in a social system provide the basis of norms, rules, regulations, and laws in any relationship.[1] For example, a law requiring equal pay for equal work is based on a shared value of equality. Values, and the norms derived from them, develop and are transmitted in the course of social interaction.

However, the simple existence of these shared prescriptive elements is not enough. Values, norms, and the like would be meaningless if participants did not comply with them. In contrast to the random responses mentioned above, participants in the relationships that constitute a social system must be able to count on each other to act *as expected* in a variety of situations. In short, the existence of norms and people's compliance with them are conditions that allow predictability of participants' actions. The more the action in a social system is predictable, the greater the stability of the system or the higher its integration. Stability and integration require that there be a level of commitment to these prescriptive components and sufficient compliance with them to meet system requirements.

Expectations may also be legitimated by persons acting in roles that allow the exercise of authority. Those in authoritative roles are expected to define system objectives and other functional requirements. Although compliance depends on participants' motivation, in the sense that their individual interests are met to an acceptable degree, compliance may have to be enforced by the exercise of power or authority. In organizations, authority structures are clearly important for the achievement of order. Although the armed services may exemplify the high priority attached to authority in organizations, business firms, hospitals, social agencies, government agencies, and other organizations also give, in greater or lesser degree, high priority to authority. This is because the people who exercise authority are the people who set objectives for the organization and are responsible for meeting them. These people must achieve and maintain the control and compliance that is necessary to generate disciplined action essential to a required level of performance. Just as authority structures may vary among societies, the authority structures of organizations may also vary.

All the actions involved in creating, modifying, and enforcing rules, in designating and allocating sanctions, and in establishing structures and processes of adjudication must be exercised by one or more members of the social system involved. Some person or persons must have the power or authority to enact rules, to judge, and to hand out rewards and punishment. This allocation of authority, at the societal level, is variable. In certain types of small societies, such authority may reside in the elders, while in other societies special roles and specific structures may be created to perform these functions. In Western democratic society, a complex political system has evolved with legislatures to make the laws, agencies, such as the police, to enforce the laws, and courts to adjudicate and apply sanctions.

An understanding of order in organizations requires an understanding of members' compliance with prescriptive elements, such as values and norms, of organizations. Such a discussion requires identification of the prescriptive elements, the authority relating to them, and the motives that result in complying or deviating action on the part of the participants. Although motivation and authority are inextricably involved in conformity and deviance, the discussion that follows is divided into sections. The first focuses mainly on motivation and the second, on authority.

COMPLIANCE

Self-motivated Compliance

Social system participants may voluntarily comply with prescriptive elements as a consequence of having internalized such components in the course of socialization and other situations of interaction. It is traditional in sociological explanations of socialization to focus on the internalization of norms and role expectations in the course of social interaction.[2] The basic idea was put forward many years ago by George H. Mead (1934). Mead said that a person, in the course of socialization, gradually perceives the norms or role expectations introduced by significant others to be part of his or her *self* and responds to those norms or role expectations as elements internally rather than externally imposed.[3] Assuming that the norms and role expectations introduced by significant others correspond to those generally approved by society, a successfully socialized person will comply closely with social role expectations and little external influence will be required to achieve full compliance. Successful socialization, then, is the most effective means of achieving compliance.

Indeed, if internally imposed compliance were not the normal state of affairs, social control would be virtually impossible. In this respect, it is worth noting that totalitarian states, despite their powerful coercive means for preventing dissent and for enforcing compliance, never rely on such means alone. Rather, they mount propaganda campaigns whose objectives are to socialize their citizens to the rulers' values, norms, and role expectations. If such societies, with their powerful instruments of state, cannot achieve a satisfactory level of compliance, surely organizations, which are much more limited social systems than societies, must depend, too, on self-motivated compliance. It has been argued (for example, Bowles and Gintis 1976) that schooling in capitalist societies is directed toward producing values and attitudes that will provide docile workers for private enterprise. However, it is also evident that many white- and blue-collar workers, despite exposure to the school systems, are not passive in relations with their superiors. It seems reasonable to assume that there are continuities and discontinuities in a person's values and attitudes in the course of a lifetime. There is evidence that values and attitudes are persistent but also that they can change. Inkeles and Smith (1974), on the basis of their comparative study of modernization, concluded that the school and the factory were the strongest forces in producing modern values and attitudes in the societies they studied. However, although self-motivated compliance is important and high levels have been observed, it is evident that there is more to compliance than self-motivation.[4]

Participants' Interests and Satisfaction

Self-motivated compliance, presumably, is self-rewarding—satisfaction comes from realizing, or even from striving to realize, the internalized value or other prescriptive element. However, compliance may also depend on participants' common interests, generated by personality and by role commitments to various collectivities, and on the expectations and actions of those who exercise authority in organizations and other collectivities. Consequently, all these components must be considered in order to understand compliance in organizations.

In the study of organizations, the most prominent concept used to guide research on the motivational aspect of compliance has been *satisfaction*. The emphasis on this concept follows from a simple model:

$$\text{rewards} \longrightarrow \text{satisfaction} \longrightarrow \text{compliance}$$

In this model satisfaction is assumed to be the consequence of rewards granted to an individual for successfully performing one or more tasks according to external criteria, such as volume and quality. If satisfaction is maintained or increased, it is assumed that an individual will continue to comply with the norms associated with the task.

Although this model has generated much research, it has also been subject to strong criticism. One critic referred to human relations research as "cow sociology" to imply that satisfaction research in the human relations perspective was motivated by employers' interests in finding incentives other than money to maintain satisfaction in their workforces. Rinehart ([1975] 1987, 143) and Kahn (1972, 169) are among many critics expressing concern that the high levels of reported satisfaction by workers in various organizations and industries may result from inadequate measures of the concept. Rinehart, for example, questioned the validity of attitudinal measures of satisfaction, which in his view do not reflect the reality of worker discontent with jobs or with the organizations that employ them. He believes that satisfaction could be more accurately assessed by behavioural measures, such as measures of absenteeism, strikes, output restriction, and sabotage (Rinehart [1975] 1987, chap. 5). For those who accept or tolerate attitudinal measures of satisfaction, the low variability of response poses a severe difficulty in testing hypotheses of either causes or consequences of satisfaction. Although Kahn expressed concern about the limitations on research on the causes or conditions associated with work satisfaction, he concluded that occupation, status, supervision, peer relationships, job content, wages and other extrinsic rewards, promotion opportunities, and physical conditions are "probable causes of satisfaction and dissatisfaction at work" (1972, 181). Kahn is even more dissatisfied with the research on the consequences of satisfaction. His report of the considerable inconsistency in findings on the relationship between satisfaction and productivity makes attempts at generalization imprudent. Kahn reported findings on the association between satisfaction and such behavioural measures as absence, turnover, and accidents to be consistent but "not rich" (1972, 192–93). Finally, the probability that many other conditions, which may not have been controlled or are difficult to measure, may affect any of these dependent variables must be considered in discussions of the methodological problems that plague research on satisfaction.

Status and Prestige

Status serves as a basic concept of one's position relative to others, derived from some consensually recognized base such as kinship or occupation. Prestige serves as a concept of rank within a position. Both status and prestige are regarded as basic components of self-image.[5] It is reasonable, then, to assume that compliance would be influenced by anticipated gains and losses to status and prestige. Stouffer et al. (1949, 251–53), for example, found that soldiers either aspiring to promotion or who were actually promoted showed higher compliance with army norms than those without such aspirations or who were not promoted. In general, salary, wages, and promotion may be perceived as means for maintaining or enhancing prestige and status. Money provides means for acquiring the possessions and standard of living symbolic of status and class expectations, whereas promotion, apart from augmented salary, provides means to membership at a given status or class level. However, an adequate assessment of the hypothesized importance of prestige and status, as motivational factors, must await research, especially research designed to include other likely influences operating simultaneously on compliance.

Interests Determined by Roles External to an Organization

The interests of members who are defined by their roles in collectivities external to an organization may also influence compliance. Depending on circumstances, individuals may have to choose between complying with norms and role expectations consistent with their external interests and those required by the organization. Spending time with one's family, for example, may sometimes conflict with one's organizational role expectations. While the resolution of such conflicts does not always favour the family, the stress reported by those experiencing such conflicts implies that complying with conflicting expectations is problematical. Coser (1974) provides documentation on the struggles between collectivities for member loyalties. While struggles between political, military, or religious organizations and families easily come to mind, conflicts are not limited to those involving the family. For example, the struggle between corporations and labour unions for workers' loyalties is a prominent form of conflict in contemporary societies.

Compliance Models

If textbook indexes are any guide, there is a tendency among organizational sociologists to avoid the problem of motivation. Others, however, have attempted to broaden the analysis by developing models of compliance. This concept provides a richer conceptualization of the problem by including both motivational and power or authority components. In addition, compliance models consider normative elements to be intrinsic to human experience, in contrast to the satisfaction model, which was developed mainly on the basis of animal experiments. Two examples of compliance models and research based on them are discussed here.

Etzioni, who contributed the first formal model, conceived of compliance as having two dimensions. First, there are the ways power and related **sanctions** are exercised to control or influence action, and second, there are the **motives** that individuals have for participating in an organization.[6] The three types he proposed for each of the two dimensions, identified in Chapter One, are described further here.

For power and related sanctions, the types are ([1961] 1975, 5):

- coercive, which refers to the use of physical sanctions that, for example, cause pain, limit movement, or control access to such requirements as food and sex;

- remunerative, which refers to various rewards, such as wages or salaries, promotion, and other economic benefits and to material punishment such as fines, pay deductions, demotion, suspension, and discharge; and

- normative, which refers to the use of non-material or *symbolic* rewards such as actions signifying agreement or support, those that contribute to prestige and status, to the realization of individual or shared values, or to self-image reinforcement or enhancement; normative punishment includes actions that violate individual or group values and that signify loss of prestige or status and result in a loss of self-esteem.

For motives, the types are ([1961] 1975, 10):

- alienative, where persons, such as prisoners and others who are confined contrary to their interests, are resistant to participation;

- calculative, where participants are involved to satisfy their own remunerative interests; and

- moral, where involvement is for reasons other than satisfying economic interests, such as a commitment to religious or political values, or to shared non-remunerative interests.

A cross-classification of the two dimensions, sanctions and motives, results in nine types of compliance. Three types are congruent:[7] coercive-alienative, remunerative-calculative, and normative-moral; and the remaining six are non-congruent. Etzioni proposed that an organization will be more effective in achieving its goals when its compliance type is congruent ([1961] 1975, 103). Etzioni further proposed that there is a strain toward congruency and that organizations characterized by incongruency will move toward congruency either by changing sanction type or by attracting participants with appropriate motives.[8]

Knoke and his associates provided a more recent formulation of the compliance model.[9] Although it is called a predisposition/opportunities model, it clearly concerns compliance since the question they sought to answer is: "Why do people contribute varying amounts of personally-controlled resources to organizations?" (Knoke and Wright-Isak 1982, 211).[10] Their answer takes the form of a model based on two concepts: **predispositions to act** and **incentive opportunities**. Each concept is formulated as a three-category typology.

The types of predisposition to act are (Knoke and Wright-Isak 1982, 228–29):

- **rational choice**—these are actions that are determined by a rational estimate of which choice will yield the maximum benefit to the participant;
- **normative conformity**—acceptable or required actions that are "grounded in individually unique and socially-instilled values"; and
- **affective bonding**—actions that are intended to achieve relationships with other participants and with symbolic representations of the collectivity.

The types of incentive opportunities are (1982, 232–33):

- **utilitarian**—these are opportunities to obtain "goods and activities which permit the calculation of benefits and costs," such as financial rewards, contributions to status and prestige, and discounts on goods purchased;
- **normative**—although not formally defined, the reference is to opportunities to obtain satisfaction from conforming to a relevant value or norm. Examples include action regarded as a civic duty, "doing one's part," giving one's "fair share"; and
- **affective**—opportunities to "foster emotional attachments among members and of the individual to the collectivity." Such opportunities include social occasions, contact with charismatic leaders, and participation in formal ceremonies.

Although Etzioni and Knoke built their models on the relation of sanctions and motives, there are differences in the content of the sanction and motive types as well as in their overall perspectives. Etzioni emphasized a narrow range—the congruent types—as the critical condition for achieving organizational effectiveness relative to goals. Although Etzioni recognized ([1961] 1975, 6, 12) that all three sanction types may be employed by organizations, he argued that a predominance of one sanction type is typical. Moreover, he believes that the three congruent types of compliance are "*found more frequently than the other six types*" (Etzioni's italics). Knoke and Wright-Isak adopted a broader congruency that takes account of the varied motives of individuals and the tendency for organizations to offer more than one type of incentive. This meaning of congruency derives from Knoke's typology of incentive systems (Knoke and Wright-Isak 1982, 234, table 2), which considers multiple as well as pure incentive types to be empirically realistic and allows for them.

Models, of course, are useful only if they provide reasonable insight into reality. In the case of compliance models, some relevant research has been undertaken. Etzioni reported on research (1975,

69–82) that confirms the assumption that a dominant compliance type is characteristic of the organizations studied, and on research (1975, 126–32) that supports the hypothesis that congruent compliance structures are effective in achieving their objectives. However, despite considerable discussion of approaches to research on compliance and organizational effectiveness, he did not cite research that explicitly includes his compliance model or that tests his hypothesis that where an organization's goals and compliance structure are incongruent, either the means of control would change or the goals would not be realized.

On the basis of research on an American national sample of voluntary associations, Knoke and Adams (1987) reported support for the congruency of the kinds of formal goals organizations embrace and the incentive types and systems offered to members (1987, 290–91, 298, 304–5).[11] They also observed that the relationship between goals and incentives is more complex than anticipated—an incentive type can support a greater variety of goals than expected on the basis of theory (1987, 299). They also reported that most associations use all three types of incentive (Knoke and Adams 1987, 300). Further analysis of these data (Knoke 1988) supports the hypothesis that congruency between the interests of members of voluntary associations and the incentives offered exerts a positive influence on the commitments of such members.

Although the research findings reported here provide support for their creators' models, it is apparent that much more information is required to sufficiently evaluate different models and the overall concept of compliance. Even though Etzioni's effort to relate research to his model was based mainly on research that was not designed as a direct test, his evidence does support a conclusion that compliance models are worth pursuing. Knoke's research, which was designed as a direct test of his model, provides much stronger evidence. On the conceptual level, work is required to refine concepts and to attempt to find conceptual unity among the models. It goes without saying that research is required to test such refined models and also to provide knowledge concerning the relative importance of the elements that make up the sanction and motive types. Such efforts could contribute to the motivational side of control in organizations and perhaps lead to a general theory of social motivation.

AUTHORITY

Although authority is frequently expressed in the form of commands, instructions, and suggestions, it is also expressed in rules and prescriptions for action.[12] As Gouldner pointed out ([1954] 1964, 166–68), rules function as remote controls substituting for direct commands from those exercising authority. To the extent that a satisfactory level of compliance with rules is achieved, they are an efficient substitute for the direct intervention of those in authority. Gouldner argued that compliance depends on who initiates the rules, whose values legitimate them, and what the consequences are for participants' values and statuses. Although Gouldner did not test his argument against research findings, it is consistent with findings reported in Chapter Five for organizations whose authority structures allow or require non-managerial employees to participate in rule-making and decision-making.

Parsons called attention to the effect of environmental conditions on norms. He proposed (1966, 42–44) that norms and role expectations that lack congruency with environmental conditions are likely to change in the direction of congruency with environmental imperatives. He illustrated this argument by drawing an example from Australian aboriginal societies. In these societies, kinship units, such as lineages or clans, are all assumed to be equal, and marriage negotiations between kinship units are based on this assumption. If environmental conditions were to change and allow significant economic differences so that stratification of kinship units resulted, the assumption of equality would have to be abandoned. There is, presumably, a period of reducing compliance with the existing norms in societies when such environmental changes occur, until new norms emerge.

Blau provided organizational examples that illustrate how compliance may vary in relation to the consequences of norms or rules for working practices ([1955] 1963, chaps. 7 and 10). In his study of a federal regulative agency, he contrasted the agents' high degree of compliance with an unofficial norm that forbade the reporting of bribes offered by business clients under investigation by the federal agency to the low compliance, close to zero, with an official norm forbidding agents to consult with each other about their cases. In the former, Blau argued that complying with the official norm, reporting the bribes, was not congruent with the agents' view that successful investigation required a positive relationship with their clients; in the latter, he argued that a pooling of expertise through peer consultation was more effective than seeking advice from a superior, a judgment apparently shared by the agents and their superiors.

Authority Structures

The most familiar type of authority structure is that identified by Weber as rational-legal and it is associated with bureaucratic organization. As noted in Chapter Two, Weber distinguished three types of authority on the basis of the nature of their legitimation—charismatic, traditional, and rational-legal—and showed how they also differed in structure and basic requirements of office. In contrast to social systems where the exercise of authority is legitimated on the basis of tradition or by certain unique characteristics of a person, Weber argued that the exercise of power in a bureaucracy is legitimized by the logical relationships between decisions and organizational objectives and by members perceiving the decisions as legal acts pertaining to the decision-maker's office. In contrast to the centralization of power that exists in traditional or charismatic authority, bureaucratic authority has a hierarchical structure. Moreover, although the scope of decision-making narrows as hierarchical levels descend, authority is decentralized and each level of authority is associated with an appropriate level of technical competence required for a given set of operations.[13] For example, a general manager, having managerial skills necessary to coordinate all organizational operations, has the authority to make decisions on a wide range of managerial issues, but may not make production-level decisions since these require the skills possessed by a line supervisor.

Weber's bureaucratic model, as noted earlier, exerted a strong influence on the study of organizations and may have led sociologists and others to equate organization with bureaucracy. When the study of organizations turned from reflective theorizing to empirical research, however, this view of organization was challenged. Gouldner (1954), for example, proposed three models of bureaucracy and also introduced the idea of bureaucratization to the study of organizations. It was, however, the focusing of research on such environmental influences as technology and values that drew attention to the considerable variation in the structures, including structures of authority, of actual organizations. Woodward ([1965] 1980) showed that variations in types of technology were systematically related to various aspects of authority, such as span of control and number of management levels. It was the work of Burns and Stalker (1961), however, that led to the understanding that organizations could have forms that were clearly non-bureaucratic.

As described in Chapter Five, Burns and Stalker (1961) proposed, on the basis of their research on a number of electronics manufacturing firms, a continuum of organizational structures whose one extreme was identified by bureaucratic structure, but which they labelled mechanistic, and whose other extreme was a bureaucratic opposite, labelled organic. Although their discussion focused on the two extremes, their argument implied that there could be an infinite variety of organizational structures ranging in form from complete bureaucratization to virtually no bureaucratization. As Burns and Stalker included both authority structure and authority style in their discussion of these variations, considerable variety in both authority structure and style are to be expected. These variations were seen to coincide with variations in the environment (specifically, with changes in market conditions) and to result in maximum efficiency. It should be noted, however, that Burns and Stalker also identified organizational variables that, depending on their values, could support or prevent the achievement of perfect compatibility of organizational structure and environmental state.

All the different participatory structures described in Chapter Five allow for a measure of participation in decision-making by organizational participants who would not exercise authority under conventional bureaucratic organization. It is also apparent that these authority structures differ in varying degrees from the hierarchical authority structure identified in Weber's bureaucratic model. Moreover, these participatory structures vary in the extent to which authority is shared by owners or managers with non-supervisory employees. Under QWL (Quality of Working Life), this happens at the workplace but does not extend to higher levels in the organization. By contrast, under co-determination, authority is shared at the top of the organization by worker and non-worker directors and also, at lower levels in the organization, through the workers' councils. In the latter case, however, shared decision-making is limited to certain areas. Workers' control gives non-supervisory employees the greatest share in authority by prescribing decision-making rights on all policy issues to the workers' councils. Even so, it must be noted that day-to-day operations of workers' control organizations are managed in the conventional hierarchical form, as is the case for most organizations whatever their level of non-managerial participation.[14] Employee stock ownership firms and cooperatives vary in their extent of employee control over policy: it is greatest in cooperatives where all employees are owners and, in the rarer instance, where employee stockholders are in the majority.

Although these forms differ from each other in various respects, a reduction of authority differences in organizational roles is common to them all. Nonetheless, despite the existence of these participatory structures, much research is required to determine how much actual authority is transferred to non-supervisory employees. As noted earlier, researchers such as Batstone (1976) questioned whether worker-directors exert much power; Batstone suggested that they are co-opted by the more experienced non-employee directors whose greater experience at the board level supports greater influence on decisions. Yugoslav sociologists (Obradovic 1976; 1972), on the basis of empirical research, have expressed scepticism about the actual degree to which workers control policy decisions, in contrast to their expectations of control. Still, a comparative study of participatory organizations in five societies (Tannenbaum et al. 1974) does show that greater devolution of authority is achieved in the countries that officially support participatory structures than in those that do not. While it must be recognized that hierarchical authority structures are to be found in most organizations, it is possible that the adoption of participatory structures is only beginning.

There are theoretical considerations that suggest that there are limits to the reduction of hierarchical authority in organizations. Robert Michels, a German sociologist and colleague of Weber, held that organizations are inherently oligarchical—the few always dominate the majority. This conclusion, which Michels referred to as "the iron law of oligarchy,"[15] is especially compelling in that it was based on his study of the German Socialist Party, which endorsed the principle of "grass-roots democracy"—the authority of the rank-and-file over the executive. As Michels required an entire book to support this conclusion, only a brief summary of his argument can be given here. He argued that once a democratic organization had grown to a size that made meetings of the total membership cumbersome, some form of representation must be adopted. Unfortunately, representatives are difficult to control and their views rather than their constituents tend to dominate. In part, this is because it is very difficult, if not impossible, to maintain effective surveillance over the representatives, but also because, in Michels' view, the membership tends to be both uninformed and apathetic about the issues requiring decision. Moreover, as organizations evolve, it becomes necessary to replace volunteers with elected or appointed officials who serve as full-time salaried staff. The expertise of these officials,[16] the experience they gain through regular dealings with the organization's matters, and their greater access to information about the organization and its situation, allow their views to prevail over those of the rank-and-file. Finally, Michels argued that the rewards of office, including the satisfaction of wielding power, are strong incentives to act to maintain office in the organization.[17] This combination of factors—representation, apathy, inferior knowledge and information, evolution to full-time officials, and the necessary rewards of office—are the basis for Michels' pessimism over the fate of democracy in organizations. Lipset, in his Preface to *Union Democracy* (Lipset, Trow, and Coleman 1956), which identifies the International Typographers Union as one of the few known exceptions to Michels' law, nonetheless admits that most empirical evidence supports Michels' law.

Certainly, there are structural features of organization that could be expected to constrain participation in decision-making. One of these is role differentiation or the division of labour, which imposes some degree of specialization of function on organizational participants. Consequently, participants tend to be limited in their knowledge of organizational affairs in proportion to their degree of specialization and their level in the organization. Moreover, role differentiation, which encourages concern with special, and perhaps narrow, interests, acts against the development of consensus, which may be necessary to maintain acceptance of a devolution of authority. To carry on routine activities, organizations also seem to require some form of managerial structure and to assign managerial functions to specific individuals. Consequently, as noted earlier, there is a measure of bureaucracy in all the participatory structures described in Chapter Five. Even if control is modified by members having the opportunity to participate in policy decisions or in creating rules that apply to the workplace or other levels of the organization, the fact that there are individuals whose roles require them to execute policy and supervise routine activities means that there is unequal access to information and unequal opportunity to take action. If an organization requires a workforce that is considerably differentiated in terms of education, rank-and-file participation in decision-making will be limited.

In addition to these structural features, it is necessary to consider the nature of the motivation required to support a devolution of authority. Evidence of low participation in organizations with participatory opportunities supports Michels' identification of apathy as an obstacle to democracy in organizations. This evidence suggests that it is unrealistic to assume that everyone experiences high satisfaction from democratic participation. On the whole, the responsibility to participate can be onerous, taking time away from activities that may be more rewarding.

EFFECTS OF VARIATIONS IN AUTHORITY STRUCTURES AND PROCESSES

Apart from the assumption of interdependence that underlies a system perspective, it is commonplace to expect authority structures and processes to influence other dimensions of action in organizations. Control over the actions of members is a fundamental requirement of collectivities, and an authority structure is expected to achieve control in an organization by establishing and maintaining the commitment of participants to the organization's objectives, rules, and procedures.

The idea that authority processes could have consequences for the achievement of organization goals and for satisfaction was prominent in research employing a human relations perspective. Early research in this perspective focused on certain dimensions of supervisory style that differentiated first-line supervisors.[18] The dimensions identified included:

- **employee orientation**—some supervisors emphasized productivity and company interests, while others, without neglecting productivity concerns, showed a strong interest in their workers' well-being (e.g., by helping workers to improve their skills, by helping to develop safety awareness, and by a readiness to discuss their workers' problems on and off the job);

- **closeness of supervision**—supervisors varied in the amount of attention given to or watchfulness over their subordinates, and in how much freedom subordinates were allowed to organize their work;

- **differentiation of supervisory role**—supervisors varied in the emphasis they gave to tasks that were distinctly different from tasks performed by subordinates, such as planning or ensuring that materials were on hand.

Associations between these dimensions of supervision and productivity and worker satisfaction were found in all three work contexts (this research is more fully described in Chapter Two). In subsequent work, three dimensions of supervisory style—close supervision, autocratic style, and employee orientation—were found to be highly intercorrelated. A supervisor whose style was autocratic was likely to supervise closely and to be productivity-oriented; a supervisor who was supportive (non-autocratic) was likely to supervise loosely and to be employee-oriented. These intercorrelations provided the basis for identifying two types of supervisor: **autocratic** or **supportive** (Argyle 1957; Stodgill and Coons 1957; Comrey et al. 1954).

While later research tends to confirm that both attitudes and behaviour are positive under supportive and negative under autocratic supervision, the analysis was strengthened by the addition of control variables. As summarized by Filley and House (1969), workers' satisfaction under supportive supervision was greater, intra-group stress was lower, and intra-group cooperation was higher than was the case for those working under autocratic supervision. In addition, the former had lower grievance rates and lower employee turnover. However, these relationships appear to depend on certain conditions (Filley and House 1969, 404) such as the nature of the decisions required by the work, the shared values of the workers, group norms, and the workers' shared perceptions of their skills. For example, employee involvement in organizational decisions is more likely where decisions are not routine, where standardized information relevant to decision-making is not available, and where there is no urgency for a decision. Participation or consultation is more likely to occur where workers share a strong commitment to independence, regard participation as legitimate, and perceive themselves as able to contribute to decisions or to work without supervision.

Gouldner ([1954] 1964) analyzed variations in rules, considering their origin, legitimation, value violation, response to deviation, and status effects (see Chapter Two), and he concluded that such variations have different effects on compliance. For example, rules that are developed jointly by management and workers and are consistent with the values of each side are more likely to minimize tensions between superiors and subordinates and to have higher levels of compliance than rules that are developed and legitimated unilaterally and that violate values held by the employees.

These early findings are supported in varying degrees by later research that reported findings on the consequences of introducing the bureaucratic alternatives described in Chapter Five. Although there are positive reports on productivity and other economic returns, there is disagreement about the direction or magnitude of such outcomes. Volvo and Saab, for example, have reported that productivity compares favourably with conventional work organization in their other plants (see, for example, Gyllenhammar 1977, 112). Co-determination has been judged to have made an important contribution to labour-management in Germany and as a result, to have contributed to Germany's economic strength (Adams and Rummel 1976, 28; Stokes 1978, 22–23). Workers' control structures and economic growth co-existed in Yugoslavia during the 1960s and 1970s. High economic performance has been reported for plywood cooperatives in the United States (Bernstein 1976, 18–19) and the Mondragon Cooperatives in Spain (Oakeshott 1978, 180–85; Stokes 1978, 34). Nightingale (1980, 40–41) described four studies,[19] including a study of companies in Canada, which found organizational performance, measured by profits, productivity, or stock prices, to be higher in employee-owned than in conventionally owned and managed companies. Mansell (1987, 3–4, 8–9, 14ff) reported improved productivity and/or economic performance for Canadian companies that have implemented job redesign, quality circles, and employee involvement and for those that have installed socio-technical systems.

Against these findings, there are more cautious assessments. Although Rothschild and Russell (1986, 318), in an extensive review of research on participatory organizations, reported that comparative studies show that the economic performance of employee "buy-out" firms compares favourably with conventionally owned firms, they also concluded that, for the range of bureaucratic alternatives, "[b]roadened participation by workers has *sometimes* improved labor motivation and productivity" (italics added). In an earlier review, Stokes (1978, 34) goes only as far as to say that "nothing . . . suggests that participation harms productivity." On cooperatives, Oakeshott (1978, xvii) concluded that "the record has been at best only modestly positive."

There is, however, research-based agreement that the devolution of authority increases satisfaction among non-supervisory employees.[20] On the basis of a summary of over twenty-five years of research, Blumberg (1968, 123) declared that "hardly a study fails to demonstrate" that increased satisfaction and other beneficial consequences result "from a genuine increase in workers' decision-making power." Rothschild and Russell (1986, 316ff) reported that alternative organizations have a positive effect on satisfaction and motivation, although there are exceptions. Mansell (1987) reported higher satisfaction for workers in various companies and government units in Canada that have implemented programs of job enrichment, employee involvement, QWL, or socio-technical systems. In a matched comparison of a sample of Canadian firms, Nightingale found perceived job satisfaction to be higher in democratic than in hierarchical firms.[21] Although criticism, as already noted, has been directed at measures of satisfaction that utilized fixed-response questionnaire items, it should be noted that, in some instances, findings of increased satisfaction are supported by reductions in such behavioural measures as absenteeism and labour turnover.

Some of the ambiguity in findings on productivity and other economic outcomes may be attributed to methodological problems (see, for example, comments by Rothschild and Russell 1986, 318–20). These include differences in measures of economic variables, differences in controls on the many other conditions that may influence economic outcomes, and sampling problems, including difficulties in matching conventional bureaucracies and bureaucratic alternatives. Before-and-after comparisons of organizations that implement change also face methodological difficulties where various conditions, such as the state of the economy, may differ in the "before" and "after" periods. Similar methodological difficulties may be faced in research on non-economic effects, although these may be concealed where a variable, such as job satisfaction, is measured by questionnaire and may not reflect the variation observed for economic variables.[22] While it would be drastic to reject such findings, methodological problems must be kept in mind so that caution is exercised in assessing the effects of organizational structure.

Although a focus on satisfaction as an outcome of organizational structure may reflect an interest in a participant's well-being, levels of satisfaction may also be interpreted as measures of the consistency between an individual's aspirations and values, and consequently, as an indirect measure of a participant's commitment to the organization. Because commitment to the organization implies some level of commitment to the organization's goals and to its rules and procedures, levels of satisfaction may be assumed to be indirect signs of changes in productivity. In short, high satisfaction suggests high productivity, and low satisfaction, low productivity. However, as is evident from the discussion of the satisfaction model, the relationship between satisfaction and productivity is influenced by a variety of other conditions. Caution is, therefore, necessary when concluding that levels of satisfaction are consistently related to levels of productivity.

Another anticipated effect of changing from a bureaucracy to one of the alternative forms of organization is a reduction in management-worker conflict since the distinction between management and non-management employees is reduced to varying extents. However, the evidence for this is ambiguous. While there are claims that the anticipated effect is realized, there is other evidence to the contrary. For example, strikes occur under workers' control in Yugoslavia (Abrahamsson 1977), and conflicts occur even in producers' cooperatives where all employees are owners (Bernstein 1976).[23]

Division of Authority

Authority, except within small organizations, is not all of one piece. It may be divided in a variety of ways. A common division of authority is in terms of operations, such as production, financial services, and human resources. Authority is customarily divided in terms of hierarchical levels that define the scope of responsibilities. It is divided up by levels that define the scope of responsibility, as has been seen for hierarchically structured authority. As it concerns the *administration* of organizations, authority is exercised in planning, execution, control, and evaluation. Stated another way, persons who exercise authority, depending on the level, must make decisions concerning objectives and the actions and resources to achieve them. They must take action to ensure that plans are implemented, including ensuring that others comply with the plans. They must assess the environmental conditions that are relevant to the planned operations, to the performances of individuals and organizational units, and to the overall performance of the organization. These responsibilities may be combined in a single role, such as the chief executive officer (CEO) of an organization or may be divided among several roles. In the latter case, the right to make decisions and issue instructions concerning these technical administrative functions may be allocated to roles and to larger role-units, such as sections, departments, and divisions.

As Woodward pointed out ([1965] 1980), the structures of authority that allocate these functions for administrative purposes have *sociological* consequences. They represent different distributions of authority but are also, as are all divisions of human beings, potential influences on conflict and cooperation. The structure of authority in terms of role and larger organizational units also has implications for status—the ordering of privilege, influence, and other rewards—and for prestige—the ranking of performance in similar and different roles. For example, in a hierarchical structure, privilege, influence, and other rewards tend to be ordered consistently with the hierarchy of authority. If changes are introduced in the authority structure that, for example, allocates rights to rank-and-file members, even if it is only a right to information, the result may be a loss of status for some authority roles and of prestige for their incumbents. This is a possible reason for the frequently reported resistance of middle managers to the introduction of QWL practices in business organizations.

Structures that allocate authority also, explicitly or otherwise, define the kinds and levels of competence required for roles in the organization. Where rational-legal authority is involved, as in bureaucracies, role incumbency is based on technical competence, that is, on possession of the skills required to do the job. These may be specific skills acquired through professional or technical training or they may be general skills, such as analytical or negotiations skills acquired through experience or education. The determination of relevant skills, however, is not always straightforward. A degree in medicine may easily be accepted as necessary for a plant physician, but the skills required by a general manager are not as easy to define and may be acquired through either experience or education. The greater the ambiguity in the definition of relevant skills for role incumbency, the greater the likelihood that conflict will result between those aspiring to such roles, but whose skills have been acquired in different ways.

Apart from hierarchical division, authority may be divided according to whether responsibilities are associated with the main activity of the organization or with activities that are seen as ancillary or supplementary to the main activity. This distinction, which has its roots in military organization, identifies the main activities of an organization as **line** activities and all other activities as **staff** activities.[24] The distinction between line and staff activities is relative—which activities are designated as line or staff depend on the objectives of the organization. Economic research will be seen as a staff activity in a manufacturing firm but as a line activity in a "think-tank" or research institute. Incumbents of positions exercising authority over a main activity, such as a production manager, are categorized as *line* officers and those exercising authority over ancillary activities, such as a personnel manager, as *staff* officers.

Early research by Dalton (1950; 1959) provided evidence of structurally generated conflict among incumbents of line and staff authority roles. Some staff officers were professionals (e.g., chemists) and, on average, staff officers had completed more years of education than line officers. Dalton provided evidence of ongoing conflict and attributed it to the different role objectives of the two kinds of authority. The objective of line officers was to maintain or increase productivity, whereas that of staff officers was to develop technological innovations or to introduce and maintain conditions such as quality control and safety, which line officers perceived or experienced as disruptive of production. However, conflict did not always persist. Compromises were made. In some instances, compromise was generated by the staff officers who were interested in moving into line positions; but compromise was also generated by a mutual interest in reducing conflict and its concomitant stress. Such compromises typically resulted in an exchange of benefits for those directly involved, but not always for interested third parties, such as the firm's customers. Cooperation often occurs between those who occupy primarily conflicting roles, such as the police and criminals, intelligence officers of different countries, or soldiers of opposing armies. Although conflict is expected to prevail in these situations, those acting in these roles may recognize that they need to cooperate with each other to achieve their objectives. Even though line and staff officers work in the same organization and are expected to cooperate, they may engage in conflict if their roles impose different conceptions of the organization and require different agenda to fulfil their organizational tasks.

Another distinction, drawn between managers and those employed as professionals, has received considerable attention from organizational sociologists.[25] Studies of professionals in organizations have focused mainly on conflict, which is perceived to be rooted in differences in the basic occupational values of professionals and managers. Professionals are perceived to demand autonomy in discharging their responsibilities and to be responsive only to peer regulation in the evaluation of their work. Thus, professionals seek to control the definition of problems in their areas of expertise and to carry out the required action to find solutions. Such expectations may run contrary to those of managers, whose priorities focus on controlling organizational resources in order to maximize contributions to the achievement of organizational objectives.

Conflict between professionals and managers dominated the study of professionals in organizations in the 1960s and 1970s (Barley and Tolbert 1991). However, such conflict, as Dalton showed in his study of staff and line managers, may not persist. Perin's research (1991), which concerned flexible time arrangements for work to be done at home and the office, reveals that professionals appear to have accepted the judgment of managers who say that presence in the office is important for organizational functioning. Bacharach et al. (1991) went further by proposing that the state of professional-managerial conflict is a function of the environment. In their view, the extent of conflict and its resolution by compromise or by the domination of one or other of the two occupational groups fluctuates in response to organizational conditions.

SUMMARY

Like all social systems, organizations must maintain a certain amount of order for the system to survive. Order in human systems is based on shared values and the norms derived from them. However, although action in social systems is governed by values, norms, and other prescriptive elements, ensuring compliance is difficult. Understanding the compliance/deviance aspect of order, then, requires the identification of the conditions that facilitate or hinder compliance. According to sociological theory and research in organizations, these conditions include self-motivation, work satisfaction, and the individual and shared interests of participants. Such conditions have been incorporated in compliance models.

The other major aspect of order concerns the exercise of authority. To understand authority in organizations, sociologists focus on the concept of structure, beginning with Weber's bureaucratic model and progressing to a conception of structural variation. This latter conceptualization embraces the ideas of bureaucratic variation and alternatives to bureaucracy. Some examples of these variations are described in the chapter. Various aspects of structural variation have interested sociologists, such as its consequences for work satisfaction and productivity, and the conflicts that may arise from varying distribution of responsibility among authoritative roles. Although the emergence of different forms of authority has stimulated research, further study is needed to understand the limits of variations as well as the anticipated and unanticipated consequences of these variable forms.

ENDNOTES

1   As used here, **norms** is a general term referring to prescriptions for action that may take the form of implicit understandings, explicit rules, regulations, and laws.

2   Socialization is a concept belonging to social psychology, which is rooted in both psychology and sociology. Although the social psychologies derived from each basic discipline have some similarities, there are marked differences. Psychological social psychology tends to be experimental in method and to focus on how the presence of others influences individual outcomes of experimental conditions. Sociological social psychology tends to involve field observation, and its purpose is to understand how the social characteristics of the situation or environment, especially values, norms, and role expectations, influence action. Consistent with this perspective, socialization is conceived to be a process by which individuals *internalize* values, norms, and role expectations.

3 *Significant* others are people who are especially meaningful or important to the person undergoing socialization. The term **self** is roughly synonymous with *personality*, or in Freudian theory, with the *Superego*. **Internalization** can be thought of as the development of conscience (although that term is not used by Mead).

4 Floyd Allport, a social psychologist, conducted a series of studies that showed **conformity**, his term for compliance, varying according to the norm and situation but revealed high levels nonetheless. The tradition of research on compliance has continued (see, for example, Alcock, Carment, and Sadava 1988, chap. 6).

5 It is assumed that participants in social interaction are able to identify their positions relative to each other so that appropriate codes of conduct will be followed. It has been reported that members of different Australian tribes, encountering each other as strangers, first exchange information on kinship affiliations to decide whether they should treat each other as friends, neutrals, or enemies. Similarly, if command has not been determined in advance, when naval vessels belonging to allied nations join unexpectedly in the course of an operation, signals giving the seniority of the commanders are exchanged to establish who is in command of the task force. Even in small informal groups, where roles and relationships may be evolving, members look for signs differentiating positions in the group (see, for example, Bales' observations (1950, 19–22) on leadership roles in experimental groups). As self-image formation is held to be based on a person's perceptions of the responses of others in situations of social interaction (see, for example, Cooley 1920; Mead 1934), and as these responses are influenced by the others' statuses and prestige positions as well as those of the person to whom the responses are directed, there is further reason to assume that status and prestige are critical concepts for understanding human action.

6 Etzioni refers to sanctions as the means of exercising power and to motives as the kinds of involvement of participants who are subject to orders and instructions.

7 That is, the sanction and motive types are assumed to be consistent with each other.

8 Etzioni is aware that intervening variables may facilitate or hinder the movement toward consistency ([1961] 1975, 121).

9 The authors regard their model as a contribution to a general theory of motivation. In their words, "Social science has yet to create" such a general theory (Knoke and Wright-Isak 1982, 212).

10 The resources referred to include a variety of forms such as material contributions, participation, and "the simple act of joining."

11 Incentive types were represented by empirically derived incentive scales and the incentive systems from Knoke's typology of incentive systems.

12 Norms, the term used to refer to explicitly stated or implicitly held prescriptions for action, include the formal rules and prescriptions characteristic of organizations as well as the informal rules and prescriptions that develop in the course of social interaction among organization participants.

13 Technical competence is the basic criterion for incumbency in a bureaucratic role of authority. By contrast, the skills required for role incumbency of traditional authority and charismatic authority are not defined independently of legitimation. Authority conferred by tradition assumes that an incumbent possesses the necessary skills, whereas charismatic authority is based on followers' perceptions of the leader as possessing unique characteristics, such as divine inspiration, or personality traits.

14 It is reasonable to suggest, as implied by the Burns-Stalker concept of a continuum of organizational variation and by the fact that organizations engage in routine activities, that most organizations will include some bureaucratic features.

15 "It is organization which gives birth to the dominion of the elected over the electors, of the mandataries over the mandators, of the delegates over the delegators. Who says organization, says oligarchy" (Michels [1911] 1962, 365).

16 Specialized function and expertise are important resources for controlling decision-making. If these resources are combined, even greater control can result. Examples are found in accounts of the power exercised by officials over elected representatives, including cabinet ministers (see, for example, MacDonald 1980), and of senior management over boards of directors.

17 Michels notes that full-time elected officials may attempt to maintain, and can succeed in maintaining, power by supporting successors whose views they share.

18 This early research was undertaken by Robert Kahn and Daniel Katz ([1953] 1960) in three different work settings: clerical operations, railroad track-laying gangs, and heavy product manufacturing. The research was rooted in the well-known leadership studies by Lippitt and White (1943).

19 One of these was Bernstein's research cited above.

20 As most of this research measured satisfaction at one interval after the change—usually soon after—it is not known if the increased level of satisfaction persists.

21 Ten democratically and ten hierarchically managed firms, matched in terms of selected criteria, such as size and technology, were compared on a variety of non-economic measures.

22 See, for example, Rinehart ([1975] 1987, 143–44) for comment on the relatively uniform high levels of job satisfaction reported when this type of measure is used.

23 In producers' cooperatives, where members are both employees and owners, the conflict is between these two roles.

24 In the military, regiments of the line (combat units) are contrasted with units that provide support, such as supplies, equipment maintenance, and engineering.

25 The distinction between managers and professionals somewhat overlaps the distinction between line and staff employees because professionals often occupy staff positions.

CHAPTER 7

CONSENSUS AND COHESION

$\mathscr{I}$t is common knowledge that members of social groups may agree and disagree about their beliefs, values, norms, and other prescriptive elements. It is also common knowledge that members of social groups may like or dislike each other. Common knowledge, however, is limited. It is common knowledge that things fall down, but centuries passed before we understood why or learned that under certain conditions things could "fall" up.

As in the case of falling bodies, we may recognize that agreement and disagreement, liking and disliking, occur without consideration of their significance for social interaction or for social systems. That significance is the subject of this chapter, which will use the concepts of consensus/dissensus and cohesion/division as a framework for discussing, respectively, agreement/disagreement and liking/disliking.

The discussion traces the use of these concepts, or their equivalents, in the analysis of social interaction and social systems from the late nineteenth century to the present. Attention to these concepts has been uneven. The periods of rising and waning interest in these concepts, as marked by theory and research, are approximately rather than precisely identified.

Following a discussion of the endurance of the concepts of consensus/dissensus and cohesion/division as analytical concepts and their relevance to sociological analysis, the discussion centres on two roughly

identifiable periods of strength for these concepts—the first was dominated by the human relations perspective, and in the second these concepts were included in a variety of perspectives that emerged in the late
1960s and thereafter.

CONSENSUS AND COHESION AS ENDURING CONCEPTS

The idea that social relationships are dependent on agreement and on
emotional ties has a long history. Weber's concept of shared values,
Marx's concept of consciousness, and Durkheim's concept of collective
conscience and of collective representations all imply that agreement, or
consensus, among participants in a social system is a fundamental condition of its functioning. Durkheim distinguished between societies that
are integrated on the basis of kinship and other traditional bonds and
those integrated by a division of labour and rational economic
exchange.[1] He also introduced the idea of non-contractual elements of
contract—understandings that regulate action, even though they may
not be expressed explicitly in a contract—in relationships that are based
on economic exchanges. Toennies distinguished between societies that
were organized about sentiments of community and those that were
formed to pursue instrumental ends. These scholars also emphasized
affective ties, or *cohesion*, as a similarly important condition. Weber
contrasted the impersonality characterizing bureaucratic relationships
with those of loyalty in traditional and charismatic relationships. Marx
stressed the concept of solidarity among those who shared interests, as
these are defined by relations of production. In his study of suicide,
Durkheim ([1897] 1951) called attention to the importance of affective
relationships as a source of support in situations of stress.

The importance for analysis of the concepts of consensus and
cohesion, however they may be labelled, has been recognized by sociological theorists who followed the founders. Cooley ([1909] 1962, chap.
3), following Toennies, distinguished between primary relationships,
which are maintained because they are intrinsically satisfying, and
those that are pursued for some external objective. Among more recent
theorists, Parsons and his collaborators (1951) include a dimension of
affectivity/affective neutrality among the shared value orientations that
they regard as fundamental regulators of social action and as basic concepts for distinguishing different forms of social relationships.[2] A recent
example is Coleman (1988). He defined social capital to include shared
expectations and obligations, affective support, etc., and uses the concept to analyze the resources that, along with physical and human cap-

ital, affect the functioning of individuals as well as social relationships. These examples demonstrate the considerable continuity in the use of consensus and cohesion to analyze social relationships.

THE RELEVANCE OF CONSENSUS AND COHESION TO SOCIOLOGICAL ANALYSIS

Consensus refers to agreed-upon or shared values, norms, and other prescriptive elements as well as to shared perceptions of situations, and it is required at some level to maintain action among participants in a relationship. Assuming that cooperation is a necessary condition for realizing the objectives of a relationship, consensus and cohesion may be seen as conditions that facilitate cooperation. If it is further assumed that relationships involve expectations and reciprocal obligations among participants, it may be hypothesized that the functioning of a relationship depends on some appropriate level of consensus about such expectations. Furthermore, it may be hypothesized that stress in a relationship is directly proportional to the level of failure of participants to meet expectations.[3]

Cohesion is rooted in the human capacity for emotional expression. Although rationality, a product of human beings' cognitive skills, is often given prominence in analyses of human action, it must be remembered that not only are people capable of emotional expression, but most action carries an emotional component.[4] In relations with others, people act to express positive emotions, ranging from liking to love, negative emotions, ranging from dislike to hate, or indifference. Moreover, humans act in different ways to attract such positive or negative emotional responses. Although most people seek to express and to receive positive emotional responses, it is reasonable to expect there to be a wide variety in people's capacity and motivation to express or seek positive, negative, or indifferent emotional responses. Moreover, circumstances may make it necessary to risk giving or receiving negative responses.[5]

Emotional exchanges between people can have serious consequences—in the extreme, a person may kill for love or hate, but even mutual dislike among members of a group may limit cooperative action. It is not surprising, therefore, that, like other action, emotional expression in social relationships is regulated by implicit or explicit expectations or norms. In many societies, for example, parents are expected to like or love their children, and in some societies, including ours, marriage is expected to be based on a shared love between the prospective bride and groom. Regulation is often directed at extreme expressions of emotions such as love, hate, grief, and even joy. Many societies have detailed norms to regulate grieving for the dead, and the literature of many societies recounts the tragic consequences of both misdirected and overstated passion—either love or hate. Although negative emotional expression, or the conditions likely to produce it, may come to mind as a prime target for control, since it is likely to generate division or conflict, normative control of positive emotional expression is also necessary to prevent or reduce any undesirable consequences for the system. For example, in societies where clans or lineages are significant kinship units, evidence of strong affection between husband and wife may be interpreted as threatening lineage or clan loyalties. Social systems, including organizations, can therefore be expected to regulate against levels of either positive or negative emotional expression that are likely to disrupt system functional requirements, such as meeting goals, responding to environmental demands, and maintaining authority.

Although consensus and cohesion are discrete concepts, research reveals them to be empirically interdependent.[6] Levels of cohesion and division may be consequences, respectively, of levels of consensus or dissensus and vice versa—persons who agree tend to like each other, and persons who like each other tend to agree. Because of this, it is difficult to separate their independent effects on other aspects of social relationships.

On the assumption that social relationships are the fundamental structural units of social systems, it is further assumed that consensus and cohesion are relevant to the analysis of all forms of social systems. It might be expected, then, that these concepts would have been prominent in the theory and research in the sociology of organizations. This chapter assesses this expectation by examining the reported effects of consensus and cohesion on organizational processes and the conditions that appear to influence levels of consensus and cohesion.

EARLY RESEARCH INTO CONSENSUS AND COHESION

Human Relations Perspective

The Western Electric studies, which employed a human relations perspective, provided evidence that friendly or hostile feelings among workers may have consequences for organizational activities. Indeed, these research findings, which characterized worker interaction as informal relations or informal groups, were viewed as a breakthrough in understanding organizations. Thus, the women of the Relay Assembly Test Room, who were regarded as independent operators, helped each other at work and also developed social ties with each other outside the workplace. The Western Electric researchers speculated that these friendly ties contributed to the upward trend of productivity during the experiment. By contrast, the researchers concluded that both friendship and hostility or conflict, observed in the Bank Wiring Observation Room, may have held productivity below management's expectations.

Other researchers within the human relations perspective contributed further evidence on the effects of cohesion and consensus. Seashore (1954) found cohesiveness to be a significant factor in determining productivity in a heavy manufacturing plant. On the basis of questionnaire data obtained from 228 work units varying in size from five to fifty workers, he showed that the variation in productivity within high-cohesive units was lower than it was in low-cohesive units. Seashore, therefore, concluded that levels of cohesion were associated with a group's influence on its members' productivity. He also found that high-cohesive unit productivity differed more than low-cohesive unit productivity from plant productivity norms. Moreover, these differences could be either higher or lower than plant norms. In other words, the more positively workers felt toward members of their work unit, the more closely workers conformed to a *group-defined* productivity norm, but such a norm could be higher or lower than the norm defined by the plant management.[7]

Paterson (1955), in a study of a Royal Air Force (RAF) station that had the highest flying accident rate in the RAF, focused, as a remedy, on developing a high level of agreement among personnel about the station's objective. To do so, Paterson defined "defeating the weather" as the station's objective in place of the traditional objective of "making contact with and destroying the enemy."[8] Paterson assumed that the new objective would be more meaningful to all personnel than the traditional objective, which related most directly to flight crews. The eventual achievement of a high level of consensus along with increased interaction among personnel, especially across status lines, was followed by a drastic reduction in the flying accident rate.

Sayles emphasizes consensus and cohesion as important conditions that provide the "internal group strength" (1958, 41) necessary to support sustained grievance behaviour. Both conditions are included as factors in his explanation of varying levels of such behaviour in various manufacturing industries.[9]

Consensus and Cohesion in Other Perspectives

Interest in consensus and cohesion also developed in research conditioned by those working in perspectives other than the human relations perspective. As discussed in Chapter Four and briefly in this chapter, the concepts of consensus/dissensus and cohesion/division are regarded as functional requirements of social systems and are established in the social system perspective. They are not singled out for further discussion here.

In the rational perspective, Weber took emotion into account in his description of the bureaucratic model that required relationships in the bureaucracy to be emotionally neutral. As actions in the bureaucracy are to be determined on the basis of rationality—giving orders or instructions or complying with them should not depend on whether superiors or subordinates like or dislike each other—emotional ties or responses, whether positive or negative, were seen by Weber as undermining rationality. Many managers subscribe to the Weberian position— for example, by adopting policies directed against employing persons related to existing employees. There are, however, varied views among organizational consultants and management on the consequences of emotional neutrality and of positive emotional ties between members of an organization. In contrast to the emphasis on emotional neutrality, some companies have promoted an image of employee relationships as familial, implying that emotional commitments, presumably positive, are desirable. At one time, a United States automobile manufacturer advertised its policy of hiring the sons of its employees as contributing to its high production quality. Unions, by adopting terms such as "brotherhood" and "sisterhood," imply that members' commitments to each other should be modelled on expectations of sibling loyalty.

Blau ([1955] 1963), a neo-Weberian, made observations and analyzed the statistical records of the work done by two sections of a state employment agency. He concluded that a lower level of competitiveness but higher productivity in one section was associated with a higher level of consensus, as revealed by high consensus on professional standards, and by high cohesiveness, as assessed by workers spending rest periods in each other's company and other observations of interaction. Blau gave greater prominence to cohesion, as measured by interaction in various situations, in his analysis of a federal regulatory agency, arguing that the high level of cohesion among the agents made an important contribution to the agency's objectives. On the basis of his observations, Blau concluded that the strong positive evidence of mutual emotional support among the agents served to reduce significantly the stress generated by their work, which otherwise would have severely reduced their effectiveness.

Some relevant sociological research is difficult to categorize in terms of perspective. Research on armed services combat units in World War II and in Korea provides evidence on the relationship between cohesion and combat motivation. Shils and Janowitz (1948) argued that cohesion made the critical difference between Wehrmacht units who continued to fight and those who surrendered toward the end of World

War II. Survey research on various United States combat units by Stouffer et al. (1949, 2: 108–9, 174) showed cohesion to be an important influence supporting combat motivation. Marshall (1947), a military historian who used sociological data-gathering procedures, such as direct field observation, in his studies of combat behaviour during World War II, concluded that cohesion was a significant factor in effective combat performance. Stated briefly, his research showed that a willingness to perform combat duties was low or absent where members of military units were strangers to each other and much higher in units whose members had associated with each other for some considerable time.[10]

Sociometry

Sociometry, a forerunner of network analysis, was founded by J.L. Moreno and attracted widespread interest in the 1950s and 1960s.[11] It provided a method for studying the structure of social relationships, based on the associational preferences of group members for each other. Although sociometric research gave attention to various bases of association, such as a person's task competence or desirability as a partner in leisure or social activities, studies based on affective bases, such as the liking or disliking of members for each other, were prominent. Thus Criswell, a prominent sociometric methodologist, perceived sociometric techniques as important means of measuring group integration. Sociometric research was often concerned with the effects of friendship or cohesion on productivity, job satisfaction, and morale (for examples, see Moreno et al. 1960, 153–80, 506–17). Goodacre studied the relation of the associational structure of six-man reconnaissance squads and their performance in training exercises that simulated combat operations (Moreno et al. 1960, 548–52). On the basis of preferences reported by squad members, measures of cohesion were determined for each squad and were found to relate positively to squad performance.

Influences on Consensus and Cohesion

Along with the research evidence that consensus and cohesion can influence action generally associated with other aspects of organizational functioning, there was also evidence of variation in levels of consensus and cohesion. Consequently, it was important to explore the reasons for such variability—are there features of organizations that are systematically related to consensus and dissensus, cohesion and division? The research evidence supports a positive answer. In their explanation of an unanticipated strike by the workers in all seven shoe factories in a New England community, Warner and Low (1947) emphasized, although not exclusively, the effects of a technological change in the industry that replaced craft workers with semi-skilled machine operators—a shift from a high to a low division of labour. Differences in perception, attitudes, and activities among workers of differing skill levels are well-documented (see, for example, Form 1976; Lipset, Trow, and Coleman 1956), and it is reasonable to suggest that the change to a low division of labour led to a greater consensus in perceptions of the work situation and that cohesiveness was increased to a level necessary to support action in the form of a general strike.

Paterson (1955) documented that status differences among RAF station personnel were associated with differences in perception of the station's overall task and that status differences inhibited interaction across status lines. There is, indeed, considerable evidence that consensus, as indicated by different perceptions of the organization and other differences in attitudes, opinions, and interests, varies in relation to organizational structure. People tend to identify the main tasks and the problems of an organization from the perspective of their own location and status in the organization. Moreover, since people tend to interact most with their co-workers, the potential for consensus or dissensus, cohesion or conflict within work units is stronger than it is between members of different work units. Although either cohesive or divisive responses seem likely, the research evidence seems to support Homans' optimistic hypothesis: the more persons interact with each other, the more they will like each other (Homans 1950). Generally, research shows that the interaction of organizational participants is rarely limited to fulfilling task requirements. Instead, the tendency is to expand the interaction to expressive interests. In specific terms, this may mean showing positive emotional commitment by helping co-workers with their job tasks, exchanging personal information, counselling on both organizational and extra-organizational problems, and engaging in extra-organizational social activities.

Dissensus and conflict may be more likely across structural locations and related status lines as Dalton (1950) has shown in his study of conflict between staff and line officers. This view is theoretically rooted in Marx and others, such as Dahrendorf ([1957] 1959), who hold that conflict results from inherently differing interests between owners and workers or between managers and the managed. Indeed, this assumption may be extended to any division drawn between human beings, such as those based on age, gender, language, and religion, as a basis for expecting prejudice, discrimination, and conflict. Organizations are especially prone to dissensus and conflict since a complex division of labour, is a fundamental aspect of their structure.[12] To the degree that dissensus and conflict contribute positively to organizational functioning, they are not problematical. However, on the assumption that a minimum level of consensus and cohesion are essential, there may be problems to overcome.

There is evidence to show that it is possible to overcome the effects of occupational and other organizational unit boundaries. Paterson (1955) was able to increase interaction across RAF ranking and occupational boundaries and so achieve a high level of consensus concerning the newly defined objective of the station. Burns and Stalker (1961) also showed that environmental pressures could push organizations toward an organic structure whose characteristics include interaction across occupational boundaries.

Technology has also been shown to influence levels of consensus and dissensus, cohesion and conflict. Gouldner ([1954] 1964) found that gypsum mineworkers showed greater cohesion than those employed in manufacturing wallboard in the gypsum plant he studied. He attributed the difference to the greater danger to which the miners, as compared to the manufacturing workers, were exposed and to the different work organization of the two operations—teams in contrast to an assembly line—imposed by the differing technologies. Studies of mining operations in Great Britain also revealed the effects of technology on work organization and cohesion among coal miners (Trist and Bamforth 1951). In an analysis of a wildcat strike by workers employed in manufacturing operations at the gypsum plant, Gouldner identified technological change among the conditions generating the strike.

Sayles (1958) provided an example of research that links technology to the frequency and success of grievance behaviour. He identified four types of response to dissatisfaction: high or low rates of grieving and high or low rates of success as the outcome of grieving. In general, frequency of grieving was associated with variations in technology. His findings are summarized in Table 7.1. Sayles' analysis allows this important inference: the level of dissatisfaction in a work group is not the most important condition for generating grievances. More important

TABLE 7.1 Structural features of the workplace as related to frequency of grieving*

Frequency of Grieving	
High	**Low**
Low division of labour	High division of labour
Medium level skills	Low or high occupational skills
Independent operations with a high concentration of workers in an area or work teams or crews	Isolated, independent jobs
Short or long assembly lines	Medium to long assembly lines

*These structural features are not necessarily all present for either high or low grievance activity.

are the presence of structural conditions that facilitate consensus and cohesion, the status of the workers derived from skill levels, and the power of work units to control the work process, especially the quality of the product.

MORE RECENT RESEARCH INTO CONSENSUS AND COHESION

Consensus and cohesion were important concepts for the organizational theory and research discussed so far. Although these concepts were not completely abandoned, the attention given to them, from the early 1970s to the present, diminished markedly.

A Change in Emphasis

There has been a continuing interest in the problems investigated in the earlier work. In a span of about thirty years, Litwak, for example, contributed articles on the different functions of bureaucratic structures and primary relations in organizations (see, for example, Litwak 1961; Litwak and Figuera 1968; Litwak and Messari 1989). The considerable interest in re-analysis of the Relay Assembly Test Room data, reported in Chapter Three, provides another example, as does the network analysis of friendships in organizations by Lincoln and Miller (1979). On the whole, however, consensus and cohesion were less prominent in research, partly as a consequence of the prominence of structural analysis during the first half of this later period. As will be recalled from Chapters Five and Six, the work of Blau, Hage, Woodward, and other prominent researchers and theorists centred on the idea of structure and on such indicators of structure as the levels of authority, numbers of sub-units, ratios of those exercising authority to those who do not, spans of control at different levels of authority, and the occupational structure of organizations (see, for example, Blau et al. 1976, 25). The research primarily related variations among such indicators to the size and the technology of organizations.

Blau's analysis of organizations over the years illustrates the shift in interest from interpersonal relations to a more impersonal structural perspective. Although his early research focused on structural variables, he also gave considerable attention to affective action in interpersonal relations among organizational participants. Indeed, the interrelated dynamics of status-oriented action and cohesion is central to his analysis of the federal agency ([1955] 1963, chaps. 8 and 9). In later work, however, this interest in interpersonal relations gave way to a more limited structural perspective.[13]

Structure is a basic concept in sociology and deserves emphasis in the sociology of organizations, but this emphasis may also be explained by the comparative ease of obtaining data for indicators of structure and for potentially explanatory variables.[14] Moreover, such indicators are compatible with survey methods of data gathering that allow many organizations to be included in an analysis rather than one organization (or possibly two or three), as is typical of research focused on interaction among participants of organizations. Although it is not impossible to use survey methods to gather data for indicators of consensus and cohesion, customary practice is to gather data by direct observation.

Although consensus and cohesion were given less and less attention within the structural perspective, other perspectives emerged. Consensus and cohesion were not, for the most part, explicit components of these emerging perspectives, but they were implicit in several that gained prominence in the later period.

Different Perspectives

Several theoretical perspectives centre on the analysis of interaction, which is viewed as generating conditions that explain the functioning of social relationships. Other perspectives are concerned with the supportive effects of social relationships, and still others, at a different level of analysis, focus on cultural elements in organizations and their environments.

Social Exchange

The analysis of interaction has a long history in sociology, but for present purposes, discussion is limited to the contributions made by Homans and by Blau prior to the 1970s. Both theories imply the concepts of consensus and cohesion. In his book, *The Human Group* (1950), Homans identified **norms** (1950, 121–25), **interaction**, **activity**, and **sentiments** as basic concepts for studying social relationships (1950, 34–40). He further identified **frequency**, **duration**, and **order** (1950, 36–37) as important variable aspects of interaction.[15] It is reasonable to assume that consensus is implied by the concept of norms since these are shared in relationships. Cohesion is implied by the concept of sentiments, which includes expressions of emotion and feelings, and by Homans' proposition that frequency of interaction and liking between participants are positively related (1950, 111).[16] In a later work (1961), he used the same concepts but added the concept **reinforcement** from psychology and the **exchange model** from economics. With this model, he formulated relationships between his concepts and so presented an exchange theory of interaction that he referred to as elementary social behaviour. Thus, individuals are viewed as participants in relationships when they engage in exchanges of resources they control for those they seek to acquire.

Blau's interest in exchange as a principal process of interaction is evident in his early analysis of federal agents ([1955] 1963) where certain actions of agents are interpreted as exchanging knowledge for status, support, or both. Blau developed this conception of interaction in a later work in which he proposed that "social exchange was a process of central significance in social life" (1964, 4). Like Homans, his theory is focused on interpersonal relations, but he sees it as a basis for understanding the social structure of more complex social systems. And like Homans, Blau sees interaction as an exchange of benefits. These benefits may be *extrinsic*, such as those where commodities or tasks are exchanged, or *intrinsic*, where the benefits take the form of approval or the satisfaction of meeting another's expectations. Blau is explicit in seeing cohesion as the outcome of social exchange (1964, chap. 2) and as an important influence on the development of consensus (1964, 60–61). Blau's perspective, much like Homans', viewed actors as exchanging resources as a means of realizing their aspirations and as a means of differentiating actors in terms of power.

In addition to Blau and Homans, and consistent with Durkheim's observations on the "non-contractual elements of contract," sociologists continue to argue that non-economic incentives are important to the maintenance and development of social relationships. Litwak (1961), for example, in a discussion of the relevance of impersonality and its opposite in organizational relationships, emphasized *trust* as an important condition in relationships in certain kinds of organizations.

Coleman (1988), writing generally about social relationships, introduced the concept of *social capital* to distinguish certain forms of resources from those referred to as *physical* and as *human* capital. Social capital refers, for example, to shared norms, expectations, obligations, and channels of communication. These shared elements are seen as social capital or resources since an actor can claim, or has the right to claim, appropriate responses from other participants in the relationship. As Cook and Emerson observed, "The tendency for commitments to form among exchange partners is a fact commonly acknowledged in the organizational literature" (1984, 16; see also p. 22). In Coleman's view, rational decisions may be based on control of social capital resources as well as control of human and physical resources.

Granovetter (1985) responded directly to the economic model by arguing for the importance of personal relations as a determinant of economic activities. Although his argument was directed primarily at the structuring of relationships between business firms, it is also pertinent to analyses of activities within firms. This is illustrated by an example taken from Dalton (1959, 31–49) that documents the influence of personal relations on internal audits, despite the expectation that they be conducted objectively and impersonally. Stated simply, Granovetter argued that all action, whether it concerns economic or other activities and objectives, is embedded in social relations. This means, as does Coleman's theory, that actions are regulated by shared prescriptive elements and may also include affective commitments that influence the content of interaction.

All these theories, whether they emphasize commitment, trust, shared norms, obligations, or general social embeddedness as important in human action, imply the importance of consensus and cohesion.

Negotiated Order

Negotiated order, another general perspective used by students of organizations, also emphasizes social interaction as the appropriate field of analysis (see Fine 1984). Basically, order and other regulative aspects of social action are seen to be determined by participants in the relationship rather than by externally imposed norms, rules, or other prescriptive elements. In effect, participants *negotiate* the terms of participation—the objectives, the benefits and costs and their distribution, and so on. Negotiation is viewed as an ongoing process that arises in response to stress in the relationship and that is invoked as a means of stress reduction. It is not the act, as when a teacher asks a pupil a question or a supervisor issues an order to a subordinate, that is the central concern but the meaning of the act. As these elements of action—gestures, signs, and symbols—must have shared meanings for the participants, it is apparent that levels of consensus and dissensus among actors, whether explicitly or implicitly assumed, must be crucial to the analysis. As **gestures**, such as a salute, **signs**, such as a t-shirt slogan, and **symbols**, such as a cross or flag, typically invoke emotion and serve to bind or divide interacting participants, levels of cohesion and divisions must also be crucial for the analysis.

Culture

A renewed interest in the culture of organizations has appeared, and it focuses on the shared values, norms, and other prescriptive elements of organizations.[17] As culture is a valuable concept for the analysis of societies, its extension to the analysis of other social systems is argued to be valid. Di Tomaso (1987), for example, regards organizational culture as a system of symbols that generates solidarity among organizational participants and he also sees culture as contributing to system stability.[18] Smircich (1983) similarly called attention to the *functions* of culture for organizations. She identified these as providing a sense of identity for organizational participants, facilitating commitment to an entity larger than self, enhancing social stability, and serving as a "sense-making" device. Obviously, if cultural elements are shared and are to perform such functions, as Smircich suggested, there must be some level of consensus involved.

The **institutional** perspective is also focused on culture. It uses the concept of **institutions**, which embraces such prescriptive elements as social norms, laws, rules, professional codes, and standards as a basis for studying organizations (see, for example, Scott and Meyer 1994). These elements may have their sources in organizational environments or in organizations themselves. For those using this perspective, attention is directed to the degree that such institutionalization is present, its effects on structural variation, and its relation to the stability and effectiveness of the organization or organizations concerned. These interests, along with the specification of the organization as the unit of analysis rather than relationships among participants, reveal this perspective as quite different from those employed in the earlier research focus on cultural or institutional elements.

Network Analysis

Network analysis, like its predecessor, sociometry, provides a means of describing and analyzing relations between individuals as well as between other social units such as organizations, communities, and societies.[19] Analysis includes testing for dependence and interdependence between relations with different bases, such as advice groups and friendship groups, and with other variables of interest, such as position in a social group and job satisfaction. Relations between units may be based on various kinds of links, such as transactions, advice, and responsibilities, but as in early sociometric research, liking and other kinds of affective bonds continue to be analyzed in network research (Burt 1980). Cohesion is effectively, therefore, an active interest in network analysis. Moreover, the relations of cohesive groups are well represented in research on social support (see, for example, Hall and Wellman 1985). Where organizations provide the ground for network research, however, there is stronger interest in inter-organizational rather than intra-organizational relationships.[20]

An interest in cohesion as an important condition in times of stress is not limited to network analysis. Durkheim's finding, for example, that suicide rates were lower for married as opposed to single individuals, and for those married with children compared to those without, could be interpreted, although not unambiguously, as evidence of the positive effects of social support. Blau's conclusion that cohesion among the federal agents provided support against the stress generated by the job has been described in Chapter Two. Litwak and Messari (1989) provide a general summary of the relevance of primary groups, hence, cohesion, for social support in relation to productivity, illness, and mortality and offer a theoretical explanation of the different effects of formal and informal organization on support.

Dissensus and Division

Although research on strikes and other forms of intra-organizational conflict was undertaken in the earlier period of consensus research, a greater emphasis on dissent and division than on consensus and cohesion may have existed in this later period. Certainly, there was a reaction to the concepts of consensus and cohesion on the ground that such concepts support conservative social analysis whereas dissent and division were more consistent with social change—especially change directed toward greater freedom of expression and to more equitable distributions of power and the economic returns of labour. In Edwards' widely read analysis of conflict in the workplace (1979), the focus is on the persistence of hierarchical control in the face of important changes in the workplace generated by large organizations. Studies of the labour process, such as Edwards' (1979, 12, 15), emphasize analysis of labour-management conflict in organizations. Zey-Farrell and Aiken (1981, 1–21) discuss twelve "criticisms" in their critique of the dominant perspectives in the study of organizations—identified as the comparative structural and structural contingency approaches. The criticisms cover a variety of topics, including, for example, a neglect to analyze the relation between organizations and their surrounding societies, and a neglect of power relationships in organizations. One of these criticisms— that mainline organizational analysis assumes **value consensus**—is relevant to the present discussion. By value consensus, Zey-Farrell and Aiken mean that mainline analysts assume that "all members of an organization share common values and attitudes and thus act in consensus" (1981, 10). Although this criticism may be overstated, it is fair in its recognition of a neglect of dissensus and of conflict in the sociological analysis of organizations.

Edwards' conflict perspective and Zey-Farrell and Aiken's critique underline the need for theory and research to be concerned with dissent and division as well as with consensus and cohesion. Both consensus/dissensus and cohesion/division identify conditions that are present in organizations and that have been shown to have functional and dysfunctional consequences for organizations. Conditions that generate cohesion/division and consensus/dissensus also require attention. In the past, Homans (1961) and Seashore (1954) were concerned with the causes as well as with the effects of these conditions. In more recent work, consensus/dissensus and cohesion/division appear to be outcomes of structural variation. It is reasonable to suggest, then, as does Granovetter, that this should be recognized in theory and research. Both consensus/dissensus and cohesion/division can be treated conceptually as the extremes of conditions or as dimensions reflecting varying support for values and for other cultural and prescriptive elements, and for varying levels and directions of affective ties and conditions in social relationships.

CONCLUSIONS

All the perspectives discussed in this chapter depend explicitly or implicitly on consensus or cohesion or their opposites, and they contribute to the understanding of organizations through their emphasis on one or the other condition as an important aspect of organizations. It would be far better if these various perspectives could be integrated under a common scheme—as has been suggested for the negotiated order and cultural perspectives (Fine 1984), and which is possible under a system perspective—but it is not appropriate to explore that possibility here. However, it is appropriate to observe that the earlier research was based explicitly on the concepts of consensus and cohesion and on data on interpersonal relations. Moreover, the earlier research was concerned with relations between consensus and cohesion and other dimensions of action. These other dimensions include:

- various aspects of motivation, such as productivity (Roethlisberger and Dickson [1939] 1947; Blau [1955] 1963; and Seashore 1954) or meeting role or task expectations (Marshall 1947; Paterson 1955; and Stouffer et al. 1949, vol. 2, chaps. 3 and 5);

- integration, such as transcendence of status and role boundaries (Paterson 1955); and

- support and stress reduction (Blau [1955] 1963).

It is well known that patterns of interaction in organizations, established for instrumental purposes, tend to develop into relationships of solidarity or conflict. The regularity of this pattern implies that it is premature to conclude that such changes can be ascribed to personality differences. As these amicable and divisive relationships have been shown by sociologists to have important positive and negative consequences for organizations, they present a challenge to those who study organizations.

Research that is explicitly concerned with consensus/dissensus and cohesion/division is needed to explain their relation to other dimensions of action in organizations. More important, answers are needed for questions that the early research generated but did not answer. For example, more must be learned about the minimum and maximum levels of consensus, cohesion, dissensus, and division that organizations may require or can tolerate, relative to their other necessary requirements. It seems important to know if these levels vary among organizations with different tasks or structures. Also, although there is convincing evidence that cohesive groups provide support for individuals experiencing stress, comparisons of individuals with and without group support do not explain why cohesion has the effects claimed for it. Insofar as organizations are concerned, while it is apparent that interpersonal relations are important, research on consensus/dissensus and cohesion/division, not necessarily identical to but in the manner of the earlier research, such as that conducted within the rational perspective, could provide continuity and contribute substantially to understanding "what goes on in organizations."

ENDNOTES

[1] The distinction refers to different types of solidarity, the one labelled *organic*, the other *mechanical*.

[2] In his formulation of the dimensions of social action (AGIL), Parsons includes consensus under the latency dimension and cohesion under integration (see Parsons, Shils, and Bales, 1953, chap. 5).

[3] See Parsons' discussion on the "complementarity of expectations" (1951, chaps. 6 and 7), which he regards as an important concept in the analysis of social interaction.

[4] The prominence of rationality is reflected by, for example, psychological research on learning, on remembering, and on perception.

[5] People generally try to attract positive and minimize negative emotional responses and, consequently, tend to respond positively rather than negatively to others. A person may, depending on circumstances, however, express negative responses to others and may seek to provoke negative responses. This latter practice, in extreme form, is perceived as pathological.

[6] See Golembiewski's summary (1965) of interpersonal relations in organizations for research examples and a discussion of relations between consensus and cohesion.

[7] Seashore claimed that the difference in the direction of deviation from management-defined productivity norms was dependent on whether the members of a work unit shared a perception of management as supportive or non-supportive.

8 The station was located in an area of northern Britain that held records for bad weather.

9 His data were obtained from work records, interviews, and observations from three hundred work groups in thirty plants in the United States.

10 See Phillips et al. (1987) for a review and discussion of research on cohesion in the armed services and in other types of organizations.

11 For those wishing to know more about sociometry, Moreno's book *Who Shall Survive?* ([1934] 1953) is an excellent source. It provides an account of the origins of sociometry, its underlying principles, and its methods. *The Sociometry Reader* (1960), which Moreno edited, provides many examples of sociometric research on a wide range of topics.

12 See, for example, Smith (1966), whose research on intra-organizational conflict includes the division of labour as one of five measures of social structure.

13 See Gordon's review (1976) of Blau's *On the Nature of Organizations* for corroboration of this assessment of a shift away from consensus and cohesion in the study of organizations. References cited by Phillips et al. in a theoretical paper (1987) also reveal that cohesion studies in non-military organizations were concentrated in the 1950s and 1960s.

14 Granovetter (1985, 504) commented, "Existing empirical studies of industrial organization pay little attention to patterns of relations, in part because relevant data are harder to find than those on technology and market structure." He also believes that the neglect of interpersonal relations in research is a consequence of the dominance of an economic perspective in which such relations are perceived as "frictional in effect." He means, presumably, inconsequential.

15 Order referred to whether an actor was the originator or the recipient of an action.

16 Homans provides three formulations of the proposition (1950, 113–17), possibly because he was aware that the stated relationship holds only under certain conditions.

17 Anthropologists, who claim a proprietary interest in the concept of culture, were studying organizations as early as the 1950s, as a perusal of the periodical, *Human Organization*, will attest. See also Jules Henry ([1963] 1965, chaps. 7 and 8) for an analysis of schools as cultural contexts for students and Elliott Jaques (1951) for a study entitled *The Changing Culture of the Factory*.

18 Fine (1984) sees the negotiated order and culture perspectives as complementary and argues for their integration.

19 Although there has been considerable development in the use of quantitative analysis within the network analysis perspective, along with an expansion of its applications, it is not apparent that there is a substantive distinction between network analysis and sociometry. Burt (1980) uses both terms in his overview of this approach.

20 See, for example, Berkowitz (1982, chap. 3) The chapter referred to, entitled "Corporations and Privilege: Economic Structure and Elite Integration," focuses exclusively on inter-corporate relations.

CHAPTER 8

ORGANIZATIONAL PERFORMANCE

PERFORMANCE ASSESSMENT: EARLY YEARS

Suppose someone wishes to know how well an organization is performing. It might seem reasonable to assume that the organization's purpose would be reflected by its activities, and that an indicator or measure of its activities would show how successful the organization was in realizing its purpose.[1] So, for example, the performance of a firm engaged in manufacturing might be assessed by some measure of productivity, the performance of a school by some measure of its students' success in their coursework, and that of a hospital by its success in treating its patients.

A perceptive reader would, of course, raise questions about the assumptions made in the foregoing paragraph. Such a reader might point out, for example, that organizations, whether engaged in business, education, health care, or any other activity, may have more than one goal and would need more than one measure to assess performance. Nonetheless, this simple common-sense approach to assessing organizational performance was typical of early research in the sociology of organizations. In the human relations perspective, for example, productivity was the primary dependent variable used in the Western Electric Researches, and it maintained its prominence in later research when the idea of organizational effectiveness was adopted. Blau's research on government agencies, which may be seen as representative of the rational perspective, similarly used productivity as a measure of organizational performance. In fact, many studies cited or described in this text included some concept of goals and related measures that could be regarded as assessing the performance of the organization studied. Although hindsight may allow criticism of such simple attempts to assess organizational performance, the idea that an organization could be assessed by the degree to which it achieves its purposes, objectives, or goals seemed straightforward.

The choice of goal-achievement as a measure of performance is supported by theory. In general sociology, the idea that organizations have goals is explicit in the concept of organizations. In contrast to "natural" collectivities, such as families, other kinship groups, and groups of friends, organizations are seen to be created as a means to achieve some purpose, objective, or goal. This concept of organizations was added to by theorists of the rational perspective who hold that the structures and processes of organizations are determined by an organization's goals and the necessity of achieving them.

This chapter is concerned with the assessment of organizational performance. It begins with a brief account of methods used to assess organizational performance in the early days of the study of organizations. These methods are shown to have led to criticism that, in turn, led to renewed efforts to improve the assessment of organizational performance. The discussion of these efforts is focused on questions concerning appropriate criteria for assessment and the identification of indicators relevant to performance. The chapter includes descriptions of current methods developed in research as solutions to this challenging problem of assessing organizational performance.

Early Challenges

In the early history of sociological research on organizations, the use of goals and criteria of goal-achievement as a means of assessing organizational performance, for the most part, went unchallenged. This situation did not last for long. Indeed, it was challenged in the early 1960s by Perrow (1961) who pointed out that serious analysis of organizational goals had been neglected. He held that researchers either ignored goals or uncritically accepted the statements of organizations as given in charters, official reports, and public statements. Such documents describe the official goals of organizations, but these "are purposely vague and general" (Perrow 1961, 855) and accepting them at face value meant that researchers could neglect the many decisions organizations make concerning the ways of achieving goals, the priorities attached to them, and the unofficial goals that an organization might pursue. He perceived such decisions as determining the *operative* goals of organizations. In Perrow's view, the way to identify operative goals was through the "intensive analysis of decisions, personnel practices, alliance and elite characteristics" of organizations (1961, 856). Moreover, such an analysis required the identification of the "dominant group"—those who control the four task areas that "[e]very organization must accomplish." These four tasks, for an organization, are to: "(1) secure inputs in the form of capital sufficient to establish itself, operate and expand as the need arises; (2) secure acceptance in the form of basic legitimation of activity; (3) marshal the necessary skills; and (4) coordinate the activities of its members, and the relations of the organization with other organizations and with clients or consumers" (Perrow 1961, 856).

Perrow's views on the study of organizational goals do not understate the complexities of goal analysis, and they show that he clearly believed that the analysis of organizational goals was essential to the understanding of organizations.

Later Criticism

Researchers in the human relations perspective also helped to develop the analysis of organizational performance by including other criteria, such as levels of job satisfaction and intra-group tension (see, for example, Georgopoulos and Tannenbaum 1957). In more recent criticism of the methods used to assess organizational performance (for example, Goodman and Pennings 1977; Scott 1977; 1992, chap. 14; Kanter and Brinkerhoff 1981), many conceptual and methodological problems have been identified that make the assessment of organizational performance far less straightforward than had been assumed.

The criticism raises questions about what aspects or conditions of organizations should be assessed and what indicators can be established for those chosen. There are questions about the availability of the data needed for assessment; about the relevance, reliability, and validity of the available data; and about the time spans the data cover. Before these issues are addressed, however, a matter of terminology requires comment.

Terminological Distinctions

There is a relevant distinction drawn between **effectiveness**, which refers to an organization's success in attaining its goals, and in the system perspective, to success in maintaining its functional conditions, and **efficiency**, which refers to the level of costs in resources and energy, including human resources and energy, expended to attain the goals and meet system requirements. Although efficiency may appear to be primarily an economic issue, it has sociological relevance within the system perspective, which identifies the acquisition and allocation of resources as a functional requirement.

Some authors use the terms **organizational effectiveness** and **organizational performance** interchangeably (for example, Scott 1977; 1992, chap. 14), but others hold the view that effectiveness reflects a concern with managerial problems or applied research (Hannan and Freeman 1977b, 108) and is inappropriate in scientific investigation. Such criticism is consistent with the view that the human relations perspective, which views organizational effectiveness as an important concept, is biassed toward management interests. Given these reservations, the term *organizational performance* might be preferred. However, the widespread use of *organizational effectiveness* makes it a difficult term to avoid in discussion.

ORGANIZATIONAL THEORY AND ASSESSMENT CRITERIA

At a general level, the question of what aspect or condition of organizations should be assessed is determined by the theoretical perspective used to study organizations. For investigators who accept the assumption that organizations are established to achieve some purpose, objective, or goal, and especially for those who adopt a rational perspective, it is appropriate to assess an organization's performance by its success in realizing its stated purpose or achieving its stated objective or goal. This assumption was also accepted by those employing an early version of the human relations perspective. For them, a purpose, such as productivity of some economic good in the case of business firms, was a prominent basis for performance assessment. As the human relations perspective expanded, goals were not considered sufficient to measure performance, and other conditions, such as organizational flexibility and intra-organizational strain, were added (Georgopoulos and Tannenbaum 1957). The first of these terms refers to the capacity of an organization to adjust to changing internal or external conditions; the second, to the extent of tension or intra-group conflict between organizational units such as work groups or sections.[2] The inclusion of conditions in addition to goals continued, and organizational effectiveness developed as an important concept within the human relations perspective as it evolved to a system perspective (see Katz and Kahn [1966] 1978). In the system perspective, because it specifies several conditions to be met in order for an organization to survive, it is logical for these conditions to be used as a basis for assessing organizational performance.

Although there is obvious disagreement about what should be assessed in evaluations of organizational performance, it must be recognized that this disagreement is an unavoidable consequence of differences in theoretical frameworks. Theories differ in the characteristics identified as critical in organizations and are, therefore, bound to emphasize different characteristics in judging how well (or badly) organizations perform.

GOALS AND GOAL-ATTAINMENT AS CRITERIA

Although the debate on organizational performance tends to be framed, for the most part, in terms of either goals or system conditions (see, for example, Campbell 1977, chap. 2), "[m]ost analysts define effectiveness as goal achievement," according to Hannan and Freeman (1977b, 131). While this may suggest that assessing goal-achievement provides a satisfactory means of assessing organizational performance, it does not mean that the problems of performance assessment have been solved insofar as sociological research is concerned. It may be that there are organizations where goals and goal-achievement are so important that other conditions of organizational functioning contribute little, but it is unlikely that this condition applies to all kinds of organizations. Whether one emphasizes goals over other indicators of performance may depend on which theoretical perspective most adequately reflects the reality of organizations. If the successful pursuit of goals is sufficiently dominant over other conditions in organizations, then limiting performance assessment to goals is a reasonable choice. However, if, for example, cooperative action, appropriate control procedures, and the acquisition and control over resources are important, a broader definition of the components of organizational performance is necessary. As most, if not all, of the people who adopt a systems perspective include goal-attainment among the conditions for system survival, this broader view of the components of assessment may provide a more complete approach to assessing organizational performance than that adopted by the rational perspective.

Regardless of whether goals and goal-attainment are included as a basis for assessing organizational performance there are problems to be recognized and, if possible, to be solved.

The overall problem is to identify goals. This requires recognizing that most organizations have multiple goals. The goals of business firms may include maximizing profits, maintaining or increasing their market share, raising productivity, and developing new products. Universities characteristically include teaching and research—the communication of existing knowledge and the creation of new knowledge—as goals, but they may also have other goals such as establishing supremacy in higher education or in research or demonstrating "fiscal responsibility." Hospitals, like universities, may include research and teaching as goals, along with successfully treating patients. Moreover, hospitals may also wish to maximize revenues or demonstrate fiscal responsibility. A goal of charitable fund-raising organizations is to raise as much money as possible for their causes, but they may also adopt a goal of minimizing administrative costs. Because the various goals are not necessarily given equal priority, it is necessary for the researcher to attempt to determine the organization's goal priorities.

An organization's goals may be distinguished as formal or informal. Formal goals are those explicitly stated in an organization's mandate or mission statement. Informal goals are those that are pursued but not mandated and may conflict severely with the organization's formal goals. It is not uncommon for organizations to proclaim explicit goals for public consumption while pursuing other goals agreed on within the organization. Prisons, reformatories, and similar organizations that deal with offenders against the law may proclaim rehabilitation of the inmates as a goal but may actually focus on custody. Some hospitals with specific populations of patients, such as those with mental or emotional problems, may similarly claim treatment or rehabilitation as goals but limit themselves to care and custody. Some schools may serve mainly custodial functions despite a mandate to educate their students. In such instances, the failure to pursue explicit or formal goals may be *rationalized* (see, for example, Scott 1977; 1992, 285–86) in terms of the abilities or motivation of inmates or patients or in terms of inadequate staffing or funding. Scott (1981, 268), citing Weick (1969, 38) and Staw (1980), notes that formal acknowledgement of goals may follow to justify or explain planned or unplanned actions taken by an organization.[3] Any of these actions make it difficult to identify organizational goals.

An important part of identifying an organization's goals is deciding who should determine what the organization's goals are. The basic choice is for the researcher either to accept the goals identified by participants in the organization or to identify the goals independently of the participants on the basis of available information. The researcher may also, of course, use a combination of these two choices. Whatever the method chosen, the information about an organization's goals, with the exception of the researcher's observations, will come from documents, such as constitutions, mandates, or memoranda, or from interviews of, or questionnaires directed to, selected members of the organization. If the analyst depends on information provided by the organization in the form of documents, interviews, or questionnaires, there may be problems of determining which of several goals are actively being pursued and whose goals they are. Reported goals may vary depending on the informant's position in the organization and may reflect personal or group interests. In mental hospitals, for example, it is not unusual to find goal conflicts between psychiatrists who pursue therapeutic goals and ward attendants whose goals are care and custody (see, for example, Jones 1973).

Instead of attempting to identify an organization's goal by asking participants or outsiders to do so, an analyst may attempt to determine what an organization is trying to achieve by observing its activities. For example, if in a mental hospital ward, patients are observed to spend their days sitting on chairs or pacing the halls of the ward, with only scheduled interruptions for meals, medication, personal hygiene, and so on, the observer may be justified in concluding that the goal of the authorities governing the ward is either care or custody or both. On the other hand, if a high proportion of patient activity involves participation in individual or group therapy and other rehabilitative activities, it is reasonable to conclude that treatment or rehabilitation is a goal of ward personnel and, possibly, of the patients. Other actions, such as the use of force or persuasion to induce patients to conform to staff expectations, or an emphasis on activities aimed at moving the patients to discharge may support the observer's conclusions. Actions may not, of course, allow unambiguous interpretation. It may not be easy to decide whether tranquilizing drugs are intended to induce states in patients that enhance responsiveness to therapy or to maintain control and order on the ward. Obviously, to infer goals from activities or from the allocation of resources requires a set of classification categories, ideally ranked in order of importance.

SYSTEM PERSPECTIVE: ASSESSMENT CRITERIA

If the analyst adopts a system perspective, the conditions necessary for survival must be used along with goal-attainment to assess performance. These conditions could include an assessment of an organization's success in limiting stress originating in group or individual conflict; of the success or failure of control and coordination procedures; and of the organization's capacity to acquire resources and modify or add value to them. However, although there is some agreement on what constitutes functional or survival conditions—support and maintenance are frequently mentioned—there certainly is no unanimity. As noted in Chapter Four, Parsons and Katz and Kahn differ in the number of dimensions or conditions identified and in the level of abstraction. Katz and Kahn's categories are much closer to actual organizational practices than Parsons' highly abstract AGIL scheme described in Chapter Four (Katz and Kahn [1966] 1978; see also Scott and Shortell [1983] 1988, 419 for a modified version of these categories).[4]

The extent of these differences suggests that a great deal of conceptual refinement is necessary before anything like unanimity can be achieved in the identification of functional conditions. However, although differences in the categorization of conditions imposes limits on the generalizations that can be made about organizations, they do not necessarily mean that useful information cannot be discovered about relations among functional conditions. Even so, the introduction of additional dimensions for assessing performance undoubtedly introduces complications not present when goal-attainment alone is the criterion of performance.

Performance Indicators

Whether goals or goals plus other system conditions provide the framework for assessing organizational performance, indicators of the *state* of such conditions must be identified. In earlier studies, productivity was used as an indicator of the performance of business organizations. Scott (1992, 319) referred to such indicators of production, whether in the form of manufactured units, treatment success, or student performance, as *output* indicators. Although output indicators are widely used to assess organizational performance, he cautioned that they are almost always subject to influence by indicators of other variables. Thus, productivity can be influenced by the internal and external activities and conditions of an organization. Other indicators, such as profits, revenues, and costs, are also subject to influences, such as market demand, or the internal actions of departments or groups responsible for sales, marketing, or financial control.

Similar problems confront researchers in hospitals, schools, and other non-business organizations. A hospital's treatment record, for example, may be influenced by the composition of the populations it serves, by its intake policies, and by the efficiency of its intake department. Indeed, the "output" of most people-processing organizations, such as schools, hospitals, and prisons, will be influenced by the characteristics of the population served and by admission policies. Certainly, these kinds of organizations have little control over the actions of clients outside the organization. Thus, patients may or may not follow post-discharge instructions, and students will vary in their degree of participation in school and non-school activities.

It is likely that outcome measures, given their theoretical support and widespread use, will continue to be used as indicators of organizational performance, but researchers must ensure that appropriate control variables and analytical designs are employed to take account of various internal and external influences. Scott (1977, 77–78) gives an example from his own research on the outcome of surgical procedures in a number of acute-care general hospitals to demonstrate the complex design required to control the effects of input variables on outcomes.

Campbell called attention to the complexity of assessing organizational performance (organizational effectiveness, as he called it) by providing a list of thirty indicators that had been used in research. He stated that at the time he wrote, only "two really rigorous" studies of organizational effectiveness had been undertaken (1977, 41). These studies by Mahoney and Weitzel (1969) and by Seashore and Yuchtman (1967) adopted a model that required large homogeneous samples of organizations or organizational sub-units,[5] information obtained from many indicators, and the application of factor analysis to reduce the data to meaningful findings. Mahoney and Weitzel used 114 questionnaire items to obtain ratings of effectiveness, which were reduced by factor analysis to twenty-four factors, including Democratic Supervision and Emphasis on Results.[6] Seashore and Yuchtman used a variety of information obtained from the records of seventy-five insurance companies, which factor analysis reduced to ten factors, including Productivity and Market Penetration. A more recent study of organizational effectiveness (Georgopoulos 1986) reveals that the complexities have not lessened. This research on emergency units in approximately thirty general hospitals in the United States is guided by the assumptions that "the concept and assessment of institutional effectiveness is complex and multifaceted rather than unidimensional" and that "the overall effectiveness of a hospital [emergency unit] is . . . the joint outcome of economic, clinical, and social performance" (Georgopoulos 1986, 75). For this study, data were obtained from hospital and community records, questionnaires, and personal interviews. The data described structures, processes, and outcomes for the three types of organizational performance. It is apparent that Georgopoulos (1986, 284) believes that his complex methodology is necessary to yield a valid, reliable, precise assessment of organizational effectiveness.

RELIABILITY AND VALIDITY

In addition to the complexity of research design and the choices concerning indicators for the various criteria used to evaluate organizational performance, problems of reliability and validity of data must also be faced. For example, job satisfaction, which may be used as an indicator of motivation or some other worker state, is bedevilled by methodological difficulties. Data for indicators of cohesion—such as frequency of contacts between organizational participants in organizational and extra-organizational contexts—are difficult to obtain, and their reliability and validity are often difficult to assess.

Single and Multiple Indicators

Doubt about the reliability of any single indicator of organizational performance encourages the identification of substitutes for those found wanting or alternative or additional measures. As it is likely that any single indicator may measure a concept imperfectly, as in the case of productivity for goal-attainment, the error may be minimized by using multiple measures for each concept (see, for example, Blalock 1969; Costner 1969; Mayer and Younger 1974). Factor analysis, particularly in the form of confirmatory factor analysis (Hauser and Goldberger 1971, 84), provides procedure for using multiple indicators.[7]

The creation of a plethora of indicators, marked by considerable variety, is not explained only by the need to replace unsatisfactory indicators. It is, as Scott argued (1992, 343–48), the result of several research-driven requirements. These include differences in theoretical perspectives guiding research, the point in time when the organization is studied. These requirements also include differences in the scope of the research target. In the case of hospitals, the research may be targeted on the wards, the hospital in its entirety, or the hospital's relation to other community agencies or to the entire community.

IMPROVING PERFORMANCE ASSESSMENT

A reading of specific attempts to measure organizational performance as well as critiques of these attempts may induce pessimism. Scott (1977, 63), following a review of the literature on organizational effectiveness, concludes "that this topic is one about which we know less and less." Abandoning the task may seem the best strategy. Indeed, there is no requirement that every study of organizations must include organizational performance as a variable. Research on the effects of organizational size and technology on organizational structure, although it ignores assessments of performance, still contributes to the understanding of organizations.[8]

If the aim of sociological analysis, regardless of perspective, is to understand how social relationships are or are not maintained in the face of various conditions, it must also aim to understand how higher configurations of social relationships, including organizations and other forms of collectivity, do or do not persist. For those who adopt a system perspective of organizations, which links organizational survival to goal-attainment and to the organization's success in responding to other requirements, the inclusion of organizational performance as a variable is mandatory.

OUTCOMES, PROCESSES, AND STRUCTURES

An approach used mainly in research on hospitals and other health care organizations is worth considering as a general approach to the assessment of organization performance.[9] It focuses on three general categories of organizational features (Donabedian 1966) relevant to performance:

- **Outcomes** refer to what the organization produces, taking into account both quantitative and qualitative aspects of production. Outcomes may be measured by indicators relevant to types of organizational activity. For example, appropriate indicators for manufacturing firms may include productivity per worker (or per organizational unit), cost-benefit ratios, and profits. For hospitals, indicators for treatment outcomes could include mortality, morbidity, and recovery rates of patient-treatment populations. Indicators for educational organizations could include rates for high grade achievement, acceptance by prestigious educational organizations, and graduate students' attainment of employment in occupations appropriate for their level and type of training.

- **Processes** refer to the procedures that organizations use in their operations and in meeting their responsibilities. Indicators for procedures could include, depending on the specific organization's activity-type, cost-benefit analyses, quality control procedures, the number and types of tests in medical care, the number of visits by caseworkers, or rates of student-faculty contact.

- **Structures** refer to such organizational characteristics as the emphasis on rules, the degree of centralization and distribution of power in organizations—the levels where decisions on purchasing, production, budget allocations, and hiring and firing of employees are made—and the degree of complexity in organizations—the division of labour as defined by differentiation in occupations and in operating and support units.

Although these categories are familiar, this formulation links them as essential components of organizational activity and broadens the basis for assessment of performance. The procedures and processes of operations, the structural context of these operations, and the resulting product or outcome are all considered in measuring performance. All three categories have limitations—for example, rules for distinguishing indicators of process and structure are needed, and indicators of all three are subject to a variety of external influences that bias measurement (see Scott 1992, 353–57). Despite their limitations, though, the categories cover important components of organizational performance, and including all three in assessments provides opportunities to investigate relationships both *between* categories via their indicators as well as among indicators *within* categories. It must be noted, however, that all three categories focus on goal attainment. This is immediately apparent in the case of outcomes, but it should be noted that only those processes and structures immediately relevant to goal-attainment are included in the other two categories.[10] For research undertaken in a systems perspective, there is still a need to broaden the assessment of performance to include other functional requirements such as consensus, cohesion, coordination, and control.[11]

THE EXAMPLE OF SOCIAL INDICATORS

While there is much room for improvement in procedures for assessing organizational performance, it must be said that the sociology of organizations differs little, in this respect, from other areas of sociology. For example, the problems described here concerning the identification of variables and their indicators apply not only to organizations but also to descriptions of total societies. Initially, studies of total societies used simple common-sense measures.[12] However, as the analysis of total societies increased, various inadequacies in available data were gradually recognized. The resulting criticism led, over the years, to a focused attempt to develop improved measures.

Much of this effort was provided by analysts (for example, Bauer 1966; Russett 1964; Taylor and Hudson 1972; Taylor, Hudson, and Jodice 1983) who proposed, during the 1960s, that societal analysis required *social* indicators analogous to those used by economists for the analysis of economic systems. These proposals fuelled a movement that included sociologists, political scientists, and other social scientists who organized conferences, often sponsored by government agencies, aimed at developing improved measures for societal analysis (see, for example, Carley 1981; Miles 1985). These efforts have achieved some success in developing social indicators that are used in policy analysis by various organizations, such as the Organization for Economic Cooperation and Development (see, for example, OECD 1976a; 1976b; 1986). Several governments, including Canada, use social indicators for social reporting and accounting.[13] Moreover, the availability of improved social indicators benefits academic study of total societies. Still, it must be admitted that improvements in social indicators have fallen short of the expectations voiced when the movement was getting underway. Familiar problems remain:

- validity—it remains necessary to establish that specific indicators do, in fact, reflect the societal conditions they are assumed to reflect;

- reliability—problems remain in ensuring that indicators are reasonably free from error and that most societies meet such a standard; and

- availability—there is need to improve coverage of world societies to ensure that comparable data are available for as many social indicators as possible.[14]

These persistent problems suggest that the focused approach used to develop social indicators will not accomplish more for students of organizations than did the more informal approaches that have so far characterized the identification of appropriate criteria and indicators of organizational performance.

WHO SHOULD IDENTIFY CRITERIA AND INDICATORS?

Despite the heavy responsibility it entails, it is desirable that the researcher, rather than the participant, define the criteria and indicators of organizational performance. Data obtained from participants, including those revealing conflicts over goals or goals defined by "dominant coalitions," should be treated as important for understanding organizations rather than for assessing their performance. If objectivity is sought in determining an organization's goals, its other functional conditions, and their indicators, the better procedure is to combine the researcher's theoretical perspective with observations of the actions of participants and of the allocation of the organization's resources, including human energy.

Researchers are, of course, fallible. They may overinterpret or misinterpret the documents they read, the interviews they conduct, and the observations they make. Some of these errors may be corrected or reduced if a research team uses comparative observations and analysis. However, even with the probabilities of researcher error, a researcher-defined approach should result in a more objective identification of the components and indicators of organizational performance than would a participant-defined approach.

Researchers should not be overly ambitious. They should heed Scott's suggestion (1992, 362) that the search for performance measures that apply to all organizations be abandoned. For the present, at least, it may be more fruitful to focus on identifying conditions that appear relevant to the organization under study.

SUMMARY

The discussion, in this chapter, provides a basis for several conclusions relating to the problem of assessing organizational performance.

It is apparent that assessing organizational performance is not a simple matter. Moreover, despite recognition of many difficulties and some admirable research efforts to improve assessment, the problems of assessment are far from solved. It is clear that performance cannot be measured by goal-achievement alone, nor by the use of a single indicator, such as productivity. Moreover, there are problems in using goal-achievement, whether as a sole dimension or as one among several dimensions. For example, an organization may pursue goals that differ from, or conflict with, its official goals. It is also possible that an organization's goals may be defined or understood differently by its members according to their position in the organization.

It is, therefore, essential for those who adopt a system perspective to identify several dimensions of performance and prudent to identify more than one indicator for each dimension, and these requirements are also likely to be true for those working within other perspectives. Finally, in the search for an acceptable method of assessing organizational performance, the better strategy at this stage in the study of organizations is to develop one that relates to a specific kind of organization rather than to aim at a single method that would apply to any kind of organization.

ENDNOTES

[1] In this chapter, "purpose" or "objective" are synonyms for "goal."

[2] In this research, goal-attainment was measured by "station productivity" on the basis of data obtained from company records. The measure of organizational strain was based on reported evidence of tension or conflict between supervisors and non-supervisory personnel rather than "between organizational sub-groups." Internal conditions included changes in technology and operating procedures; external conditions included changes in demand (Georgopoulus and Tannenbaum 1957, 537–38).

3 This idea is elaborated on and somewhat modified in Wieck (1979, 18–21).

4 Katz and Kahn's formulation is usually regarded as an example of an "open-system" approach, which emphasizes environmental influences. It is contrasted with Parsons' model of a social system, which is characterized as a "closed system." This characteristic of Parsons' scheme seems to arise from a misunderstanding. Parsons' adaptive dimension refers specifically to cross-boundary transactions—responses to environmental influences—and it includes actions relevant to the acquisition and transformation of resources as well as their disposal as output.

5 Organizations had to be the same type—all manufacturing firms or all hospitals.

6 Referring, respectively, to the extent that subordinates participated in decision-making, and to the degree of emphasis on results or outcomes versus procedures. The relationship of the twenty-four factors to an overall measure of effectiveness was also estimated.

7 The objective of factor analysis is to reduce quantitative information obtained for various indicators of a subject of study—persons, communities, societies, and collectivities, such as organizations—to a relatively small number of factors. Factor analysis allows a hunt and find expedition in the sense that it is used to search the data to identify any coherent relationships among indicators.

By contrast, confirmatory factor analysis is used to confirm or disconfirm propositions formulated prior to the analysis. This form of factor analysis is seen to be more consistent with the principles of scientific investigation (see Jöreskog and Lawley 1968).

8 It is possible that our understanding of organizations would be enhanced if performance measures were included. A study by Armandi and Mills of the relations between size and Blau-Hage measures of structure, which also included economic performance measures (according to the authors this was the first such study to do so), found support for only one of four hypotheses concerning the effect of structure on economic performance (1982, 43–44, 55, table 5).

9 See, for example, Dornbusch and Scott (1975). The research and theory presented in this book concerns organizations whose activities include health care, education, manufacturing, news reporting, recreation, religion, and scientific research. The focus is on the effects of evaluation on role performance rather than on the performance of organizational units or of the total organization.

Other relevant research includes work by Georgopoulus (1986, 80–84), Kanter and Brinkerhoff (1981, 321–34); Money, Gillfillan, and Duncan (1976, 32–33); Scott (1977; 1981); Scott, Forrest, and Brown (1976, 72, 77); Shortell (1976, 7–8); and Shortell and Kaluzney ([1983] 1988, 427–29).

10 See Scott's evaluation of indicators, based on outcomes, processes, and structures, for assessing organizational effectiveness (1992, 353–57).

11 Georgopoulus responded to this need in his design for research on hospital emergency units. He assumed that "overall effectiveness" resulted from economic, clinical, and social performance (1986, 75), and he used a variety of indicators of these forms of performance (1986, chaps. 4 and 5) as well as indicators of the structure of the emergency units (1986, chap. 3). He regarded his research design as integrated with "open system theory" (1986, xv).

¹² An example is Lipset's comparative research ([1960] 1963, 35–38) on the correlates of political democracy, which used indicators of wealth (such as per capita income, thousands of persons per physician, and persons per motor vehicle); means of communication (telephones, radios, and newspaper copies per thousand persons); industrialization (percentage of males in agriculture, per capita energy consumed); education (literacy rate, enrolments per thousand persons in primary, secondary, and higher education); and urbanization (percentage of population in cities over 20 000, over 100 000, and in metropolitan areas). Lipset included footnotes to identify the limitations of these various indicators. Cutright's research (1963; 1965; 1967), which continued the investigation of this topic, provides an example of attempts to improve indicators and statistical procedures.

¹³ Statistics Canada explicitly regarded the social statistics published in *Perspectives Canada* (Statistics Canada 1974; 1977b; 1980), which was released occasionally between 1974 and 1980, as bases for identifying social indicators, defined as "barometers of social change." More recently, Statistics Canada began publishing *Canadian Social Trends* (Statistics Canada 1981), which includes tables of economic and social indicators as well as articles on various topics based on socio-economic indicators. See also Michalos (1980–82); and Henderson (1974).

¹⁴ For specific problems with social indicators, see, for example, Carley (1981, chap. 4). For a broad discussion of the advantages and disadvantages of social indicators, see Miles (1985), especially the Introduction and chapters 1 through 4.

REFERENCES

Abrahamsson, Bengt. 1977. *Bureaucracy or participation*. Beverly Hills, CA: Sage Publications.

Adams, Roy J., and C.H. Rummel. 1976. *Workers' participation in management in West Germany: Impact on the worker, the enterprise, and the trade union.* McMaster Faculty of Business Research Series No. 117. Hamilton, ON: McMaster Faculty of Business.

Adizes, Ichak. 1971. *Industrial democracy: Yugoslav style*. New York: The Free Press, Collier-Macmillan.

Ahrne, Göran. 1994. *Social organizations: Interaction inside, outside and between organizations*. London: Sage Publications.

Alcock, J.E., D.W. Carment, and S.W. Sadava. 1988. *A textbook of social psychology*. Scarborough, ON: Prentice Hall.

Aldrich, Howard. 1979. *Organizations and environments*. Englewood Cliffs, NJ: Prentice Hall.

Allport, F.H. 1934. The J-curve hypothesis of conforming behavior. *Journal of Social Psychology* 5:141–83.

Argyle, Michael. 1953. The relay assembly test room in retrospect. *Occupational Psychology* 27:96–103.

———. 1972. *The social psychology of work*. London: Allen Lane The Penguin Press.

Argyle, Michael, Godfrey Gardner, and Frank Cioffi. 1957. The measurement of supervisory methods. *Human Relations* 10:295–313.

———. 1958. Supervisory methods related to productivity, absenteeism and labor turnover. *Human Relations* 11:23–40.

Armandi, B.R., and E.W. Mills Jr. 1982. Organizational size, structure and efficiency: A test of a Blau-Hage model. *American Journal of Economics and Sociology* 41:43–60.

Ashford, J.R., and R.R. Sowdon. 1970. Multivariate probit analysis. *Biometrics* 26:535–46.

Bacharach, Samuel B., Peter Bamberger, and Sharon C. Conley. 1991. Negotiating the "see-saw" of managerial strategy: A resurrection of the study of professionals in organizational theory. *Research in the Sociology of Organizations* 8:217–38. Greenwich, CT: JAI Press Inc.

Bales, Robert F. 1950. *Interaction process analysis*. Cambridge, MA: Addison-Wesley Press.

Barley, Stephen R., and Pamela S. Tolbert. 1991. Introduction: At the intersection of organizations and occupations. *Research in the Sociology of Organizations* 8:1–13. Greenwich, CT: JAI Press Inc.

Baritz, Loren. 1960. *The servants of power*. Westport, CT: Greenwood Press.

Baron, James N. 1984. Organizational perspectives on stratification. *Annual Review of Sociology* 10:37–69. Palo Alto, CA: Annual Reviews Inc.

Batstone, Eric. 1976. *Industrial democracy and worker representation at board level: A review of the European experience*. London: HMSO.

Bauer, Raymond, ed. 1966. *Social indicators*. Cambridge, MA: MIT Press.

Bellas, Carl J. 1972. *Industrial democracy and the worker-owned firm*. New York: Praeger Publishers.

Berkowitz, S.D. 1982. *An introduction to structural analysis*. Toronto: Butterworths.

Bernstein, Paul. 1976. *Workplace democratization: Its internal dynamics*. Kent, OH: Kent State University Press.

Bertalanffy, Ludwig. 1933. *Modern theories of development*. Translated by J.H. Woodger. London: Oxford Univerity Press.

———. 1968. *General system theory*. New York: George Braziller.

———. 1975. *Perspectives on general system theory: Scientific philospohical studies*. New York: George Braziller.

Blalock, H.M. Jr. 1969. Multiple indicators and the causal approach to measurement error. *American Journal of Sociology* 75:264–72.

Blau, Peter M. [1955] 1963. *The dynamics of bureaucracy*. Chicago: University of Chicago Press.

———. 1964. *Exchange and power in social life*. New York: John Wiley and Sons.

———. 1970. A formal theory of differentiation in organizations. *American Sociological Review* 35:201–18.

Blau, Peter M., Cecelia M. Falbe, William McKinley, and Phelps K. Tracy. 1976. Technology and organization in manufacturing. *Administrative Science Quarterly* 21:20–40.

Blau, Peter M., and Otis D. Duncan. 1962. *The American occupational structure*. New York: Wiley and Sons.

Blau, Peter M., and W. Richard Scott. 1962. *Formal organizations*. San Francisco: Chandler Publishing Company.

Blauner, Robert. 1964. *Alienation and freedom*. Chicago: University of Chicago Press.

Blumberg, Paul. 1968. *Industrial democracy: The sociology of participation*. London: Constable.

Bolweg, Joep F. 1976. *Job design and industrial democracy*. Leiden: Martin Nijhoff.

Bowles, Samuel, and Herbert Gintis. 1976. *Schooling in capitalist America*. London: Routledge and Kegan Paul.

Bramel, Danel, and Ronald Friend. 1981. Hawthorne, the myth of the docile worker and class bias in psychology. *American Psychologist* 36:867–78.

Brayfield, A.H., and W.H. Crockett. 1955. Employee attitudes and employee performance. *Psychological Bulletin* 52:396–424.

Burns, Tom, and George M. Stalker. 1961. *The management of innovation*. London: Tavistock Publications.

Burt, Ronald S. 1980. Models of network structure. *Annual Review of Sociology* 6:79–111.

Campbell, Angus, and Philip E. Converse. 1972. *The human meaning of social change*. New York: Russell Sage Foundation.

Campbell, John P. 1977. On the nature of organizational effectiveness. Chap. 2 in Goodman and Pennings (1977).

Carey, Alex. 1967. The Hawthorne studies: A radical criticism. *American Sociological Review* 32:403–16.

Carley, Michael. 1981. *Social measurement and social indicators*. London: George Allen and Unwin.

Carroll, Glenn R. 1984. Organizational ecology. *Annual Review of Sociology* 10:71–93.

Carroll, Glenn R., and Yangchung Paul Huo. 1986. Organizational task and institutional environments in ecological perspective: Findings from the local newspaper industry. *American Journal of Sociology* 91:838–73.

Case, J., and R.C.R. Taylor, eds. 1979. *Co-ops, communes & collectives: Experiments in social change in the 1960s and 1970s*. New York: Pantheon.

Child, J., and R. Mansfield. 1972. Technology, size and organization structure. *Sociology* 6:369–93.

Cohen, Albert. 1955. *Delinquent boys: The culture of the gang*. Glencoe, IL: The Free Press.

Cohen, Sheldon, and S. Leonard Syme. 1985. *Social support and health*. New York: Academic Press.

Cole, Robert E. 1979. *Work, mobility and participation*. Berkeley, CA: University of California Press.

Coleman, James S. 1988. Social capital in the creation of human capital. *American Journal of Sociology* 10:239–62.

Comrey, A.L., J. Pfiffner, and W.S. High. 1954. *Factors influencing organizational effectiveness*. Los Angeles: University of Southern California Bookstore.

Cook, Karen S., and Richard M. Emerson. 1984. Exchange networks and the analysis of complex organizations. *Research in the Sociology of Organizations* 3:1–30.

Cooley, Charles H. [1909] 1962. *Social organization of the larger mind*. New York: Schocken Books.

———. 1920. *Social organization*. New York: Scribners.

Coser, Lewis. 1974. *Greedy institutions*. New York: The Free Press.

Costner, Herbert L., ed. 1971. *Sociological methodology*. San Francisco: Joosey-Bass.

Costner, Herbert L. 1969. Theory, deduction and rules of correspondence. *American Journal of Sociology* 75:245–63.

Crozier, Michel. 1964. *The bureaucratic phenomenon*. Chicago: University of Chicago Press.

Cutright, Phillips. 1963. National political developments: Measurement and analysis. *American Sociological Review* 28:253–64.

———. 1965. Political structure, economic development and national social security programmes. *American Journal of Sociology* 70:527–50.

———. 1967. Inequality and cross-national analysis. *American Sociological Review* 32:562–68.

Dahrendorf, Ralf. [1957] 1959. *Class and class conflict in industrial society.* Stanford, CA: Stanford University Press.

Dalton, Melville. 1950. Conflicts between staff and line managerial officers. *American Sociological Review* 15:342–51.

———. 1959. *Men who manage.* New York: John Wiley and Sons.

Davis, Alison. 1946. The motivation of the underprivileged worker. Chap. 5 in Whyte (1946).

Davis, Kingsley. [1949] 1965. *Human society.* New York: Macmillan.

Di Tomaso, Nancy. 1987. Symbolic media and social solidarity: The foundations of corporate culture. *Research in the Sociology of Organizations* 5:105–34.

Donabedian, Avedis. 1966. Evaluating the quality of medical care. *Milbank Memorial Fund Quarterly* 44, part 2:166–206.

Donaldson, Lex. 1985. *In defence of organization theory: A reply to critics.* Cambridge: Cambridge University Press.

Dore, Ronald. 1973. *British factory Japanese factory.* Berkeley, CA: University of California Press.

Dornbusch, Sanford M., and W. Richard Scott. 1975. *Evaluation and the exercise of authority.* San Francisco: Joosey-Bass.

Downs, Anthony. 1967. *Inside bureaucracy.* Boston: Little, Brown and Company.

Dubin, Robert, et al. 1965. *Leadership and productivity.* San Francisco: Chandler Publishing Company.

Durkheim, Emile. [1893] 1933. *On the division of labor in society.* Translated by George Simpson. New York: Macmillan.

———. [1897] 1951. *Suicide.* Glencoe, IL: The Free Press.

———. [1912] 1947. *The elementary forms of the religious life.* Translated by George W. Swain. Glencoe, IL: The Free Press.

Edwards, Richard. 1979. *Contested terrain.* New York: Basic Books Inc.

Emery, Fred, and Einar Thorsrud. [1964] 1969. *Form and content in industrial democracy.* London: Tavistock.

———. 1976. *Democracy at work.* Leiden: Martinus Nijhoff.

Etzioni, Amitai. [1961] 1975. *A comparative analysis of complex organizations.* New York: The Free Press.

Evan, William M. 1993. *Organization theory: Research and design.* New York: Macmillan.

Evans-Pritchard, E.E. 1962. *Social anthropology and other essays.* Glencoe, IL: The Free Press.

Fienberg, Stephen E. 1977. *The analysis of cross-classified categorical data.* Cambridge, MA: The MIT Press.

Filley, Alan C., and Robert J. House. 1969. *Managerial process and organizational behavior.* Glenview, IL: Scott, Foresman and Company.

Filley, Alan C., Robert J. House, and Steven Kerr. 1976. *Managerial process and organizational behavior.* Glenview, IL: Scott, Foresman and Company.

Fine, Gary Alan. 1984. Negotiated orders and organizational cultures. *American Sociological Review* 10:239–62.

Firth, Raymond. [1951] 1961. *Elements of social organization.* Boston: Beacon Press.

Form, William H. 1976. *Blue-collar stratification.* Princeton, NJ: Princeton University Press.

———. 1979. Comparative industrial sociology and the convergence hypothesis. *Annual Review of Sociology.* 5:1–25.

Fox, J.B., and J.F. Scott. 1943. *Absenteeism: Management's problem.* Cambridge, MA: Harvard University Graduate School of Business Administration.

Franke, Richard H. 1980. Worker productivity at Hawthorne. (Reply to Schlaifer). *American Sociological Review* 45:1006–27.

———.1979. The Hawthorne experiments: Re-view. *American Sociological Review* 44:861–67.

Franke, Richard H., and James D. Kaul. 1978. The Hawthorne experiments: First statistical interpretation. *American Sociological Review* 43:623–42.

Freeman, John. 1973. Environment, technology and the administrative intensity of manufacturing organizations. *American Sociological Review* 38:750–63.

Freeman, John, and Michael T. Hannan. 1975. Growth and decline processes in organizations. *American Sociological Review* 40:215–28.

Freeman, John, and J.E. Kronenfeld. 1973. Problems of definitional dependency: The case of administrative intensity. *Social Forces* 52:108–21.

Georgopoulus, B.S. 1986. *Organizational structure, problem solving, and effectiveness.* San Francisco: Jossey-Bass.

Georgopoulus, B.S., and A.S. Tannenbaum. 1957. A study of organizational effectiveness. *American Sociological Review* 22:534–40.

Globe and Mail. 1992. Vaccine technicality bars boy from school. 30 Sept.

Goh, Swee Chua, and Martin G. Evans. 1985. Organization growth and decline: The impact on direct and administrative components of a university. *Canadian Journal of Sociology* 10:121–38.

Golembiewski, Robert T. 1965. Small groups and large organizations. In *Handbook of Organizations,* edited by James G. March. Chicago: Rand McNally.

Goodacre, Daniel M., III. 1960. The use of a sociometric test as a predictor of combat unit effectiveness. In Moreno et al. (1960, 548–52).

Goodman, P.S., and J.M. Pennings, eds. 1977. *New perspectives on organizational effectiveness.* San Francisco: Jossey-Bass.

Gordon, Gerald. 1976. Review of *On the Nature of Organizations. Contemporary Sociology* 5:474–76.

Gouldner, Alvin. [1954] 1964. *Patterns of industrial bureaucracy.* New York: The Free Press of Glencoe.

——. 1954. *Wildcat strike.* Yellow Springs, OH: Antioch Press.

Granovetter, Mark. 1984. Small is bountiful: Labor markets and establishment size. *American Sociological Review* 49:323–34.

——. 1985. Economic action, social structure and embeddedness. *American Journal of Sociology* 91:481–510.

Gross, Edward, and Amitai Etzioni. 1985. *Organizations in society.* Englewood Cliffs, NJ: Prentice-Hall.

Gruneberg, Michael M. 1979. *Understanding job satisfaction.* London: MacMillan.

Gyllenhammar, Pehr. 1977. *People at work.* Reading, MA: Addison-Wesley.

Hage, Jarrald. 1965. An axiomatic theory of organizations. *Administrative Science Quarterly* 10:289–320.

Hall, Alan, and Barry Wellman. 1985. Social networks and social support. In *Social Support and Health*, edited by Sheldon Cohen and S. Leonard Syme. New York: Academic Press.

Hall, Richard H. 1982. *Organizations: Structure and process.* Englewood Cliffs, NJ: Prentice-Hall.

Hall, Richard H., J. Eugene Haas, and Norman Johnson. 1967. Organizational size, complexity, and formalization. *American Sociological Review* 32:903–12.

Hannan, M.T., and J. Freeman. 1977a. The population ecology of organizations. *American Journal of Sociology* 82:929–64.

——. 1977b. Obstacles to comparative studies. Chap. 6 in Goodman and Pennings (1977).

Hassard, John. 1993. *Sociology and organization theory.* New York: Cambridge University Press.

Hauser, Robert M., and Arthur S. Goldberger. 1971. The treatment of unobservable variables in path analysis. In Costner (1971).

Hawley, Amos. 1950. *Human ecology.* New York: Ronald Press.

Heise, David R., ed. 1974. *Sociological methodology.* San Francisco: Joosey-Bass.

Henderson, D.W. 1974. *Social indicators: A rationale and research framework.* Ottawa: Information Canada.

Henry, Jules. [1963] 1965. *Culture against man.* New York: Random House, Vintage Books Edition.

Hickson, David J. 1987. Decision-making at the top. *Annual Review of Sociology* 13:165–92.

Hickson, David J., C.R. Hinings, C.J. McMillan, and J.P. Schwitter. 1974. The culture-free context of organization structure: A tri-national comparison. *Sociology* 8:59–80.

Hickson, D.J., D.S. Pugh, and Diana C. Pheysey. [1969] 1980. Operations technology and organization structure: An empirical reappraisal. In *A sociological reader on complex organizations*, edited by A. Etzioni and Edward W. Lehman. New York: Holt, Rinehart and Winston. Originally published in *Administrative Science Quarterly* 14:378–97.

Hodson, Randy, and Robert E. Parker. 1988. Work in high technology settings: A review of the empirical literature. *Research in the Sociology of Work* 4:1–29.

Hofstede, Geert. 1980. *Culture's consequences: International differences in work-related values*. Beverley Hills, CA: Sage Publications.

Homans, George C. 1950. *The human group*. New York: Harcourt Brace.

———. 1961. *Social behavior: Its elementary forms*. New York: Harcourt Brace.

Hughes, Everett C. 1958. *Men and their work*. Glencoe, IL: The Free Press.

Hummon, Norman P., Patrick Doreian, and Klaus Teuter. 1975. A structural control model of organizational change. *American Sociological Review* 40:813–24.

Inkeles, Alex, and David Smith. 1974. *Becoming modern*. Cambridge, MA: Harvard University Press.

Jaques, Elliott. 1951. *The changing culture of a factory*. London: Tavistock.

Jones, Frank E. 1954. The infantry recruit: A sociological analysis of socialization in the Canadian army. Unpublished Ph.D. thesis, Harvard University.

———. 1956. A sociological perspective on immigrant adjustment. *Social forces* 35:39–47.

———. 1968. Structural determinants of consensus and cohesion in complex organizations. *Canadian Review of Sociology and Anthropology* 5:219–40.

———. 1973. Psychiatric centres as therapeutic communities: Some implications for participatory management of organizations. In Pusic (1973).

———. 1984. The comparative analysis of organizations: Toward the construction of a general model. Chap. 2 in *Work, Organizations and Society*, edited by M. Brinkerhoff. Westport, CT: Greenwood Press.

Jones, Stephen R.G. 1990. Worker independence and output: The Hawthorne studies reevaluated. *American Sociological Review* 55:176–90.

———. 1992. Was there a Hawthorne effect? *American Journal of Sociology* 98:451–68.

Jöreskog, K.G., and D.N. Lawley. 1968. New methods in maximum likelihood factor analysis. *British Journal of Mathematical and Statistical Psychology* 21:85–96.

Kahn, Robert L., and Daniel Katz. [1953] 1960. Leadership practices in relation to productivity and morale. Chap. 29 in *Group Dynamics: Research and Theory*, 2nd edition, edited by D. Cartwright and A. Zander. Evanston, IL: Row, Peterson and Company.

———. 1972. The meaning of work: Interpretation and proposals for measurement. Chap. 5 in *The Human Meaning of Social Change*, edited by Angus Campbell and Philip E. Converse. New York: Russell Sage Foundation.

Kanter, Rosabeth M., and Derick Brinkerhoff. 1981. Organizational performance: Recent developments in measurement. *Annual Review of Sociology* 7:321–49.

Katz, Daniel, and Robert L. Kahn. [1966] 1978. *The social psychology of organizations*. 2nd ed. New York: John Wiley.

Kimberly, J.R. 1976. Organizational size and the structuralist perspective. *Administrative Science Quarterly* 21:571–97.

Kingsley, J.D. 1944. *Representative bureaucracy*. Yellow Springs, OH: The Antioch Press.

Kluckhohn, Clyde. [1944] 1967. *Navaho witchcraft*. Boston: Beacon Press.

Knoke, David. 1988. Incentives in collective action organizations. *American Sociological Review* 53:311–29.

Knoke, David, and Richard E. Adams. 1987. The incentive systems of associations. *Research in the Sociology of Organizations* 5:285–309. Greenwich, CT: JAI Press Inc.

Knoke, David, and Christine Wright-Isak. 1982. Individual motives and organizational incentive systems. *Research in the Sociology of Organizations* 1:209–54. Greenwich, CT: JAI Press Inc.

Kolaja, Jiri. [1960] 1973. *A Polish factory*. Westport, CT: Greenwood Press.

Kroeber, Alfred L., and Clyde Kluckhohn. 1963. *Culture: A critical review of comments and definitions*. New York: Vintage Books.

Kuhn, Alfred, and Robert D. Beam. 1982. *The logic of organization*. San Francisco: Jossey-Bass.

Kühne, Robert J. 1980. *Co-determination in business: Workers' representatives in the boardroom*. New York: Praeger.

Labour Canada. 1991. *Provision in collective agreements*. Unpublished survey data.

Lammers, Cornelis J., and David J. Hickson. 1979. *Organizations like and unlike*. London: Routledge and Kegan Paul.

Landsberger, Henry. 1958. *Hawthorne revisited*. Ithaca, NY: Cornell University.

Lawler, Edward, and Lyman W. Porter. 1967. The effect of performance on job satisfaction. *Industrial Relations* 7:20–28.

Leibow, Elliot. 1967. *Tally's corner*. Boston: Little, Brown.

Lincoln, James R., and Kerry McBride. 1987. Japanese industrial organization in comparative perspective. *Annual Review of Sociology* 13:289–312.

Lincoln, J. R., and Jon Miller. 1979. Work and friendship ties in organizations: A comparative analysis of relational networks. *Administrative Science Quarterly* 24:181–99.

Lippitt, R., and R. White. 1943. The social climate of children's groups. In *Child behaviour and development*, edited by R.G. Barker, J. Kounin, and H. Wright. New York: McGraw-Hill.

Lipset, Seymour M. [1960] 1963. *Political man*. New York: Doubleday & Company.

Lipset, Seymour M., Martin A. Trow, and James S. Coleman. 1956. *Union democracy*. Glencoe, IL: Free Press.

Litwak, Eugene. 1961. Models of bureaucracy that permit conflict. *American Journal of Sociology* 67:177–84.

Litwak, Eugene, and Josephina Figuera. 1968. Technological innovations and theoretical functions of primary groups and bureaucratic structures. *American Journal of Sociology* 73:468–81.

Litwak, Eugene, and Peter Messari. 1989. Organizational theory, social supports, and mortality rates: A theoretical convergence. *American Sociological Review* 54:49–66.

Locke, E.A. 1976. The nature and causes of job satisfaction. In *Handbook of industrial and organizational psychology*, edited by M.D. Dunnette. Chicago: Rand McNally.

Long, Richard J. 1978. The relative effects of share ownership vs control on job attitudes in an employee-owned company. *Human Relations* 31:753–63.

MacDonald, Flora. 1980. Cutting through the chains. *The Globe and Mail*, 7 November.

Mahoney T., and W. Weitzel. 1969. Managerial models of organizational effectiveness. *Administrative Science Quarterly* 14:357–65.

Malinowski, Bronislaw. [1922] 1961. *Argonauts of the Western Pacific*. New York: E.P. Dutton.

———. [1929] 1932. *The sexual life of savages in North-Western Melanesia: An ethnographic account of courtship, marriage, and family life among the natives of the Trobriand Islands, British New Guinea*. London: Routledge and Kegan Paul.

———. [1948] 1984. *Magic, science and religion*. Glencoe, IL: The Free press. Reprinted 1984 by Westport, CT: Greenwood Press.

Mansell, Jacquie. 1987. *Workplace innovation in Canada*. Ottawa: Economic Council of Canada, Supply and Services Canada.

Marsh, Robert M., and Hiroshi Mannari. 1976. *Modernization and the Japanese factory*. Princeton: Princeton University Press.

Marshall, S.L.A. 1947. *Men against fire*. New York: William Morrow and Company.

Maslow, Abraham. 1954. *Motivation and personality*. New York: Harper and Row.

Mayhew, Bruce. 1983. Hierarchical differentiation in imperatively coordinated associations. *Research in the Sociology of Organizations* 10:153–229.

Mayer, Lawrence R., and Mary S. Younger. 1974. Multiple indicators and the relationship between abstract variables. In Heise (1974).

Mayo, Elton. 1933. *The human problems of an industrial civilization*. New York: The Macmillan Company.

———. 1945. *The social problems of an industrial civilization*. Cambridge, MA: Harvard University Press.

Mayo, Elton, and G. Lombard. 1944. Teamwork and labor turnover in the aircraft industry of southern California. *Business Research Studies* no. 32. Cambridge, MA: Harvard University.

McKelvey, Bruce. 1982. *Organizational systematics*. Berkeley: University of California Press.

Mead, George H. 1934. *Mind, self and society*. Chicago: University of Chicago Press.

Mercier, Jean. 1985. "Le phénomène bureaucratique" et le Canada français: Quelques données empiriques et leurs interprétation. *Canadian Journal of Political Science* 18:31–55.

Merton, Robert. 1949. *Social theory and social structure*. Glencoe, IL: The Free Press.

———. 1957. *Social theory and social structure*. Revised and enlarged edition. Glencoe, IL: The Free Press.

Michalos, Alex C. 1980–1982. *North American social report*. Vols. 1–5. Dordrecht, Holland: D. Reidel Publishing Company.

Michels, Robert. [1911] 1962. *Political parties*. New York: The Free Press.

Miles, Ian. 1985. *Social indicators for human development*. London: Frances Porter.

Miller, James G. 1978. *Living systems*. New York: McGraw-Hill.

Money, William H., David P. Gilfillan, and Robert Duncan. 1976. A comparative study of multi-unit health care organizations. In Shortell and Brown (1976).

Moore, Wilbert E. 1965. *The impact of industry*. Englewood Cliffs, NJ: Prentice Hall.

Moreno, J.L. 1934. *Who shall survive?* New York: Beacon House.

Moreno, J.L., et al. 1960. *The sociometry reader*. Glencoe, IL: The Free Press.

Morse, Nancy C. 1953. *Satisfactions in the white collar job*. Ann Arbor, MI: University of Michigan.

Morse, Nancy, and E. Reimer. 1956. The experimental change of a major organizational variable. *Journal of Abnormal and Social Psychology* 52:120–29.

Mungall, Catherine. 1986. *More than just a job: Worker cooperatives in Canada*. Ottawa: Steel Rail Publishing.

Nightingale, Donald V. 1980. *Profit sharing and employee ownership*. Don Mills, ON: Profit Sharing Council of Canada.

———. 1982. *Workplace democracy*. Toronto: University of Toronto Press.

Oakeshott, Robert. 1978. *The case for worker's coops*. London: Routledge and Kegan Paul.

Obradovic, Josip. 1972. Distribution of participation in the process of decision-making on problems related to the economic activity of the company. In *Participation and self-management*. Zagreb, Yugoslavia: First International Conference on Participation and Self-Management.

———. 1976. Sociology of organization in Yugoslavia. *Acta Sociologica* 19:23–35.

Organization for Economic Co-operation and Development. 1976a. *Measuring social well-being*. Paris: OECD

———. 1976b. *Measuring social well-being: A progress report on the development of social indicators*. Paris: OECD.

————. 1986. *Living conditions in OECD countries*. Paris: OECD.

Ouchi, William G., and Alan L. Wilkins. 1985. Organizational culture. *Annual Review of Sociology* 11:457–81.

Park, Robert E., E.W. Burgess, and R.D. McKenzie, eds. 1925. *The city*. Chicago: University of Chicago Press.

Parsons, Talcott. [1937] 1949. *The structure of social action*. Glencoe, IL: The Free Press.

————. 1951. *The social system*. Glencoe, IL: The Free Press.

————. 1960. *Structure and process in modern societies*. Glencoe, IL: The Free Press.

————. 1966. *Societies*. Englewood Cliffs, NJ: Prentice-Hall.

————. 1971. *The system of modern societies*. Englewood Cliffs, NJ: Prentice-Hall.

————. 1977. *The evolution of societies*, edited by Jackson Toby. Englewood Cliffs, NJ: Prentice-Hall.

Parsons, Talcott, Robert F. Bales, and Edward A. Shils. 1953. *Working papers in the theory of action*. New York: The Free Press.

Parsons, Talcott, Edward A. Shils, and others. 1951. *Towards a general theory of action*. Cambridge, MA: Harvard University Press.

Parsons, Talcott, and Neil J. Smelser. 1956. *Economy and society*. Glencoe, IL: The Free Press.

Paterson, Tom T. 1955. *Morale in war and work*. London: Max Parrish and Company.

Pennings, J.M., and Paul S. Goodman. 1977. Towards a workable framework. Chap. 8 in Goodman and Pennings (1977).

Perin, Constance. 1991. The moral fabric of the office: Panopticon discourse and schedule flexibilities. *Research in the Sociology of Organizations* 8:241–68. Greenwich, CT: JAI Press Inc.

Perrow, Charles. 1961. The analysis of goals in complex organizations. *American Sociological Review* 26:856–66.

————. 1986. *Complex organizations: A critical essay,* 3rd ed. New York: Random House.

Phillips, Robert L., John D. Blair, and Neal Schmitt. 1987. Beyond group cohesion: The concept of synergy and its impact on performance. *National Journal of Sociology,* spring:140–71.

Powell, Walter W., and Paul J. Dimaggio, eds. 1991. *The new institutionalism in organizational analysis*. Chicago: University of Chicago Press.

Presthus, Robert. [1962] 1978. *The organizational society*. New York: St. Martin's Press.

Pusic, Eugen, ed. 1972–73. *Participation and self-management*, 6 vols. Zagreb, Yugoslavia: The Institute for Social Research, University of Zagreb.

Radcliffe-Browne, A.R. 1933. *The Andaman Islanders*. Cambridge: Cambridge University Press.

————. 1935. On the concept of function in social science. *American Anthropologist* 37:394–402.

Rankin, Tom. 1990. *New forms of work organization.* Toronto: University of Toronto Press.

Ray, Larry J., and Michael Reed. 1994. *Organizing modernity: New Weberian perspectives on work, organization and society.* London: Routledge.

Rinehart, James W. [1975] 1987. *The tyranny of work,* 2nd ed. Toronto: Harcourt Brace Jovanovich.

————. 1986. Improving the quality of working life through job redesign: Work humanization or work rationalization. *Canadian Review of Sociology and Anthropology* 23:507–30.

Roethlisberger, F., and F.J. Dickson. [1939] 1947. *Management and the worker.* Cambridge, MA: Harvard University Press.

Rosner, M. 1973. Worker participation in decision-making in kibbutz industry. In *Israel: Social structure and change,* edited by M. Curtis and M.S. Chertoff. New Brunswick, NJ: Transaction Books.

Rothschild, Joyce, and Raymond Russell. 1986. Alternatives to bureaucracy: Democratic participation in the economy. *Annual Review of Sociology* 12:307–28.

Rothschild-Whitt, Joyce. 1979. The collectivist organization: An alternative to rational bureaucratic models. *American Sociological Review* 44:509–27.

Russett, Bruce M. 1964. *World handbook of political and social indicators.* New Haven, CT: Yale University Press.

Sayles, Leonard. 1958. *The behaviour of industrial work groups: Prediction and control.* New York: Wiley.

Schlaifer, Robert. 1980. The relay assembly test room: An alternative statistical interpretation. *American Sociological Review* 45:995–1005.

Scott, W. Richard. 1977. Effectiveness of organizational effectiveness studies. Chap. 4 in *New perspectives on organizational effectiveness,* edited by Goodman and Pennings. San Francisco: Jossey-Bass.

————. [1981] 1987. *Organizations: Rational, natural, and open systems.* Englewood Cliffs, NJ: Prentice-Hall.

————. 1992. *Organizations: Rational, natural, and open systems.* Englewood Cliffs, NJ: Prentice-Hall.

Scott, W. Richard, William H. Forrest Jr., and W. Brown Jr. 1976. Hospital structure and postoperative mortality and morbidity. In Shortell and Brown (1976).

Scott, W. Richard, and John W. Meyer. 1994. *Institutional environments and organizations: Structural complexity and individualism.* Thousand Oaks, CA: Sage Publications.

Scott, W. Richard, and Stephen M. Shortell. [1983] 1988. Organizational performance: Managing for efficiency and effectiveness. In Shortell and Kaluzny ([1983] 1988).

Seashore, Stanley F. 1954. *Group cohesiveness in the industrial work group.* Ann Arbor, MI: University of Michigan Press.

Seashore, Stanley F., and E. Yuchtman. 1967. Factorial analysis of organizational performance. *Administrative Science Quarterly* 12:377–95.

Selznick, Philip. [1949] 1966. *TVA and the grass roots*. New York: Harper and Row.

Shepard, Jon M. 1971. *Automation and alienation: A study of office and factory workers*. Cambridge, MA: MIT Press.

Shils, Edward A., and Morris Janowitz. 1948. Cohesion and disintegration in the Wehrmacht in World War II. *Public Opinion Quarterly* 12:29–42.

Shortell, Stephen M. 1976. Organization theory and health services delivery. In Shortell and Brown (1976).

Shortell, Stephen M., and Montague Brown, eds. 1976. *Organizational research in hospitals*. Chicago: Blue Cross Association.

Shortell, Stephen M., and Arnold D. Kaluzny, eds. [1983] 1988. *Health Care Management*. New York: John Wiley and Sons.

Sills, David. 1957. *The volunteers*. Glencoe, IL: The Free Press.

Slater, Robert O. 1985. Organization size and differentiation. *Research in the Sociology of Organizations* 4:127–80.

Smircich, Linda. 1983. Concepts of culture and organizational analysis. *Administrative Science Quarterly* 28:339–58.

Smith, Adam. 1884. *An inquiry into the nature and the wealth of nations*. London: Thomas Nelson.

Smith, Claggett. 1966. A comparative analysis of some conditions and consequences of intra-organizational conflict. *Administrative Science Quarterly* 10:504–29.

Statistics Canada. 1974. *Perspectives Canada I*. Ottawa: Statistics Canada.

———. 1977a. *Vital statistics*. Ottawa: Statistics Canada.

———. 1977b. *Perspectives Canada II*. Ottawa: Statistics Canada

———. 1980. *Perspectives Canada III*. Ottawa: Statistics Canada.

———. 1981. *Canadian social trends*. Ottawa: Statistics Canada.

———. 1992. *1991 census dictionary*. Ottawa: Statistics Canada.

Staw, Barry M. 1980. Rationality and justification in organizational life. *Research in organizational behavior* 2:45–80.

Stodgill, R. M., and A. E. Coons, eds. 1957. *Leader behavior: Its description and measurement*. Research Monograph 88. Columbus, OH: Bureau of Business Research, Ohio State University.

Stokes, Bruce. 1978. *Worker participation: Productivity and the quality of work life*. Washington, DC: World Watch Institute.

Storey, Robert. 1987. The struggle to organize Stelco and Dofasco. *Relations Industrielles* 42:366–85.

Stouffer, Samuel A., et al. 1949. *The American soldier*, 2 vols. Princeton: Princeton University Press.

Tannenbaum, Arnold S., ed. 1968. *Control in organizations*. New York: McGraw-Hill.

Tannenbaum, Arnold S., et al. 1974. *Hierarchy in organizations.* San Francisco: Joosey-Boss.

Taylor, Charles L., and Michael C. Hudson. 1972. *World handbook of political and social indicators,* 2nd ed. New Haven, CT: Yale University Press.

Taylor, Charles L., Michael C. Hudson, and David A. Jodice. 1983. *World handbook of political and social indicators,* 3rd ed. New Haven, CT: Yale University Press.

Taylor, Frederick W. 1947. *Principles of scientific management.* New York: Harper and Brothers.

Tepperman, Lorne. 1973. The effect of court size on organization and procedure. *Canadian Review of Sociology and Anthropology* 10:346–65.

Trist, E.L., and K.W. Bamforth. 1951. Some social and psychological consequences of the long wall method of coal-getting. *Human Relations* 4:3–38.

United States Department of Health, Education and Welfare. 1973. *Work in America.* Cambridge: MIT Press.

Vroom, Victor H. 1964. *Work and motivation.* New York: Wiley.

Walker, Henry A., and Mary L. Fennell. 1986. Gender differences in role differentiation and organizational task performance. *Annual Review of Sociology* 12:255–75.

Walton, R.E. 1979. Work innovations in the U.S. *Harvard Business Review* 57:88–98.

Warner, W. Lloyd, and J.O. Low. 1947. *The social system of the modern factory.* New Haven, CT: Yale University Press.

Warriner, C.K. 1977. Empirical taxonomies and the comparative study of organizations. Paper presented at the annual meeting of the American Sociological Association.

Weber, Max. [c1904–5] 1930. *The protestant ethic and the spirit of capitalism,* trans. Talcott Parsons. New York: Charles Scribner's Sons.

———. [1922] 1963. *The sociology of religion,* trans. Ephraim Fischoff. Boston: Beacon Press.

———. [1925] 1947. *The theory of economic and social organization,* trans. L.J. Henderson and Talcott Parsons. New York: Oxford University Press.

———. 1978. *Economy and society,* 2 vols., trans. E. Fischoff et al. Berkeley: University of California Press.

Weick, Karl E. 1969. *The social psychology of organizing.* Reading, MA: Addison-Wesley.

———. 1979. *The social psychology of organizing.* Reading, MA: Addison-Wesley.

White, Ralph, and Ronald Lippitt. [1953] 1960. Leader behaviour and member reaction in three 'social climates.'" Chap. 28 in *Group dynamics: Research and theory,* 2nd ed., edited by D. Cartwright and A. Zander. Evanston, IL: Row, Peterson and Company.

Whitehead, T.N. 1938. *The industrial worker,* 2 vols. Cambridge, MA: Harvard University Press.

Whyte, William F. 1946. *Industry and society*. New York: McGraw-Hill.

———.1955. *Money and motivation*. New York: Harper and Bros.

———. [1955, 1966] 1981. *Street corner society*. Chicago: University of Chicago Press.

———. 1972. Elton Mayo. *International Encyclopedia of the Social Sciences*, vols. 9 and 10, edited by David L. Sills. New York: Macmillan and The Free Press.

Winship, Christopher, and Sherwin Rosen. 1988. Introduction: Sociological and economic approaches to the analysis of social structure. *American Journal of Sociology* 94 Supplement:S1–S16.

Wolff, Kurt. 1950. *The sociology of Georg Simmel*. Glencoe, IL: The Free Press.

Woodward, Joan. [1965] 1980. *Industrial organization: Theory and practice*, 2nd ed. Oxford: Oxford University Press.

Worthy, Joseph C. 1950. Organizational structure and employee morale. *American Sociological Review* 15:169–79.

Wrege, Charles D. 1976. Solving Mayo's mystery: The first complete account of the origin of the Hawthorne studies—the forgotten contributions of C.E. Snow and H. Hibarger. *Proceedings of the Academy of Management* 36:12–16.

Young, Ruth. 1988. Is population ecology a useful paradigm for the study of organizations? *American Sociological Review* 94:1–24.

Zey-Farrell, Mary, and Michael Aiken, eds. and contributors. 1981. *Complex organizations: Critical perspectives*. Glenview, IL: Scott, Foresman and Company.

Zucker, Lynne G. 1987. Institutional theories of organization. *Annual Review of Sociology* 13:443–64.

Zwerman, William L. 1970. *New perspectives in organization theory*. Westport, CT: Greenwood Publishing Corp.

INDEX